KT-590-196

GREEN PERSUASION

ALSO BY JEFFREY K. STINE

Living in the Anthropocene:
Earth in the Age of Humans (coeditor)

America's Forested Wetlands:
From Wasteland to Valued Resource

Going Underground:
Tunneling Past, Present, and Future (coeditor)

Twenty Years of Science in the Public Interest:
A History of the Congressional Science
and Engineering Fellowship Program

Mixing the Waters:
Environment, Politics, and the Building
of the Tennessee-Tombigbee Waterway

Technology and Choice:
Readings from Technology and Culture (coeditor)

A History of Science Policy in the United States, 1940–1985

GREEN PERSUASION

ADVERTISING, VOLUNTARISM, AND AMERICA'S PUBLIC LANDS

JEFFREY K. STINE

A Smithsonian Contribution to Knowledge

Smithsonian
Scholarly Press
WASHINGTON, D.C.
2021

Published by SMITHSONIAN INSTITUTION SCHOLARLY PRESS
P.O. Box 37012, MRC 957
Washington, D.C. 20013-7012
https://scholarlypress.si.edu

Cover images: Front (*clockwise, from top left*)—View from Sunset Point toward the Aquarius Plateau in Bryce Canyon National Park (photo by Ben Turnbull/Unsplash); Figure 12; giant sequoias at Yosemite National Park (photo courtesy of Library of Congress); and Figures 16, 7, 8, 6, and 10. Back cover (*from top*)—Figure 11; button lampooning Interior secretary James Watt (photo courtesy of National Museum of American History, Smithsonian Institution); and Figures 5 and 15. See captions in text for figure credits.

Compilation copyright © 2021 Smithsonian Institution

The text by Jeffrey K. Stine is in the public domain. The rights to all other text and images in this publication, including cover and interior designs, are owned either by the Smithsonian Institution or by third parties.

This work is licensed under a Creative Commons Attribution-NonCommercial 4.0 International (CC BY-NC 4.0) License.

Library of Congress Cataloging-in-Publication Data

Names: Stine, Jeffrey K., author. | Smithsonian Institution Scholarly Press, issuing body.
Title: Green persuasion : advertising, voluntarism, and America's public lands / Jeffrey K. Stine.
Other titles: Advertising, voluntarism, and America's public lands | Smithsonian contribution to knowledge.
Description: Washington, D.C. : Smithsonian Scholarly Press, 2021. | Series: A Smithsonian contribution to knowledge | Includes bibliographical references and index.
Identifiers: LCCN 2021025893 | ISBN 9781944466466 (paperback) | ISBN 9781944466459 (epub)
Subjects: LCSH: Take Pride in America—History. | Advertising Council—History. | Public lands—United States—Management—History. | Volunteer workers in conservation of natural resources—United States—History. | Recreation areas—Maintenance—United States—History. | Advertising, Public service—United States—History. | Green marketing—United States—History.
Classification: LCC HD216 .S78 2021 | DDC 333.10973—dc23 | SUDOC SI 1.60:L 23
LC record available at https://lccn.loc.gov/2021025893

ISBN-13: 978-1-944466-45-9 (online)
ISBN-13: 978-1-944466-46-6 (print)

Publication date (online): 31 August 2021

Printed in the United States of America

∞ The paper used in this publication meets the minimum requirements of the American National Standard for Permanence of Paper for Printed Library Materials Z39.48–1992.

For Marcel, again.

CONTENTS

INTRODUCTION

For much of the twentieth century, environmental policy in the United States advanced through bipartisan coalitions. Major legislative acts dealing with natural resources conservation, public health, and pollution abatement were signed into law by Republican and Democratic presidents alike. Congressional champions of environmental causes sat on both sides of the aisle. Local and national environmental organizations reflected a wide political spectrum and often set aside their differences to collaborate on projects with overarching appeal. Democrats and Republicans may have quarreled over the best approaches to conserve natural resources, reduce pollution, and protect public lands, but there was general agreement that the goals themselves represented the national interest.

The strength of this bipartisan consensus was tested repeatedly during the 1970s as Republican support for environmental causes waned. That trend accelerated after Ronald Reagan's election in 1980, when the GOP's conservative wing shifted the party further toward curtailing the size and power of the federal government, expanding economic development on public lands, and reducing environmental regulations. Although the measures undertaken by James Watt at the Department of the Interior and Anne (Gorsuch) Burford at the Environmental Protection Agency dominated press coverage and enflamed critics, the Reagan administration's anti-environmental proclivities found expression across the executive branch. At first, the intensity of the public backlash caught the White House off guard. The president's political advisors endured the unabated criticism until it threatened Reagan's reelection, at which point Watt and Burford were quickly dropped. Still, the administration refused to modify its environmental agenda, so the attacks continued.

In response, the new Interior secretary, Donald Hodel, launched a public relations initiative—an amiable, well-orchestrated bit of green persuasion directed toward changing the public's image of the Reagan environmental choices. Sold to the nation via a sophisticated advertising campaign devised by the Ad Council, the patriotically themed program Take Pride in America called upon individuals to donate their own time and labor to care for and protect public lands. Appealing to the generosity of citizens to help meet the challenge of managing the roughly 700 million acres of federal lands was a reasonable and inspired approach, especially given the country's rich tradition of voluntarism. Americans have long volunteered their time, energy, and money to all sorts of worthy causes, from food banks and clothing drives to watershed cleanups and neighborhood safety patrols. Take Pride in America's call for volunteer assistance was meant to signal the administration's environmental sensitivity, while the emphasis it placed on personal (rather than governmental) responsibility for looking after the nation's commonly owned lands sought to deflect attention from the administration's unaltered environmental policies and weak commitment to federal land management agencies.

The Take Pride in America program, and its various iterations under successive presidents, took advantage of the appreciation Americans had for the beauty, diversity, and bounty of the country's lands, an appreciation that drew on iconography and messaging derived from Native Americans' reverence for nature. It also drew on the nation's long-standing civic reliance on voluntarism and volunteer organizations. Whether in the nineteenth-century landscape paintings of Thomas Moran or twentieth-century advertisements for suburban housing developments, the value of a surrounding environment, both aesthetic and commercial, has long infused American culture. Those attitudes had been tapped before in government advertising programs like the Smokey Bear forest fire prevention campaign, and the Reagan initiative built on their techniques. The Take Pride program exploited the widespread fascination with Hollywood by recruiting three actors known for their tough-guy cinematic personas—Clint Eastwood, Charles Bronson, and Louis Gossett Jr.—to serve as the ad campaign's celebrity spokespersons. And later iterations of the program developed friendly fictional icons to serve as mascots.

Green Persuasion traces the evolution of this volunteer-based, public lands stewardship program from its initial development in the Reagan era through the ways it was revised, neglected, and readopted by subsequent presidencies. Take Pride's role in federal environmental policy turned out to be fraught with problems, resulting in frequent shifts in its political support within the government. Nevertheless, its basic goal to engage citizens as volunteers on public lands survived across multiple administrations, and that history offers valuable insights into how (and why) Americans have expressed care of the nation's landed inheritance in their collective political choices.

CHAPTER 1

THE RISE OF PUBLIC SERVICE ADVERTISING

From colonial newspaper notices for salt, sugar, and soap to the signs and shingles outside businesses today, advertising has permeated American culture, provoking interest and amusement, with its catchy slogans and songs later incorporated into our daily discourse. Long before the Internet's pervasive pop-ups, commercial and political enterprises used advertising to increase sales of goods and services, pique interest in new products, and persuade customers to adopt new styles or change behavior. As nineteenth-century industrialization produced more manufactured goods, the techniques for selling them became more specialized. Lighted signs, sparkling designs, clever jingles, and fictional characters turned heads, promoted innovation, and became ubiquitous parts of modern life, from Main Street department stores to City Hall, and eventually as essential tools in environmental and natural resources campaigns.[1]

In the early twentieth century, U.S. government entities increasingly employed advertising techniques to sell policies and shift public attitudes. The Woodrow Wilson administration, for example, created the Committee on Public Information (CPI) in April 1917, with the explicit goal of shaping Americans' opinions on the European war. The federal government, observed journalist John Maxwell Hamilton, needed to persuade citizens "to serve in the military or, if they stayed at home, to conserve precious resources, pay higher taxes, buy war bonds and patriotically stick with the war as it dragged bloodily along."[2] Toward this end, CPI seasoned its domestic propaganda with a liberal mixture of cultural references, iconography, and nationalism. The result was a banquet of notable advertising campaigns, such as the posters promoting Liberty Loans. Those "unifying emblems" helped "to mobilize a disparate and contentious population," historian Jackson Lears explains; World War I was the first time that government policies were "systematically promoted through commercial techniques of mass persuasion."[3]

Although the flood of government public service advertising subsided with the armistice, it was replaced in the mass media during the 1920s by insistent corporate promotion, a tide somewhat slowed by the 1929 stock market crash. Commercial and nonprofit entities continued to use advertising, even as the economic depression eroded public confidence in big business. Troubled by the profusion of deceptive claims and the unbridled entreaties to buy, buy, buy at a time of desperate social hardship, consumer advocates lobbied Congress to regulate advertising firms and their practices.[4] In reaction, industry leaders touted the singular utility of advertising to society at large. As Gerd Horten recounts, when representatives of the major advertising associations met in November 1941 to hammer out a collective strategy to avoid unwanted government intervention, they concluded that "with little to sell or to advertise, advertising should sell itself, as well as American business and free enterprise."[5] The advertising industry realized it must prove that advertising could be a useful public service, not just a tool for selling goods.

THE WAR ADVERTISING COUNCIL

World War II presented the advertising industry with an opportunity to reassert its social value in a tangible, patriotic, conspicuous manner and to offer a positive, nondefensive retort to the industry's critics. President Franklin D. Roosevelt had created the Office of Facts and Figures (OFF) in October 1941 to facilitate "the dissemination of factual information to the citizens of the country on the progress of the defense effort and on the defense policies and activities of the Government" and appointed the Librarian of Congress, Archibald MacLeish, to head the initiative.[6] Shortly after the 7 December Pearl Harbor attack and the U.S. declaration of war, the Association of National Advertisers and the American Association of Advertising Agencies offered their services to help the government. The OFF quickly embraced the idea, agreeing to oversee a new volunteer-based War Advertising Council created in February 1942.[7]

Three months later, the Office of War Information (OWI) absorbed OFF, MacLeish became assistant director to OWI's head, and the War Advertising Council became a special external unit of OWI, charged with developing public service advertising campaigns for the war effort. As coordinator of propaganda and information campaigns, OWI reviewed and prioritized government agency petitions for media coverage, forwarding approved projects to the War Advertising Council. The council then assembled teams of volunteer managers and advertising agencies for the campaigns it deemed feasible.[8]

The council's membership comprised advertising executives from across the country, all of whom donated their services. It initially represented six national organizations: the Association of National Advertisers, American Association of Advertising Agencies, National Publishers Association, Bureau of Advertising of the American Newspaper Publishers Association, National Association of Broadcasters, and Outdoor Advertising Association of America. The council thus served as a coalition of the industry's three key groups—the advertising agencies, their business clients, and the print and broadcast media—with the goal of showing how advertising benefitted the nation. Council campaigns employed established commercial advertising methods, but rather than selling merchandise or services, they sought to shape public opinion, encourage citizen engagement, and change behavior.[9] Their topics ranged widely—from war bonds and victory gardens to the conservation and salvaging of resources to the recruitment of millions of women workers.[10]

In an upbeat style befitting a Madison Avenue copywriter, the War Advertising Council's first annual report declared that the group had "one purpose and only one—to help win the war by using the power of advertising to inform, clarify, and persuade," adding that "wars are won by a unified citizenry taking common action toward a common goal. Advertising can help secure that action." Explaining that its task required "dogged, arduous spade work—the results of which will only be apparent during the months to come," the report's text exemplified the industry's colorful imagery and metaphors: "A basic job of education has had to go on many fronts. Missionary work within government, within industry, and within the ranks of advertising itself has been necessary before advertising had a chance to flex its muscles. Mental handcuffs had to be removed from many minds."[11] The council's patriotic rhetoric soared, buoyed by the claim that if advertising "plays the part it is capable of playing, fewer American men will die." Advertising would be asked "to help recruit housewives by the millions to leave their kitchens for the jobs men left behind" and to inspire Americans "to learn to conserve—to eat it up, wear it out, make it do."[12]

The belief that home-front actions and attitudes could expedite military success permeated the Roosevelt administration's decision-making. And yet Americans were independent thinkers. Civilian social, political, and financial support could not be commanded at will. The need to sell millions of dollars of war bonds, for example, made government officials eager to embrace the advertising profession's assistance. And the benefits flowed two ways. The War Advertising Council kept corporate names before the public at a time when many of the nation's largest firms had diverted their production lines from consumer to military goods. Advertising agencies also kept their own skills honed by creating innovative campaigns for war bonds, blood donations, scrap salvage drives, victory gardens, women's war work, and forest fire prevention. Historian Roland Marchand argues that World War II "endowed postwar advocacy advertising with a threefold bequest: it enhanced advertising's reputation for selling ideas; it schooled advertisers in subtle methods of infusing advocacy for greater business autonomy into public-spirited messages; and it passed on an institutional legacy in the form of the Advertising Council."[13]

On 9 August 1945, as the world envisioned peace, the War Advertising Council's board of directors discussed an internal report titled "Plan to Sell the Post-War Council." As advertising professionals, they knew a successful appeal would have to convince the federal government, business community, major public relations and advertising firms, mass media, *and* the public that their work had social benefit. The council's directors even weighed the merits of developing "a nation-wide [radio] broadcast, either open or closed circuits, in which the President and top national figures would participate," with the goal of underscoring "the wartime information job and the part the people have played in speeding victory."[14]

High-visibility, public service advertising was thus perceived as a way to reinforce both the industry's social respectability and its economic sustainability. The group removed the word *War* from its title, becoming simply the Advertising Council. Next, as Griffith explains, the council "sought to broaden its activities and to avoid any restraints that the government might impose on it," no longer automatically accepting government proposals, but reserving the right "to accept or reject messages as they saw fit."[15] The council also entertained requests for public service advertising campaigns from both government and private nonprofit organizations.[16]

The council repeatedly stressed that it was a nonprofit organization created to bring American business, advertising, and communications industries together to promote voluntary citizen actions addressing national problems. Some campaigns, such as the first nongovernmental initiative, involved matters of life and death, like reducing traffic accidents. Begun in 1946, the National Safety Council–sponsored campaign was still going strong 16 years later, when the council's annual report claimed credit for helping to change behavior: "Traffic fatalities were expected to rise after the war, with unlimited gasoline supplies and millions of old, prewar automobiles on the highways. Instead, the death rate has been cut to less than half the rate of 1941."[17]

The peacetime approach endeavored to secure assistance from "informed, judicious, and public-spirited leaders of opinion," asking them to "decide whether campaigns considered by the Council were in truth in the interest of all the people."[18] Created in 1947, a Public Policy Committee—more than 30 members representing business, labor, education, medicine, law, banking, agriculture, and social services—advised the council's board of directors on whether proposed campaigns seemed sufficiently national, nonpartisan, and in the public interest. Acceptance of new campaigns required approval by both the board of directors and the Public Policy Committee, with the latter providing cover for the council's ultimate decisions.[19] Paul Hoffman, who chaired the Public Policy Committee for many years, described the goal as informing "the American people that the means to many worthy ends are in their own hands, not in the hands of some agency of the federal government."[20] This combination of self-reliance, voluntarism, and private-sector initiative has remained the Advertising Council's operational formula ever since.

Another constant has been the Ad Council's reliance on its constituent groups' voluntary contributions. The council's operating budget has always paid for staff salaries and office expenses but never the direct costs of the campaigns themselves.[21] Campaign development costs (including the work of creating the ads—the writing, design, drawing, still photography, film and video editing, and the like—and distribution of materials) are provided gratis by each campaign's volunteer advertising agency, whereas council staff arrange with mass media outlets for donated space or time for publishing, posting, and broadcasting the public service ads.

The American Association of Advertising Agencies and the Association of National Advertisers played a critical role by lending the Ad Council credibility

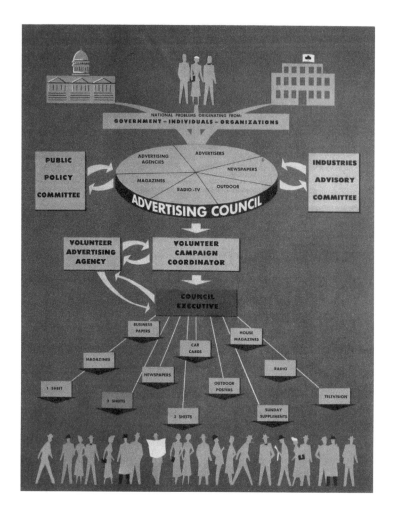

FIGURE 1. Organizational schematic of the Ad Council's public service campaigns as published in the council's 1952 annual report. Courtesy of Ad Council Archives, University of Illinois Archives, record series 13/2/202.

within the advertising industry as a whole. For each public service campaign, the American Association of Advertising Agencies appointed a volunteer advertising agency to provide the creative talent, while the Association of National Advertisers assigned a volunteer coordinator (typically an advertising or communications executive chosen from the business corporations that fund the council) to supervise the volunteer ad agency and liaise with the Ad Council and campaign sponsor.[22] At no time did the admen forget that "their weapons are words and pictures." Thus, as the council explained, "Campaigns to gain public cooperation in highway safety or in forest fire prevention, or support for Radio Free Europe, [are] given the same advertising 'know-how' as a campaign to sell soap or washing machines or automobiles."[23]

The council's efforts to avoid offending any branch of government, political party, or business community have inevitably influenced campaign selections and approaches, yet the council's goal of promoting excellence in advertising has meant that its products could be visually and conceptually daring, pushing boundaries to gain attention. Through the years, campaigns centered on a handful of themes, such as education, health, citizenship, anti-crime, highway safety, religion in American life, and economics. From the outset, perhaps because of the visual potential, environmental concerns have been popular topics, beginning with victory gardens and forest fire prevention during World War II. The number of environmentally oriented campaigns also increased during the 1970s and thereafter because of the interest of government sponsors like the Department of the Interior, Environmental Protection Agency, and Department of Energy, with support from private organizations like Keep America Beautiful, the Environmental Defense Fund, and the Alliance to Save Energy. The council's board of directors likewise recognized the growing need to secure clean water supplies, curb pollution, check urban sprawl, and meet the expanding demands for outdoor recreational areas.[24]

SMOKEY BEAR AND THE FOREST FIRE PREVENTION CAMPAIGN

No Ad Council campaign subject proved more dramatic or durable than forest fire prevention. U.S. concern about wildfires grew during the early twentieth century, especially in the mountainous expanses of the West, where commercial forestry had established itself as a major industry, but a national fire prevention advertising campaign did not emerge until World War II, when firefighting needs merged with civil defense goals. The strategic importance of woodland resources had elevated the priority assigned to protecting Western forests. As ever more trained firefighters joined the armed forces or went to work in defense plants, the state and federal forest agencies stepped up recruitment of volunteer replacements and began promoting civilian awareness of forest fire safety.[25]

National defense officials also feared that arsonous saboteurs might target forest preserves. When a Japanese submarine fired more than a dozen shells at a coastal oil depot near Goleta, California, and the Los Padres National Forest in 1942, direct enemy attack became an added concern. Apprehension of deliberately ignited wildfires had already aggravated the racism underpinning the government's relocation of nearly 120,000 people of Japanese descent (roughly two-thirds of them U.S. citizens) from their homes near the Pacific Coast to inland internment camps.[26] Although federal planners rationalized the unconstitutional detention of Japanese Americans as a preventative measure to lower the risk of arson and other acts of sabotage, they knew that the nation's timberlands faced a far greater threat from mundane carelessness, such as untended campfires and discarded cigarettes and matches.[27]

Defense-related fears were worsened when the Japanese military engaged in a scheme to pepper the U.S. mainland with balloon-delivered incendiary bombs. Released from Japan, the unmanned, hydrogen-filled, mulberry paper balloons ascended to more than 30,000 feet and rode the easterly jet stream winds 5,000 miles across the north Pacific before dropping their payloads. In his history of this meticulously planned offensive, Robert Mikesh estimated that about 1,000 of the 9,000 balloons launched in 1944 and 1945 reached North America.[28] Despite their potential for igniting wildfires, the unguided devices ultimately inflicted minimal damage on the forests. The most dangerous threat was the potential psychological impact of news about the bombing attempts. To avert panic, as well as deny the encouragement such information might give the enemy, government officials worked to muzzle the media.[29] Meanwhile, print and broadcast outlets were pushed to persuade Americans to be vigilant about campfires and smoking.

To assist their response to such potential threats, the U.S. Forest Service and the National Association of State Foresters created the Cooperative Forest Fire Prevention Program in 1942 and petitioned the War Advertising Council for help. The council agreed, enlisted the Los Angeles office of Foote, Cone & Belding Communications to serve as the volunteer advertising agency, and made forest fire prevention its second public service advertising campaign.[30]

Their first forest fire prevention posters leaned heavily on patriotic, war-related themes, as exemplified by their early slogans "Careless Matches Aid the Axis" and "Your Match, Their Secret Weapon." When Disney Studios released its animated film *Bambi* in August 1942, the War Advertising Council successfully sought the studio's permission to incorporate the Bambi character (a fawn that had lost its mother to a hunter and later escaped the horror of a human-kindled wildfire) in family-oriented ads. Disney consented to a one-year loan, allowing Bambi to appear on numerous posters, with such taglines as "Please, Mister, Don't Be Careless. Prevent Forest Fires. Greater Danger Than Ever!"[31]

The immediate popularity of the Bambi posters convinced leaders of the Cooperative Fire Prevention Campaign to develop a successor animal symbol once the Disney licensing contract expired. After internal debate over the most representative type of woodland creature to adopt, the Forest Service settled on a bear. In August 1944, campaign director Richard Hammett summarized

FIGURE 2. The artist Albert Staehle in 1947 holding the image of Smokey Bear he created for the U.S. Forest Service. Courtesy of U.S. Forest Service.

the group's suggested features for the anthropomorphized mascot: "nose short (Panda type), color black or brown; expression appealing, knowledgeable, quizzical; perhaps wearing a campaign (or Boy Scout) hat that typifies the outdoors and the woods."[32]

For an illustration, the council turned to artist Albert Staehle, whose paintings of cocker spaniels and other animals had long appeared in advertisements and on the covers of such mass-circulation magazines as the *Saturday Evening Post*. He accepted the volunteer assignment on behalf of the war effort and created one of the most iconic public service advertising symbols of all time: Smokey Bear. Staehle clothed his version of the bipedal ursine firefighter in blue jeans and a forest ranger's hat. Campaign officials named the bear "Smokey" in honor of Joseph B. "Smokey Joe" Martin, who, as assistant chief of the New York City Fire Department from 1919 to 1930, gained widespread renown for his firefighting skill and repeated willingness to risk his life to rescue people from burning buildings.[33]

Basing its design work on Staehle's painting, Foote, Cone & Belding developed the first Smokey Bear poster, which it printed in late 1944 for distribution in early 1945. Two years later, the admen crafted Smokey's signature message, "Remember, Only You Can Prevent Forest Fires."[34] While Foote, Cone & Belding handled the creative work and fabrication and the Ad Council distributed the public service advertisements, the Forest Service began producing supplementary material featuring Smokey, most of it fashioned by two Forest Service artists, Rudolph "Rudy" Wendelin and Harry Rossoll. The Ad Council campaign made use of the Foote, Cone & Belding artwork, leaving the Forest Service to undertake its own separate and complementary effort to promote the forest fire prevention message. In this parallel exercise, Wendelin devoted himself to generating images for Forest Service posters, publications, and licensed products, whereas Rossoll drew weekly Smokey comics for syndicated publication in the United States and Canada.[35]

FIGURE 3. Poster depicting the National Zoo's Smokey passing the forest fire prevention mantle to the rescued cub, Little Smokey, in 1971. Courtesy of Smithsonian Institution Archives.

The real test of the forest fire protection campaign came after World War II, when recreational use of woodlands surged. The Smokey Bear character became an essential part of the government educational effort, and to control possible commercial exploitation of the symbol—as well as to avert perversion of his fire-fighting message—Congress passed the Smokey Bear Act in 1952, which required anyone wanting to manufacture or sell Smokey Bear products to obtain a license from the secretary of Agriculture and pay a 5% royalty on each

FIGURE 4. Rudolph Wendelin painting of Smokey Bear and family welcoming their new neighbors to the National Zoo in April 1972. The giant pandas Ling-Ling and Hsing-Hsing quickly eclipsed Smokey as the zoo's most popular attraction. Courtesy of Smithsonian Institution Archives.

item's wholesale price. Only products deemed in "good taste" and conveying a forest fire prevention message won approval. Unauthorized use of the character or name "Smokey Bear" would expose the offender to a fine not to exceed $250 or imprisonment not to exceed six months or both.[36]

Over time, the Smokey icon merged in American culture with efforts to prevent human-caused wildfires *and* to promote healthy forests as sources of water, recreation, timber, and wildlife. It also succeeded because the anthropomorphized bear resonated with children as well as adults. Ads for the Forest Service's Junior Forest Ranger program were pitched at kids in the hope that they would then press Smokey's message on their parents. That decision proved to be an advertising gold mine when, in 1950, firefighters found an injured black bear cub gripping the charred remains of a tree in the aftermath of the Capitan Gap Fire in New Mexico. State officials nursed the orphaned cub back to health, christened him Smokey, and relocated him to the Smithsonian's National Zoological Park in Washington, D.C. Ad Council and Forest Service officials realized that the real bear cub with its sympathetic backstory provided the advertising campaign with a ready-made creation myth for its cartoon bear. Newspapers from coast to coast snapped up the story, illustrating it with endearing photographs of the bandaged cub.[37]

Next, the admen commissioned a jingle to heighten the appeal of radio and television spots, choosing in 1952 "Smokey the Bear," a song cowritten by Steve

Nelson and Jack Rollins, authors of such holiday compositions as "Here Comes Peter Cottontail" and "Frosty the Snowman." The song's soaring popularity lent added fame to both the living and animated Smokey. At the Smithsonian's zoo, Smokey's abode became the facility's most visited animal display. Meanwhile, kids from around the country penned so many letters to Smokey that, in April 1964, the U.S. Postal Service assigned him his own ZIP code, 20252.[38]

To keep the hype rolling, Smithsonian and Forest Service publicists announced in September 1962 that the 12-year-old Smokey would be "married" to an 18-month-old black bear named Goldie, who was flown in from New Mexico to be his mate. Like Smokey, Goldie (later known as "Mrs. Smokey") had been orphaned at a young age; a logger in the Cibola National Forest near the town of Magdalena found her in August 1961.[39] Smokey and Goldie failed to produce offspring, leading Smithsonian and Forest Service officials to arrange for the ursine couple to "adopt" Little Smokey, another rescued black bear cub from New Mexico's Lincoln National Forest, in 1971. Of course, like all living creatures, Smokey slowed down with age. When the Forest Service and zoo cohosted a gala retirement ceremony in May 1975 for the graying bear, radio star Jackson Weaver, the longtime broadcast "voice" of Smokey, served as master of ceremonies. Although the Smithsonian proposed returning the two elderly bears to New Mexico, Congress refused to fund the project, so Smokey and Goldie remained in Washington, where they were moved to low-key quarters, allowing their more prominent accommodations to be occupied by Little Smokey, who was rechristened Smokey Bear II.[40]

The original Smokey died of old age in November 1976, and the zoo, Forest Service, and Ad Council saturated the media with a carefully worded news release, resulting in obituaries in hundreds of newspapers across the country.[41] The symbolic character, though, lives on. Indeed, the animated Smokey has yet to cease delivering his forest fire prevention message. For the Ad Council, the Smokey Bear project provided a model for subsequent environmentally oriented public service advertisement campaigns, especially in a character that appealed across generations and communities. In the short term, children might sway their parents' actions, whereas in the long run the values and awareness absorbed by young people might carry forth into adulthood. The forest fire prevention campaign had also demonstrated the expediency of combining advertising and voluntarism, especially when the goal is to encourage behavioral change for the public good via individual self-policing and self-regulation.[42]

CHAPTER 2

KEEP AMERICA BEAUTIFUL

The Advertising Council's volunteer-based operational structure and its emphasis on first-class public service announcements proved an effective model, building on the continuing support of the advertising industry and a steady influx of fresh talent. In general, the admen who bristled with creativity tended to be young, whereas the industry's managerial leaders were seasoned veterans attuned to their profession's long-term goals and political connections. Together, the two talent pools ensured that the council's campaigns mirrored changes in American culture and social values while remaining sensitive to evolving media techniques and consumer patterns.

The evolution of the council's Keep America Beautiful campaign exemplified how, over the course of two decades, advertising professionals responded to society's maturing environmental awareness. Post–World War II economic prosperity had intensified public concerns about quality of life. Concurrent with the baby boom population spike, there was an explosive growth in automobile ownership and use and a proliferation of consumer packaging and single-use products (epitomized by disposable diapers, paper towels, nonreturnable cans and bottles, and the ubiquitous plastic wrappings enveloping food, gum, cosmetics, and tobacco products), all of which contributed to an unprecedented rise in municipal trash and roadside litter, along with swelling numbers of complaints to local governments. Political divisions exacerbated the debate over solutions. Conservative critics blamed the problem on individual thoughtlessness, lack of public education, and declining social mores; liberal commentators pointed to inadequate provision of public trash receptacles and the staunch opposition of major canning and bottling companies to regulations requiring container deposits, reuse, and recycling.[1]

Seeking to avoid government intervention, corporations and industry groups representing canning, bottling, and packaging manufacturers—together with large businesses using and selling those products—formed the advocacy group Keep America Beautiful (KAB) in 1953. As a national nonprofit organization underwritten by an interrelated set of industries, KAB sought to shift public attention away from the production of "wasteful" packaging and toward littering, that is, to shape the perception of the discarded trash problem as being caused by individual behavior, not industry practice. As Ad Council vice president George Ludlam explained, KAB was "financed in large part by glass, tin and paper container manufacturers who are aware that thoughtless disposal of their products is one of the most obvious causes of the Nation's litter problem."[2] Keep America Beautiful's focus on improving the aesthetics of public corridors in communities across the country (their streets and sidewalks, parks and playgrounds, parking lots and theaters) was highly appealing. Tidiness, if not cleanliness, tapped into the nation's sense of self-worth. So, too, did the focus on personal responsibility, which helped KAB expand its sponsorship base beyond business and industry, eventually to include labor unions, trade associations, government agencies, and professional groups.[3]

Keep America Beautiful gained broad public visibility thanks to the Ad Council's clever anti-littering campaign. As it turned out, the council and KAB had much in common, from their creation by leading business interests to their cardinal philosophy of advancing social improvement through inspiring behavioral changes in individuals. The two organizations even shared several corporate sponsors. Keep America Beautiful's 1960 petition for the development of an anti-littering advertising campaign had proved irresistible to the Ad Council. With a nod to the Smokey Bear ads, the council observed that "it isn't fire alone that can waste and destroy natural beauty," which is why it was working "to persuade Americans not to litter our cities and countryside with trash."[4] The advertising packet distributed to media outlets in June 1962 highlighted the campaign slogan "Every Litter Bit Hurts," adding that "working together we can help keep America beautiful."[5]

The 1961 television spot "It Happens in the Best of Places" became one of the KAB campaign's most memorable ads. As the Museum of Television & Radio described it, "With the Statue of Liberty looking on, Susan Spotless, on an outing with her family to Liberty Island, reminds her dad, after he drops a paper

FIGURE 5. Public affairs officials at the Bureau of Land Management used the fictional character Johnny Horizon to promote voluntary stewardship of public lands. Courtesy of Department of the Interior.

wrapper, not to litter because keeping America beautiful is a family affair. After he picks up his wrapper and drops it in a basket she sings the famous 'Please, don't be a litter bug.'"[6] The 18-minute anti-littering film *Heritage of Splendor* reinforced the message. Produced in 1963 by the Richfield Oil Corporation for KAB, the film—narrated by actor (and future politician) Ronald Reagan—extoled the majesty of America's landscapes and stressed the obligation of individuals to handle their trash responsibly.[7]

Keep America Beautiful and the Ad Council were not alone in developing anti-littering public service announcements, especially after the passage of the Highway Beautification Act of 1965, which had benefited from Lady Bird Johnson's passionate promotion.[8] When Boyd L. Rasmussen became director of the Bureau of Land Management in 1966, following a 31-year career with the USDA Forest Service, he sought to cultivate greater environmental responsibility within the agency. Attuned to the goodwill that Smokey Bear had generated for the Forest Service, he pressed the bureau to build support for the agency's public lands stewardship mission by creating its own symbol. The result was another appealing fictional character, the square-jawed cowboy mascot Johnny Horizon, whose anti-littering campaign—epitomized by the message "It's your land, it's my land—Keep it clean!"—was introduced in 1968. Burl Ives became the volunteer spokesperson for the Johnny Horizon campaign, which was endorsed by a host of other celebrities, including Johnny

FIGURE 6. The U.S. Forest Service began using the pollution-fighting mascot Woodsy Owl in 1971. Courtesy of Forest History Society, Betty Conrad Hite Papers.

Cash, Arthur Godfrey, Eddie Albert, Dinah Shore, Johnny Carson, and Captain Kangaroo.[9] With his eye on the nation's upcoming bicentennial celebration in 1976, President Gerald Ford proclaimed the period 15 September through 15 October 1974 as Johnny Horizon '76 Clean Up America Month, an action he used to encourage organizations and private citizens to work together to promote environmental awareness and beautify America for the yearlong events.[10]

At the time of the first Earth Day, the Forest Service had been loath to dilute Smokey Bear's focus on forest fire prevention. So in September 1971, it unveiled another anthropomorphized mascot, the pollution-fighting Woodsy Owl, who enjoined everyone to "Give a Hoot—Don't Pollute!" Like the era's public service announcements for KAB and Johnny Horizon, the Woodsy Owl ads invited volunteers to help clean up the countryside.[11]

FIGURE 7. Forest Service illustrator Rudolph Wendelin emphasized the complementary messages of the agency's two advertising icons. Courtesy of Forest History Society, Rudy Wendelin Papers.

From the beginning, KAB encouraged Americans to leave environmental politics and policy decisions to elected officials, government agencies, and the affected industries. The Ad Council's anti-litter advertisements bolstered this conservative goal by focusing on the visual and the aesthetic and by fingering users of disposable items rather than producers and marketers of throwaway packaging. *Waste* per se remained unaddressed, thereby relegating it to out of sight, out of mind. Realizing that approach ran counter to growing environmental concerns in many parts of the country, the advertising team eventually convinced KAB of the advantages of morphing the anti-litter campaign into a broader antipollution campaign. Robert Keim recalled in his memoir of his 21-year tenure heading the Advertising Council, "When I came aboard as president in 1966 one of the campaigns I inherited was an anti-littering effort for Keep America Beautiful (KAB). It featured what I considered an obnoxious brat, a little girl called Suzy Spotless who skipped down the street lisping the jingle, 'Don't be, don't be a litterbug'. She was either throwing paper litter around or picking it up, I don't remember. Anyway I hated it." Aside from the campaign being "an embarrassment," Keim said, "the press had started to circle the wagons saying the campaign was a dodge by industry to cover up its pollution sins."[12]

Recognizing that the campaign's fixation on the reduction of roadside litter was too narrow and self-serving in light of the nation's environmental crisis, the Ad Council turned to a new volunteer advertising agency, Marsteller, Inc., charging it with the task of broadening the campaign into an antipollution effort, one that implicated not just individuals, but society as a whole—business, industry, and government alike.[13]

THE CRYING INDIAN
AND THE HELP FIGHT POLLUTION CAMPAIGN

In October 1969, the Ad Council's Public Policy Committee advised holding the Keep America Beautiful campaign "in abeyance until the staff can explore the possibility of expanding it to include the total environment." Committee members reasoned that "in the light of the [worldwide] environmental crisis we must get beyond litter." The majority supported revising the campaign's goals, although skeptics cautioned that the public service announcements should remain "personally meaningful." The admen did not question the scale and complexity of the environmental challenges; instead, they believed that "people will be more concerned if it involved them as individuals." The committee's minutes recorded a strong "view that our country needs the ability of each person to identify with this problem. Not littering the highway will help the larger problem."[14]

Progress proved halting, given KAB's initial hesitancy to shift the advertising focus from littering to pollution. At its September 1970 meeting, the Public Policy Committee reiterated its skepticism, this time recommending that the initiative be suspended altogether, "pending a broadening of objectives." Believing that the campaign needed to expand "to an overall environmental pollution effort," committee members were pleased by KAB's eventual willingness to incorporate the concerns of ecology. To advance that effort, the committee suggested developing a booklet on "100 Things You Can Do to Stop Pollution."[15]

The Ad Council and KAB settled the matter in 1971, agreeing to refashion the initiative into the Help Fight Pollution campaign.[16] The council's quarterly *Magazine Service Bulletin* described environmental pollution as "a threat to everyone" and a subject of personal responsibility, thus the theme "People start pollution. People can stop it."[17] An ad in the bulletin titled "Pollution Can Be Taxing" implied that opposition to pollution-reduction measures often hinged on counterproductive resistances to pay for remedies like sanitary landfills, sewage treatment plants, and modern recycling facilities. Citizens, the ad declared, should "recognize that it costs money to fight pollution."[18]

Coming from the Ad Council, these were bold words. Yet their impact on the council's products was minimal. Instead of addressing the actions of organizations, businesses, corporations, or government agencies, the council's updated campaign remained focused on individuals, encouraging citizens to combat the scourge of pollution through their own independent efforts. The campaign's most potent image became the "Crying Indian," portrayed by actor Iron Eyes Cody, who dressed in stylized Chippewa apparel—beaded moccasins, fringed leather pants and jacket, and a braided wig—and delivered the emotional tagline "Pollution: It's a Crying Shame." Released in April 1971 for the first anniversary of Earth Day, the public service ads struck a responsive chord with the American public and won two Clio Awards from the advertising industry. The Ad Council soon boasted that "Chief Iron Eyes Cody sheds a tear for America's deteriorating environment."[19] The Help Fight Pollution campaign included a parallel set of public service ads titled "Daddy, what did you do in the war against pollution?" that drew on the general context of the Vietnam War and exemplified the emphasis on individual voluntary actions. A magazine ad featuring a photograph of a young, ponytailed girl read,

> Of course you can always try to change the subject.
>
> But one answer you can't give is that you weren't in it. Because in this war, there are no 4F's and no conscientious objectors. No deferments for married men or teen-agers. And no exemptions for women.
>
> So like it or not, we're all in this one. But as the war heats up, millions of us stay coolly uninvolved. We have lots of alibis:
>
> What can one person do?
>
> It's up to "them" to do something about pollution—not me.
>
> Besides, average people don't pollute. It's the corporations, institutions and municipalities.
>
> The fact is that companies and governments are made up of people. It's people who make decisions and do things that foul up our water, land and air. And that goes for businessmen, government officials, housewives or homeowners.

What can one person do for the cause? Lots of things—maybe more than you think. Like cleaning your spark plugs every 1000 miles, using detergents in the recommended amounts, by upgrading incinerators to reduce smoke emissions, by proposing and supporting better waste treatment plants in your town. Yes, and throwing litter in a basket instead of in the street.

Above all, let's stop shifting the blame. People start pollution. People can stop it. When enough Americans realize this we'll have a fighting chance in the war against pollution.[20]

The council's spring 1972 magazine ads pursued a similar approach, with dramatic close-ups of Iron Eyes Cody's face, a tear rolling down his right cheek. The version titled "The Environment: An American Tragedy" commented, "But it's not too late to do something about it. Something as simple as acquainting yourself with local anti-pollution ordinances and abiding by them will help." A sister ad, "Pollution: It's a Crying Shame," also suggested that there were actions readers could take, "something as simple as attending local community meetings and inquiring about pollution control plans can be a big help."[21] The council released a second set of magazine ads that summer. "Clean Water: An American Dream" showed the bow of a canoe gliding through serene waters, with a tagline declaring "Our rivers don't have to lose the fight with pollution. Not if we all help." An image of discarded trash surrounding Iron Eyes Cody's feet drove home the message of an accompanying ad that insisted that litter would not be "an American symbol" if people became "concerned enough to do something about it. Like carrying litterbags in cars. Or placing trash in receptacles. Or cleaning up after picnics."[22] The moral of the ads was simple: the solution to pollution rested with individual voluntary actions, not government intervention.

This theme continued throughout the KAB campaign. The March 1975 television spot opened with a long-distance view of a person riding through a scenic forest. As the camera zoomed in on Iron Eyes Cody, the announcer stated that "the first American people loved the land. They held it in simple reverence." The scene then shifted to horse and rider following paths lushly framed with evergreens and on gorgeous trails near still waters: "This is South Coast Botanic Garden in

FIGURE 8. Poster featuring Iron Eyes Cody, from the Ad Council's Keep America Beautiful campaign. Courtesy of Ad Council Archives, University of Illinois Archives, record series 13/2/203, box 1.

California," the announcer explained. "Once this was a dumping ground for trash and litter. Community volunteers cleaned, planted and reclaimed it. And there the land is good again." When, in the next scene, horse and rider meandered through landscapes littered with trash, the viewers were reminded of "how far we still have to go . . . everyone must get involved. Now." The ad concluded with the money shot: a close-up of Iron Eyes Cody, a tear falling from his eye. The emotional power of that image was embellished with dramatic music and the announcer's final words: "People start pollution. People can stop it."[23]

Print and broadcast ads for the Help Fight Pollution campaign ran through the early 1980s. By then, the campaign had acquired an eminent endorsement, one proudly highlighted in the Ad Council's 1980–1981 annual report: a photograph

FIGURE 9. President Reagan meeting with Iron Eyes Cody in the Oval Office on 28 July 1981. Courtesy of Reagan Presidential Library.

of Iron Eyes Cody embracing President Ronald Reagan in the Oval Office. The caption read,

> President Reagan renews his ties with The Pollution Campaign during a meeting in the Oval Office with Iron Eyes Cody, the "Crying Indian" in the Ad Council's public service advertising, and Keep America Beautiful president Roger W. Powers. President Reagan's early involvement with KAB was as narrator of the film, "Heritage of Splendor," filmed in the early 1960s. His affiliation with Iron Eyes Cody goes back even further; the two appeared in three Western movies together. More recently Iron Eyes rode in the President's Inauguration Parade.[24]

FIGURE 10. Magazine advertisement from the Ad Council's Environmental Defense Fund campaign. Courtesy of Ad Council Archives, University of Illinois Archives, record series 13/2/215.

The Help Fight Pollution campaign reflected the Ad Council's efforts to address a range of environmental challenges during the 1970s, from forest fire safety to pollution reduction to energy conservation, with each campaign emphasizing the role of voluntary work by individuals, not corporate or governmental actions. When Robert Keim retired as Ad Council president in

1987, he sent an open letter to his successor, Ruth Wooden. The "indelible lesson," he advised, was that "doing good was not enough. You have to make people feel good about their doing good and you have to do it consistently and tastefully and often, if you're going to go the distance. And for supporters and volunteers to feel good about doing good you have to let it be known that something positive has happened as a result of their labors, contributions or endorsements, and that results have been achieved."[25]

CHAPTER 3

VOLUNTARISM IN AMERICAN HISTORY AND CULTURE

The Advertising Council's public service campaigns have always contained powerful subtexts about voluntarism—the willingness of ordinary people to donate time, labor, and/or material goods to advance a collective activity or social purpose. The notion of volunteering for civic activities, although not original or unique to the United States, has flourished so readily and in such profuse and varied ways that it is often considered a signature characteristic of American society. The traditions and assumptions, in fact, long predated the establishment of the country. Native Americans had thrived and survived for centuries through mutual alliances and support. The continent's early European settler-colonists cooperated among themselves in clearing land, planting crops, and erecting buildings. By the mid-eighteenth century, towns across the colonies had formed voluntary groups to provide an array of social welfare services supplementing those of government. British America's first volunteer fire department appeared in 1736 when Benjamin Franklin cofounded the Union Fire Company in Philadelphia.[1] Civilian volunteers supported the Revolutionary War by raising funds, organizing boycotts of British imports, and recruiting unpaid militia for the battlefield. In the 1830s, French diplomat and political scientist Alexis de Tocqueville marveled at the tendency of the new nation's citizens to form voluntary associations to solve problems and reinforce their shared values. As he declared in his groundbreaking book, *Democracy in America*, "In no country in the world has the principle of association been more successfully used or applied to a greater multitude of objects than in America."[2]

Voluntary organizations proliferated during the late nineteenth and early twentieth centuries, as exemplified by the establishment of the Red Cross, Young Men's Christian Association (YMCA), Young Women's Christian Association (YWCA), Volunteers of America, American Public Health Association, National Tuberculosis Association, National Society for the Prevention of Blindness, Goodwill Industries, Planned Parenthood, and scores of others.[3] Scouting for both girls and boys came to involve thousands of volunteers across the country.[4] Explaining why the Boy Scouts of America blossomed into one of the nation's largest volunteer-oriented organizations, historian Benjamin René Jordan found that more than 99% of adults overseeing the hundreds of scout troops during the 1910s and 1920s "remained unpaid volunteers, which made the organization cost efficient to run."[5]

Having succeeded in coupling voluntarism to patriotism during World War I, the federal government sought to strengthen that linkage during World War II. Millions of women were enlisted as unpaid workers, donating their time and labor to the Red Cross, United Service Organizations (USO), Office of Civilian Defense, and other groups. They volunteered as nurses, collected blood and plasma donations, arranged social events for service members, and acted as air-raid wardens. They assisted with the cultivation of some 18 million victory gardens from coast to coast and—through the U.S. Department of Agriculture— joined the Women's Land Army to work on farms, which were in desperate need of labor to make up for the men siphoned in military service.[6]

The volunteer spirit remained fervent after the war, with donation of time and effort rewarded socially, perceived as an admirable expenditure of leisure time, especially for women who were not employed outside the home. Commentators drawn to defining the American character often pointed to the strong current of voluntarism.[7] Nonprofit organizations increasingly relied on volunteers, primarily to reduce their expenses and secondarily to cultivate potential financial donors. The Census Bureau's 1974 survey of volunteers in the United States revealed "one out of four Americans over the age of 13 does some form of volunteer work" and that "a hallmark of American voluntarism is that all strata of economic, educational and social levels contribute their share."[8]

The contours of American voluntarism have varied over time, as have the types of volunteer organizations, each of which reflected the values and circumstances of its associated community. The roles played by individual volunteers have been correspondingly diverse, engaging people from all walks of life, all income levels, and all backgrounds, and incorporated into the agendas of all religious organizations from the national to local level. Given voluntarism's broad appeal and its entrenched place in American society, no cause or partisan faction has been able to resist tapping into the impulse, converting "community service" into a tool for achieving a political goal.[9]

VOLUNTARISM AND SCIENCE

Voluntarism has also played an important role in the advancement of science. In the United States, the contributions of volunteers working under the direction of professional scientists has proven especially valuable in areas heavily dependent upon extensive observations and monitoring, such as archaeology, astronomy, and natural history. The Smithsonian Institution built on the volunteer spirit from its earliest years, engaging in outreach as a way to implement founder James Smithson's bequest to further "the increase and diffusion of knowledge."[10] A year after the institution's establishment in 1846, its first head, the physicist Joseph Henry, launched an ambitious weather-monitoring initiative, the Smithsonian Meteorological Project. To assist with this large-scale undertaking, Henry recruited scores of volunteer observers, providing them with calibrated instruments and standardized blank forms to be filled out monthly. By 1860, the number of observers around the United States had grown to more than 600. The Civil War disrupted the Smithsonian's weather-monitoring efforts, which continued in a diminished fashion through 1870, when Congress transferred responsibility for taking meteorological observations to the U.S. Army Signal Corps. Like the Smithsonian, the Signal Corps relied heavily on volunteer observers. In 1890, the monitoring responsibility shifted to the newly established—and more robustly funded—U.S. Weather Bureau within the Department of Agriculture.[11]

The Smithsonian's use of volunteers has continued, with individuals donating their time and talent to assist in myriad activities—from acquiring objects and specimens for the permanent collections to translating texts to interacting directly with the public as information providers, docents, and educators. During the Cold War, Operation Moonwatch assembled an international network of thousands of amateur sky watchers to track artificial Earth satellites.[12] The Friends of the National Zoo (FONZ) was founded in 1958 to raise private funds for the Smithsonian's zoological park. Within a few years, FONZ had expanded its charge by recruiting volunteers. In 1965, zoo director Theodore Reed celebrated the dedicated FONZ assistants, who ranged from high school students to retirees, for having received "nothing in return" for their contributions "other than the satisfaction of having performed a public service."[13] By the early 1970s, hundreds of zoo volunteers were logging thousands of hours of service each year, including as animal observers in the zoo's popular "Preg Watch" program.[14] Throughout the Smithsonian, volunteers eventually came to outnumber paid staff within the institution's museums and research centers.

As many similar organizations have recognized, voluntarism allows people to contribute to causes near and dear to their hearts, regardless of their financial resources. The National Audubon Society, for example, inaugurated its Christmas bird count in 1900, and annual counts (which are undertaken by tens of thousands of amateur birdwatchers) continue to this day, generating valuable long-term data sets for ornithologists. With the maturation of ecology in the late twentieth century, volunteer observers assumed increasingly important roles in other large-scale monitoring projects, leading public policy analysts to begin to label these volunteer participants "citizen scientists."[15]

For environmental conservation, park philanthropy gained increased currency during the twentieth century, most famously publicized through the support of Laurance Rockefeller and other wealthy donors, but also through more modest private philanthropy.[16] Private donations began supplementing the National Park Service's congressional appropriations from the first decades of the agency's founding in 1916. The Park Service's first director, Stephen Mather, used his own money to purchase buildings, equipment, and tools and even subsidized the salaries of his assistant, Horace Albright, and other administrative staff members.[17] Individuals and groups formed conservancies to acquire, manage, preserve, and (sometimes) deed to government agencies land for public enjoyment. The Nature Conservancy developed the largest portfolio, but legions of smaller, more tightly focused conservancies sprouted up across the country.[18] Urban dwellers also became engaged in preserving and caring for local green spaces. During the 1980s, for example, individual donors underwrote the establishment of the Central Park Conservancy in Manhattan. This nonprofit organization worked to maintain and improve the high-visibility, internationally significant park. A decade later, the Friends of the Hudson River Park organized as a nonprofit entity dedicated to expanding Manhattan's second-largest park, Diller Island.[19]

By the time it merged with the Bureau of Fisheries in 1940 to form the U.S. Fish and Wildlife Service, the Bureau of Biological Survey had accrued a successful record of using volunteers in the collection and organization of data on North American birds. In his history of the bureau's work during the 1920s and 1930s, Etienne Benson found that information "from thousands of volunteers banding millions of birds helped ornithologists map migratory flyways and census bird populations on a continual scale."[20]

The diverse and profuse contributions of volunteers to the scientific enterprise and natural resources conservation are but a small reflection of the incalculable types of assistance volunteers have rendered to virtually all sectors of society. Not every circumstance, however, proceeded smoothly. Given the complexity of motivations for (and benefits of) volunteering and the fact that volunteers decide to work on their own volition and often come to volunteer activities with strong opinions, contradictory objectives have occasionally led to conflict among voluntary organizations.[21]

VOLUNTARISM AND PUBLIC LANDS STEWARDSHIP

When he was secretary of the Interior Department during the Kennedy administration, Stewart Udall pointed to the indispensable assistance of volunteer organizations in preserving and caring for public lands. From its establishment in 1936, one of the nation's largest conservation organizations, the National Wildlife Federation, had played a significant role in this effort, joined by groups like the Sierra Club, Garden Club of America, Resources for the Future, Desert Protective Council, and Conservation Foundation.[22] By purchasing land, advancing research and education, or planting trees, Udall wrote in 1963, the groups "have broadened our understanding of the American earth, and together they can form a rising chorus for the conservation cause."[23] Later, as President Lyndon Johnson's secretary of the Interior, Udall worked with Lady Bird Johnson on various environmental initiatives, including those that encouraged voluntary neighborhood beautification projects.[24]

Another source of human effort and generosity came from the hiking clubs that grew in number and popularity between the 1860s and 1940s. Club members built and maintained trails, erected and repaired camps and shelters, and advocated for land protection. During the early twentieth century, volunteers constructed hundreds of miles of trails in New Hampshire's White Mountains, opening the remote, rugged New England terrain to recreational hikers.[25] Beginning in the 1920s, the hiking community embarked on an even more ambitious project, the Appalachian Trail, which, when completed in 1937, stretched more than 2,180 miles from Maine's Mount Katahdin to Georgia's Springer Mountain. Beyond building and maintaining the trail, volunteers have through the years erected shelters, published maps and guidebooks, and worked with adjoining landowners to ensure ongoing permission to cross their properties. The National Trails System Act of 1968 placed the Appalachian Trail within the National Park Service, but the agency continues to rely on volunteers in the complicated land acquisition process, as well as for trail maintenance and monitoring.[26]

As the number of conservation organizations increased in tandem with the rising popularity of outdoor recreation in postwar America, so did the need for volunteers. At the end of World War II, the Fish and Wildlife Service listed 56 nongovernmental wildlife organizations; by the mid-1970s, the total exceeded 300.[27] Such growth had been fueled by the political energy surrounding the first Earth Day in April 1970, one of the largest demonstrations of any type in U.S. history and an event that sprang from the grassroots involvement of tens of thousands of volunteers across the country.[28] In the months that followed, memberships of environmental organizations soared, and many groups turned to public service advertising to recruit new members, reinforce the loyalty of existing members, and frame the political debate on environmental matters. A decade later, environmental organizations expanded yet again in response to the election of Ronald Reagan, who was perceived as opposing many of their key tenets.[29]

Although less centered on political activism, public lands stewardship also tapped into the nation's spirit of voluntarism. In 2014, Randall Wilson noted that in a country "more committed to commercial enterprise than any other in the world," one that holds private property among its "most cherished national values," Americans had chosen to set aside nearly a third of its total acreage for public ownership.[30] With such vast holdings and the burgeoning appeal of outdoor recreation in the decades after World War II, the National Park Service

FIGURE 11. Lady Bird Johnson (left), National Park Service Director George Hartzog (center), and secretary of the Interior Stewart Udall (right) lead a hiking party on Big Bend National Park's Lost Mine Trail in April 1966. Courtesy of U.S. National Park Service.

(NPS) faced a monumental task of caring for the lands and resources under its charge.[31] When Elizabeth Cushman wrote her 1955 Vassar College senior thesis on the merits of developing a student conservation corps to recruit high school and college volunteers to aid the NPS during the summer months, her teachers, family, and friends encouraged her to pursue her idea after graduation. She did, wasting little time in securing financial support from the Garden Club of America and the National Parks Association. In 1957, Cushman convinced the

FIGURE 12. Volunteer laborers from St. Paul Lutheran Church in Fullerton, California, working on Kings Canyon National Park's Grant Tree Trail in June 1974. Courtesy of U.S. National Park Service.

NPS to authorize demonstration projects in Olympic and Grand Teton national parks for what she called the Student Conservation Program. Under Park Service supervision, the student volunteers assisted with trail maintenance, building and renovating hiking shelters, and visitor information and interpretive services. The program proved an immediate success, and other park units soon opened their arms to the summer volunteers. In 1964, the program incorporated itself as the nonprofit, tax-exempt Student Conservation Association, which continues to this day to bring volunteers into the parks and to provide a model for other national youth conservation groups.[32]

Student volunteers were helpful, but their seasonal labors and limited dispersal were no match for NPS's towering needs, which continued to outpace the agency's federal appropriations. In 1967, when Park Service Director George Hartzog asked his special assistant, Ronald Lee, to assess the situation, Lee responded that "of all the conservation and management problems facing the National Park System . . . balancing the claims of rapidly mounting public use and the requirements of preservation is probably the most pervasive and difficult."[33] Two years later, following Hartzog's recommendation, Interior secretary Walter J. Hickel requested congressional authorization for an expanded, NPS-administered volunteer program. "Volunteer work is a traditional and basic value of American life"

FIGURE 13. Citizen science volunteers studying frogs in Mount Rainier National Park in August 2018. Courtesy of National Park Service.

and needed, he said, for assistance "in interpreting the parks and providing other visitor services." Hickel assured Congress that the Park Service would be able to recruit teachers, conservationists, naturalists, historians, and outdoor enthusiasts to donate their time and expertise toward jobs that would complement—and not "diminish"—the tasks of the agency's paid, career employees.[34]

Congress agreed, sanctioning the Park Service to develop its own Volunteers in Parks (VIP) program to supplement Cushman's privately run Student Conservation Program.[35] The new NPS initiative allowed the agency to accept and utilize a much larger and more experienced corps of volunteers. The program began experimentally in Washington, D.C., during fall 1970, before spreading out to other parts of the country. At remote parks and monuments, VIP participants undertook assigned tasks in exchange for temporary room and board. The program grew increasingly important after 1981, when a series of budget cuts forced a steady decline in park employees.[36] Describing the work of VIP volunteers at Washington, D.C.'s most frequented memorials, park ranger Jason Cangelosi said, "Basically, they're a docent like you'd expect at a museum— someone to be there and greet visitors and give a little history and answer questions."[37] In her tribute to the national parks on the occasion of the Park Service's centennial, author and conservation activist Terry Tempest Williams acknowledged "the 200,000 volunteers nationwide who are giving their time and hearts to our national parks. They are largely seniors, veterans, and young people. Without them, our national parks could not function."[38]

From the very beginning, Hartzog had been careful to stress the significance of the VIP program to NPS's field directors, telling them that "many other bureaus have indicated an interest in the results of Volunteers in Parks, and the use you make of the program will affect not only the National Park Service, but other agencies and departments as well."[39] His advice proved prescient. Encouraged by the success of the Park Service's VIP program, Congress passed the Volunteers in the National Forest Act of 1972, which empowered the Forest Service to recruit and train volunteers to engage with such activities as campground management and archaeological digs. The popular summer-oriented program grew in size over the next two decades.[40] Noting that "budget and staffing cuts over the last decade have challenged the ability of professionals to meet recreation needs in a responsive way," the President's Commission on Americans Outdoors reported in 1987 that public lands agencies were increasingly turning to volunteers for needed assistance.[41] The U.S. Fish and Wildlife Service exemplified that trend. Having had long made use of citizen volunteers, it formalized its public-private initiatives under the Volunteer and Community Partnership Enhancement Act of 1998, further expanding them with the help of the National Wildlife Refuge Volunteer Improvement Act of 2010.[42]

VOLUNTARISM AND THE ADVERTISING COUNCIL

Such reservoirs of talent, good will, and government support were prime targets for Advertising Council public service campaigns, and the council excelled in channeling a similar spirit of donations of time, expertise, and labor by its members. A small salaried staff has guided operations, but the burden of campaign development and execution has always been shouldered by individuals, advertising agencies, businesses, media outlets, and celebrity spokespersons working pro bono. The council's board of directors consists of volunteer members drawn

FIGURE 14. Since its founding, the U.S. Fish and Wildlife Service has made extensive use of citizen science volunteers, such as this one collecting stream data at Pinnell Creek near Kodiak, Alaska. Courtesy of National Conservation Training Center, U.S. Fish and Wildlife Service.

from advertising firms, media (newspapers, magazines, radio, television), and the business community. Acknowledging the extent to which its public service advertising initiatives have relied upon the generosity of others, the council has often portrayed itself as the "Volunteer Agency," an emphasis that infused its public service advertising campaigns, which typically solicited involvement by individual citizens and community organizations.[43]

It was understandable, therefore, that the council's successful track record captured the attention of the Nixon administration when it sought to follow through on a 1968 campaign promise to develop a wide-ranging voluntary action program.[44] In 1969, the White House announced the establishment of the National Program for Voluntary Action, a low-cost federal program supported by the nonprofit National Center for Voluntary Action (NCVA), which was responsible for raising private funds and serving as a public clearinghouse. Nixon's staff asked the Ad Council to undertake a national advertising campaign promoting the new program as a public-private partnership designed to appeal to all Americans, "be they rich or poor, urban or rural, young or old, black or white."[45]

Many of the activities developed for the NCVA (later renamed ACTION), such as an annual volunteer awards gala and National Football League involvement, resurfaced in the Reagan administration's Take Pride in America initiative. The voluntary action campaign also represented a tightening of connections between the Ad Council and potential White House political goals.[46] As Susan Ellis and Katherine Campbell explained in their historical overview of volunteerism in the United States, "The Nixon administration launched the first peacetime effort to stimulate a major American volunteer force."[47] Six citizen service volunteer agencies, which together counted for more than 24,000 volunteers, came together to form ACTION. The groups included the Peace Corps, Volunteers in Service to America (VISTA), the Foster Grandparents Program, Retired and Senior Volunteer Program (RSVP), the Service Corps of Retired Executives (SCORE), and the Active Corps of Executives.[48]

The first national volunteer awards gala was held in February 1972 at the John F. Kennedy Center for the Performing Arts.[49] The advertising elements of the Voluntary Action campaign, with its tagline "We Need You," hit markets in late summer 1972, with different media phased in through 1973. In terms of broad public exposure, the campaign's big breakthrough came in January 1973, when televised public service announcements during the Super Bowl attracted more than 53 million viewers.[50] During football's regular season, the Voluntary Action television spots included 24 players from across the National Football League. For the championship game, which pitted the Miami Dolphins against the Washington Redskins, the public service announcements appearing during commercial breaks featured Washington players Jerry Smith and Brig Owens discussing volunteer service, followed by the voice-over plea "What we need, money can't buy. We need you."[51]

As a complement to the Voluntary Action campaign, Nixon issued two presidential proclamations on 20 April 1974, which together linked environmental stewardship and voluntarism. The first designated the week beginning on 21 April as "Earth Week, 1974," and the second designated the same period as "National Volunteer Week, 1974." To commemorate Earth Week, the president asked "that special attention be given to personal voluntary activities and educational efforts toward protecting and enhancing our life-giving environment."[52] The companion proclamation establishing National Volunteer Week declared that "the spirit of voluntarism, one of the hallmarks of American life, has rarely been stronger than it is today. It has been estimated that one out of every five Americans is contributing time and talent in some kind

FIGURE 15. The U.S. Postal Service's 1983 commemorative stamp honoring the Ad Council's Volunteer–Lend a Hand campaign. Courtesy of National Postal Museum, Smithsonian Institution.

of voluntary service," and it claimed that more than 90,000 people were then serving in ACTION-sponsored programs.[53]

Quite unexpectedly, the Ad Council's Voluntary Action campaign struck advertising gold in the wake of President Nixon's August 1974 resignation, when Barbra Streisand—one of many prominent figures included in the infamous Nixon White House "enemies" list[54]—agreed to serve as the campaign's celebrity spokesperson. Streisand drew on the continuing popularity of her rendition of "People" from the 1964 Broadway musical *Funny Girl* to produce several "People Who Need People" spots for the campaign. The high-visibility coverage continued in 1975, when the campaign succeeded in placing a television spot in association with Super Bowl IX, the most watched television event up to that time. The Ad Council had sent Volunteer TV packages to all stations in cities with NFL teams; at least 20 stations reported airing the public service announcements in the run up to the game.[55]

With the nation celebrating is bicentennial anniversary in 1976, volunteerism offered a safe and popular theme for activities. The Ad Council convened a National Congress on Volunteerism and Citizenship as "an opportunity for all Americans to have a voice in determining ways in which individuals and institutions can most effectively contribute to the solution of major social problems in the next decade and beyond," whether those problems concern jobs, housing, crime, education, racial conflict, health, or the environment.[56] At that stage, the NCVA was chaired by George Romney, former governor of Michigan (1963–1969) and secretary of Housing and Urban Development (1969–1973), who stressed the Republican Party's focus on individual rather than government action: "The volunteer side of our nation should not wait for government to initiate such cooperative action."[57]

For years, the Ad Council had maintained that the common thread running through all of its campaigns was "the promotion of independent volunteer actions to solve America's problems,"[58] and that message dovetailed with the new administration's goals, as Ronald Reagan took office in January 1981. Reagan wanted to harness the growing dissatisfaction with federal programs to promote private support of public causes, so in December 1981, the Ad Council's Public Policy Committee pitched just such an approach to the president's staff and the Association of Junior Leagues. Although the administration did not join forces with the Ad Council on that project, the discussions contained the seeds for what became the Take Pride in America campaign during Reagan's second term.[59]

CHAPTER 4

RONALD REAGAN'S ENVIRONMENTAL RECORD

Prior to Ronald Reagan's election in 1980, U.S. environmental policymaking tended to flow from bipartisan alliances.[1] Legislation signed into law by Presidents Johnson, Nixon, Ford, and Carter had reflected a consensus among concerned Democrats and Republicans about the need to decrease pollution, protect human health, and preserve natural resources, with minor quibbling over the administrative and regulatory strategies to achieve those goals. Reagan abandoned this approach. Striving to shrink the overall size of the federal government, accelerate the development of natural resources on public lands, and reduce regulation of business, his administration emphasized economic growth and the relaxation of health, safety, and environmental rules.[2]

Toward this end, Reagan sought to expand government reliance on market forces. Doing so, he contended, would meet more of society's needs without causing undue harm to the natural environment and public health. In the absence of public or congressional approval, however, this shift in federal priorities and direction provoked considerable controversy and political outrage. Reagan's aversion to direct confrontation with Congress led him to depend on administrative fiat rather than legislation. In addition to weakening the enforcement of federal regulations, he reorganized executive branch agencies, significantly trimmed or reallocated their budgets and personnel, and appointed like-minded loyalists to key positions throughout the bureaucracy. Resources for the Future analyst Paul Portney observed that "there is a price to pay for inattention to legislative change" because subsequent presidents could more easily reverse administrative policies.

"Fundamental change," he said, "is much more likely if an administration takes the time to work closely with Congress in redirecting policy," something the Reagan White House consistently avoided.[3] Instead, the president promoted his agenda through positive publicity, working the levers of public relations like a Hollywood agent.

CALIFORNIA DREAMING

To understand the anger that greeted President Reagan's environmental policies, it is useful to look back at his record as governor of California. Although his tenure in Sacramento, from 1967 to 1975, overlapped with the coming of age of the Golden State's environmental movement, he never championed the causes of conservation and environmental protection. Buoyed by the rejuvenating solitude of his spacious properties in the Santa Monica Mountains north of Los Angeles (during the 1950s and 1960s) and the Santa Ynez Mountains northwest of Santa Barbara (after 1974) and informed by his travels throughout the West, Reagan came to view the United States as containing a superabundance of land, beauty, and natural resources. His environmental perspectives were also tempered by his innate political values, values that paralleled those of prodevelopment factions in the West, which chafed at government restrictions yet demanded government assistance in gaining access to public resources. Nevertheless, as governor of a state renowned for the strength of its citizenry's environmental concerns, he charted a middle-of-the-road course, aided throughout his eight years in office by his proenvironmental secretary of Resources, Norman "Ike" Livermore Jr.[4]

Reagan was among a cohort of governors who were in office when the first big wave of federal environmental legislation took effect. But unlike Jimmy Carter, who led the state of Georgia from 1971 to 1975, Reagan did not initiate state environmental protection efforts. As long as he believed legislative proposals would not unduly burden the business sector, Reagan endorsed them. In this respect, his environmental policy approach resembled President Nixon's.[5] Reagan's gubernatorial record thus came to include breakthrough legislation associated with coastal zone protection and air and water pollution control. He signed into law the wide-ranging California Environmental Quality Act, whereas his fiscal conservatism and antagonism toward large federal projects led him to oppose the U.S. Army Corps of Engineers' massive Dos Rios Dam, which had been proposed for the middle fork of the scenic Eel River and which had ignited vigorous opposition from conservation organizations.[6]

When he vacated the governor's mansion in 1975, however, Reagan left behind the associations he had forged with various proenvironment advisors in Sacramento. Now casting his politically ambitious gaze away from the environmentalist-leaning West Coast toward the nation as a whole, Reagan's views on natural resources came to be increasingly influenced, as biographer Lou Cannon observes, by "prodevelopment friends in business and industry" who opposed in principle federal environmental regulations and preservation programs.[7]

Reagan's 1980 presidential campaign neither emphasized nor ignored environmental concerns. His platform stressed the goal of reducing the size of the federal government and taming the inflationary economy that had plagued the nation throughout Carter's presidency. Reagan promised to cut taxes, limit federal domestic spending, and increase military expenditures. He also pledged to lighten the regulatory burden placed upon business and to transfer appropriate federal responsibilities to state and local government, an approach that worked against prioritizing environmental values. To the extent that Reagan discussed natural resources and environmental policy at all during the campaign, he placed them within the framework of his pragmatic political goals, not as social or ethical imperatives.[8]

This marginalization of environmental concerns persisted throughout the presidential race, with neither the Carter nor the Reagan campaign emphasizing environmental policy. In the face of rampant inflation and soaring interest rates, Reagan made the economy his top priority and criticized his opponent for not following suit. Carter focused on personal qualities, stressing his own honesty and integrity and, by implication, casting doubts upon Reagan's trustworthiness. These campaign strategies, in fact, reflected leading polls, which consistently showed voters failing to list natural resources and the environment among their top 10 concerns.[9]

Hampered by tepid support among Democratic leaders, persistently high levels of unemployment and inflation, and the Iran hostage crisis, Carter suffered a landslide defeat. This defeat spurred Reagan to portray his decisive electoral victory as a mandate from the people, a ringing endorsement of his call for a thorough reorientation of public policy, which the new administration extended to environmental and natural resources decision-making.[10]

The 1980 election results stunned environmentalists. They were suddenly confronted with an administration hostile toward their core values. Political scientist Norman Vig has called Reagan "the first president to come to office with an avowedly anti-environmental agenda," one based on a belief that conservation was "fundamentally at odds with economic growth and prosperity."[11] Lewis Regenstein of the Fund for Animals quipped at the time that he felt as if he had "one foot in the grave and the other on a banana peel."[12] These concerns became reality during the first months of Reagan's presidency, as the White House announced its selections for the top environmental posts, moved to slash budgets and personnel at the Environmental Protection Agency (EPA), and gutted the Council on Environmental Quality. Environmental regulations across the board appeared threatened by the administration's drumbeat assertion that environmental protection and economic growth were incompatible.[13]

The White House pursued these goals by initially focusing on EPA and the Department of the Interior, even though authority to execute environmental policy also resides within such departments and independent agencies as the Tennessee Valley Authority, Army Corps of Engineers, Department of Agriculture, Department of Commerce, and Department of Energy. The Interior Department, created in 1849, has served as the central player in the management of the nation's natural resources, accumulating through the years a complex patchwork of duties and constituencies. Some of these responsibilities were preservationist in orientation, whereas others were developmental, resulting in internal bureaucratic tensions and competing public expectations. By 1981, the department's preservationist side encompassed the National Park Service, Fish and Wildlife Service, and Wilderness Area activities, whereas the developmental side included the Bureau of Reclamation, Bureau of Mines, and Bureau of Land Management.[14]

The nomination of James G. Watt as secretary of the Interior buttressed Reagan's standing within the right wing of the Republican Party, especially with those in the West. The 43-year-old Watt had been born and raised in Wyoming and earned both bachelor's (1960) and juris doctor (1962) degrees from the University of Wyoming, before joining the staff of Senator Milward Lee Simpson (R-WY). From 1966 to 1969, he worked as a lobbyist for the U.S. Chamber of Commerce, opposing clean air and water legislation, until appointed by President

Nixon as deputy assistant secretary of Water and Power in the Department of the Interior. After three years in that post, he moved up the agency's hierarchy to head the Bureau of Outdoor Recreation. President Ford appointed him to the Federal Power Commission in 1975, where he served for two years. In 1977, Watt became the first president and chief legal officer of the Mountain States Legal Foundation. That ultraconservative organization, founded and financially supported by beer magnate Joseph Coors, specialized in litigation challenging federal programs designed to conserve natural resources on public lands.[15]

Later, as Reagan's Interior secretary, Watt brazenly advanced elements of the president's proindustry, anti-regulation political agenda. His high-profile, confrontational style and his often-extreme official actions generated media coverage and the ire of environmentalists. As a personality, he proved easy to ridicule, dislike, and even despise, and he came to symbolize the administration's environmental insensitivity. Watt cultivated his bad-boy, in-your-face persona. As a self-designated lightning rod for the White House, he kept environmental criticism from directly striking Reagan, a strategy that seemed to work during the new administration's opening months.[16]

Rather than pursuing a time-consuming legislative approach as Interior secretary, Watt worked internally, appointing trusted abettors to key administrative positions, realigning strategic priorities, and reprogramming the agency's budget to shape policy. When describing his emphasis on embedding like-minded civil servants within the department, he explained, "I will build an institutional memory that will be here for decades."[17]

Reagan had entered office determined to give his cabinet secretaries a prominent voice in governing the nation, and he pursued that intent by establishing a system of cabinet councils. Questions of energy, environment, and natural resources fell under the Cabinet Council on Natural Resources and Environment, whose chairman pro tempore was the secretary of the Interior.[18] Heading this executive group expanded Watt's influence, allowing him to cast his shadow over other agencies like EPA, the Department of Energy, and the Department of Agriculture.[19]

Watt's first bundle of policy directives in spring 1981 triggered an avalanche of protests. Conservationists were particularly galled by the Interior secretary's moratorium on new land acquisitions for the national parks, his push to open more federal land to mining and logging, his program to increase offshore oil and gas leases, and his proposal to transfer strip-mining regulations to the states. These actions represented just the tip of the iceberg, for Watt went on to block the listing of new endangered species, promote the acceleration of oil and gas leasing in Alaska, reorient the Land and Water Conservation Fund, and oppose the creation of urban national parks. He replaced the Carter era directors of every agency within Interior except for one: the National Park Service. There he left in place Russell Dickenson, a career parks administrator selected in 1980 by Interior secretary Cecil Andrus. During Watt's confirmation hearing, he told the Senate that he wanted to keep Dickenson as a sign of his intention to professionalize National Park Service leadership; he did not reveal that he had gotten to know Dickenson when they had worked together at Interior during the Nixon administration or that Dickenson had expressed his wholehearted agreement with Watt's desire to freeze the acquisition of new park lands.[20]

Retaining the National Park Service's director may have eased anxieties within that agency, but it did little to calm the swelling waves of public protest or congressional resistance. Arguing that the Park Service had grown too quickly, Watt sought to reallocate money earmarked for land procurement to upgrade and repair roads and hotels within existing parks. Congress, however, objected and restored funds into the agency's land acquisition budget.[21]

Watt's suspension of new parkland acquisitions paled in comparison to his talk of disposing of other federal lands—either through sale to the private sector or through transfer to the states—when it came to rubbing many outdoor recreationalists, such as hunters and anglers, the wrong way. As political scientist Richard Ganzel observed in 1984, "The obvious glee experienced by James Watt in taunting environmentalists transformed their skepticism into angry resistance."[22] Land ownership was one thing, but Watt also continued to downplay protection and to facilitate development of the vast public land holdings overseen by the Department of the Interior, knowing full well that this would further provoke environmental activists. In July 1981, the National Wildlife Federation (NWF)—the nation's largest (at 4.5 million members) and most politically conservative environmental organization—called for Watt's dismissal, something already being pushed by the smaller, more combative Sierra Club and Wilderness Society. Since its founding in 1936, NWF had never lobbied for the dismissal of a White House appointee, yet it now publicly opposed Watt, charging him with paying "lip service to environmental protection" while "working to undermine or circumvent many of our basic environmental protection laws."[23]

Although the Reagan administration's environmental and natural resources policies drew a wide range of objections, the most impassioned critiques were directed to actions on public lands. No federal office received more venomous criticism than the Department of the Interior. Its antagonistic secretary openly sympathized with the "Sagebrush Rebellion," a loosely knit political movement whose adherents advocated that much of the federal land holdings (especially those in the West) be transferred to the states or sold outright. Recreational users of public lands were understandably apprehensive, especially in light of Watt's action in February 1981 to abolish the Heritage Conservation and Recreation Service (formerly the Bureau of Outdoor Recreation).[24]

Watt also drew fire from opponents of offshore oil development. During his 1980 presidential campaign, Reagan had signaled his desire to expand oil exploration under the nation's coastal waters. Soon after his installation as Interior secretary, Watt filed a proposal to designate 111 tracts, totaling 5,100 acres, in the Santa Maria Basin off California's San Luis Obispo County coast. As a follow-up, he called for the additional lease of more than 150,000 acres farther north. National environmental organizations questioned the Outer Continental Shelf lease sales in Northern California, but their outcry paled in comparison to the protests raised by the state's elected officials and congressional delegation, who complained that the administration's heavy hand on this matter contradicted Reagan's campaign promise to delegate more authority to state and local government. In March 1981, a bipartisan group of California members of the House of Representatives formally requested that the president reconsider the proposed sale.[25] Meanwhile, the state of California, together with 19 local governments and several environmental groups, challenged Watt's decision in court. Federal District Judge Mariana Pfaelzer blocked the oil leases in July 1981, ruling that the Coastal Zone Management Act of 1972 authorized the prohibition of such drilling if it conflicted with the state's coastal management plan.[26]

In July 1982, Alaska and California and seven environmental organizations elevated their opposition of Watt's five-year coastal oil and gas leasing program proposal to the U.S. Court of Appeals. In October, the court ruled in favor of the plaintiffs, ordering the Interior Department "to give greater weight to 'environmental and social costs' in carrying out its offshore leasing program."[27] Watt announced another plan that summer to develop almost a billion acres off both coasts. Faced with the well-publicized complaints of 28 members of Congress, the secretary retorted that "it is much easier to explain to the American people why we have oil rigs off our coast than it would be to explain to the mothers and fathers of this land why their sons are fighting on the sands of the Middle East as might be required if the policies of our critics were to be pursued."[28]

Environmental organizations made political hay from such controversies. The Sierra Club, for example, used a "remove James Watt" theme for its 1982 membership drive. As executive director Michael McCloskey stated in his widely distributed recruitment letter, "Unless you and I act immediately, we will surely see the destruction of lands

FIGURE 16. Environmental button lampooning Interior secretary James Watt. Courtesy of National Museum of American History, Smithsonian Institution.

needed for our national parks, the invasion of our irreplaceable wilderness lands, and the demise of habitat for our nation's wildlife." He described the club's successful "Dump Watt" campaign and announced a new and similar "Replace Watt" petition. "As soon as we have the signatures of 1,000,000 more friends—people like you—we will again take the REPLACE WATT petitions to Washington," he said. "Imagine the effect a total of *two million* signatures will have on the Congress, the press, and on President Reagan. Nothing of this magnitude has occurred in recent years in the conservation movement!"[29] Arguing that "Watt's reign of environmental terror electrified and reinvigorated the environmental movement," former National Park Service director George Hartzog believed that Watt was unquestionably "the most successful spur to increased membership ever to serve the citizen conservation organizations. Their memberships skyrocketed while he was secretary of the interior."[30]

The political waves Watt so gleefully generated began to have a ripple effect on the whole administration. The increased revenues generated from their anti-Watt campaigns enabled environmental organizations to build their professional staffs to unprecedented levels, and Democratic Party strategists perceived the Interior secretary as a highly useful foil in the forthcoming election campaigns. As Philip Shabecoff of the *New York Times* observed, Democrats were publicly calling for

Watt's resignation, even while privately admitting "they have more political profit to make by having him remain in office."[31] An aide to House Speaker Thomas P. O'Neill Jr. joked, "Watt is the best thing we have going for us."[32]

As the 1984 campaign season drew near, polls suggested that Watt's mounting unpopularity might harm the president's prospects for reelection. Following his lifelong pattern of dissociating himself from unpleasant controversy, Reagan had not engaged personally in debates over his administration's natural resources and environmental policies, preferring instead to let Watt take the lead—and the heat.[33] As a pragmatist, however, Reagan understood that the time had come for him to compromise and retreat. The Interior secretary's words and actions were alienating too many potential voters, endangering not only the president's reelection but also the reelection bids of several Republican congressional members. When the White House forced Watt to resign in October 1983, even the editors of the *New York Times* opined that it was Watt's "indiscretions, not his—or Mr. Reagan's—policies, that did him in."[34]

Many commentators speculated that Reagan would choose a new secretary committed to advancing the same agenda. They were surprised when he selected someone with little experience in the areas encompassed by Interior. The choice of National Security Advisor William P. Clark showed that Reagan was not taking any chances. Unlike Watt, who had been recommended to him and whom Reagan barely knew, Clark was a longtime confidant who had served Reagan faithfully as both gubernatorial and presidential troubleshooter. The president completely trusted him to straighten out the controversies at Interior while keeping the agency's basic policy orientation in line with the administration's.[35]

Clark had proved himself up to tough administrative challenges, as he had had minimal foreign policy experience before being named national security advisor. Although his meager background in environmental and natural resources matters posed little concern for the White House, it did alarm the administration's critics. Environmental Policy Institute president Louise Dunlap observed that Clark's appointment "shows the White House understands they are in deep political trouble over the environmental issue." Wilderness Society executive vice president William Turnage labeled the choice "a tragedy," adding, "the President clearly doesn't care about the environment and has delivered another insult to the environment." Even House Republican Leader Robert Michel of Illinois called Clark's nomination "incredible and baffling."[36] The *New York Times* editorialized about Clark's lack of qualifications but concluded that he was likely to "take less extreme positions on fundamental questions like how fast to exploit oil and coal resources on public lands."[37]

THE 1984 PRESIDENTIAL CAMPAIGN

During the first two and a half years of Reagan's presidency, the negative publicity and political animus engendered by James Watt's direction of the Department of the Interior were exacerbated by the controversies surrounding another presidential appointee, Anne (Gorsuch) Burford, administrator of EPA.[38] As media criticism of these two agencies (and the White House's environmental policies in general) became more strident, Reagan and his advisors came to see the administration's environmental record as a political liability that could hamper a reelection bid.[39] The environment had "emerged, if only temporarily, as a dominant feature on the nation's political landscape," wrote Philip Shabecoff; "it was an issue that captured and held the public's attention for weeks and preoccupied the Government at its highest levels."[40] Such circumstances encouraged even more acrimonious criticism by environmental leaders. With polls indicating that the majority of Americans *favored* environmental protection, the administration's detractors gained greater purchase within Congress and the news media.[41] The political climate became so heated—with the EPA administrator and 20 other senior officials at the agency resigning in the spring and Interior secretary Watt attracting relentless media scrutiny—that the environment remained a front-page story throughout most of 1983.

Andy Pasztor of the *Wall Street Journal* reported in March 1983 that "the White House is trying to project a new image as a tougher foe of polluters, hoping to limit the political fallout enveloping the Environmental Protection Agency."[42] The shift in Reagan's stance on natural resources and environmental policy was not so much a reconsideration of his basic priorities as it was an acknowledgment of political realities. Some modest compromises and a softening of the administration's image—made clear by a variety of deliberate messages relayed by the news media—seemed the least that was necessary for the White House to repair its relations with Congress and deny Reagan's Democratic opponents a potentially explosive campaign issue.

On 11 June 1983, the president devoted his weekly radio address to a defense of the administration's environmental track record. Claiming critics had distorted his accomplishments, Reagan said America was becoming "more healthy and more beautiful each year" and that he personally favored "a sound, strong environmental policy that protects the health of our people and a wise stewardship of our nation's natural resources."[43] However, rather than subduing the discord surrounding his administration's policies, Reagan's radio address merely stirred the embers of controversy, providing an opportunity for his critics' views to be restated in the media whenever they countered the president's assertions with harsh assessments of his record on wilderness issues, national parks, natural resources development, and air and water quality.[44]

Such criticism notwithstanding, the controversy ultimately had little effect on the presidential election. Confident that voters who placed the environment high on their list of political concerns would automatically lend him their support, the Democratic presidential nominee, Walter Mondale, did not elevate that issue in his campaign. During his televised debate with Reagan in October 1984, for example, Mondale eschewed the opportunity to criticize the president's environmental record, choosing instead to question Reagan's political and economic sensibilities.[45] Three out of four Mondale voters told pollsters that the environment was a key concern, yet those voters represented only 4% of all those who went to the polls.[46] As Reagan's landslide victory attested, Americans may have cared about the environment, but at that time, other matters carried more influence in the voting booth.[47]

REAGAN'S FIRST-TERM LEGACY

Environmental and natural resources policy had been thoroughly intertwined with broader policy concerns during Reagan's first term. Despite his high hopes to redirect federal programs, Reagan had failed to achieve fundamental reforms in this area.[48] Much of his inability to bring about long-term change can be attributed to his decision to follow an administrative rather than legislative approach, although other factors also played a role. One was the White House's miscomprehension of the public's growing appetite for environmental quality and amenities. As R. Shep Melnick has observed, "The public now expects the federal government to protect it from a wide variety of hazards."[49] Thus, although Reagan's push to curb government expenditures had broad appeal, Americans also considered safeguarding human health from environmental hazards a vital federal function.

Another major factor limiting Reagan's lasting influence was the successful public relations efforts of environmental organizations, which reinforced popular concern for the environment. By providing contradictory interpretations of the administration's actions and supplying colorful quotations and protests, they helped keep the issue on the front page. Media attention, in turn, fueled a climate of political opinion that constrained Reagan's reforms, primarily by sustaining congressional opposition to White House policies and encouraging career bureaucrats to resist the radical reorientation of their agencies. Taken together, the public, the press, and congressional Democrats effectively moderated the administration's influence. Reagan's attempt to maneuver around existing environmental laws and soften the enforcement of protections enacted during the 1960s and 1970s was ultimately thwarted by deep-seated public support for such protection.

Asking how the administration justified "such a radical departure from the bipartisan consensus that had characterized environmental policies throughout the 1970s," political scientist Michael Kraft concluded that Reagan and his aides were blinded by their overwhelming victory over Carter, which they misinterpreted as legitimizing the entirety of their political agenda. Thus, they "seriously misjudged the public's commitment to environmental policy." Kraft then paraphrased William Ruckelshaus's acknowledgment (made after his installment as EPA administrator in 1983), stating that the Reagan White House had confused "the public's wish to improve the way environmental and public health programs were administered with a desire to change the goals of the programs themselves. When it attempted to change some of those goals through deregulation, this caused the 'perception' that the administration was hostile to environmental programs."[50]

After the mounting controversies involving EPA, the administration softened its approach, and a kinder and gentler attitude toward environmental matters lasted through the 1984 presidential election and into Reagan's second term. White House officials had learned that it made little sense to provoke environmentalists on their basic values, and that knowledge permeated throughout the agencies. As a result, the administration adopted a less confrontational style, one that sought to achieve change through public relations and a new volunteer program called Take Pride in America.

CHAPTER 5

TAKE PRIDE IN AMERICA

Ronald Reagan wasted little time in assembling his second-term cabinet. For the Department of the Interior, he selected Donald Paul Hodel, who had already served in the administration as James Watt's under secretary of Interior (1981–1982) and, later, as secretary of the Department of Energy (1982–1985). He was also a long-standing friend of Watt. Hodel was a young, Portland-based attorney managing Oregon's Reagan for President Committee when he and Watt first met in 1968, and the two Westerners immediately found common ground in their conservative politics and evangelical religious beliefs. Soon after President Nixon installed Watt as deputy assistant secretary of Water and Power in the Department of the Interior in 1969, Watt secured Hodel's appointment as Interior's Deputy Administrator of the Bonneville Power Administration (BPA), the agency responsible for marketing the electricity generated by 31 federally built hydroelectric dams on the Columbia River and its tributaries. Hodel flourished in that job, eventually serving as BPA administrator from 1972 to 1977. He returned to the private sector during the Carter presidency, founding the energy consulting firm Hodel Associates, Inc. When Watt again recruited Hodel to government service in 1981, the duo focused on expanding energy exploration and development on federal lands, increasing leases for offshore oil drilling, and restricting wilderness designations.[1]

At the 1985 Senate hearing on Hodel's nomination to head Interior, Hodel said that President Reagan had instructed him to pursue two main goals: "preserving the Nation's national park, wilderness and wildlife resources" and "enhancing America's ability to meet our energy and mineral needs with domestic resources."[2] Senator Howard Metzenbaum (D-OH) asked Hodel how he planned to balance "the pressures for development" with "the national mandate to preserve those unique elements of our national heritage." Reminding the nominee "we all remember too well the cynical and destructive reign of Jim Watt," Metzenbaum emphasized that Congress and the public did not want "such a travesty to be repeated."[3]

Hodel's confirmation in February 1985 did not sit well with the environmental community. Sierra Club executive director Michael McCloskey, who had been Hodel's classmate at Harvard and the University of Oregon Law School, recalled meeting with Watt and Hodel at Interior headquarters four years earlier, shortly after their installment as secretary and under secretary. "At Harvard he [Hodel] had been president of the Young Republicans, while I had been president of the Young Democrats," McCloskey wrote. "We always seemed to be on opposite sides, and this time was no exception. As I tried to get specifics from Watt and Hodel about what they planned to do, they blurted out that they were so clever that they planned to 'fix' things in the Interior Department so that their adversaries would never be able to reverse them."[4]

Nevertheless, as Interior secretary, Hodel initially cultivated cordial relationships with the leadership of mainstream environmental organizations. His respectful, unassuming demeanor (Hodel's stylistic yin to Watt's yang) had been one reason Reagan had chosen him.[5] William P. Clark's leadership in the two years after Watt had not eased the political damage or repaired relations with the environmental community. Hodel thus found himself in a delicate position. To openly denounce his old friend's reckless posturing would risk being perceived as disloyal and as criticizing White House policies—policies that he himself wholeheartedly espoused.[6] The real problem, he believed, rested with his predecessor's abrasiveness. And so he adopted a cautious, nonconfrontational, under-the-radar approach. Barely two weeks into his Interior job, secretary Hodel told the National Conference of State Legislatures that he intended to follow the same low-profile course he had taken at the Department of Energy. Explaining why, he deadpanned, "If you'd been Jim Watt's number two man for 21 months, you'd want to keep a low profile, too."[7] In an hour-long call-in interview on C-SPAN in April 1985, Hodel reiterated his adherence to Reagan's contention that the United States could obtain adequate domestic supplies of energy, minerals, and natural resources while simultaneously improving the nation's environmental quality. The nation, he asserted, did not face an either/or proposition.[8]

When Hodel appeared before the Senate Committee on Energy and Natural Resources in February 1985, he stuck to that script until New Mexico's Democratic Senator Jeff Bingaman raised a simple but unexpected question. Expressing dismay at "the theft of several large petrified logs from one of our wilderness areas because of lack of adequate monitoring," the senator asked whether the administration's budget request was sufficient to carry out Interior's mandate to protect the public lands within its jurisdiction. Unprepared for that line of inquiry, Hodel improvised, testifying in a long-winded manner that he was "not particularly optimistic we can protect all of the time all of the resources that are under our management in the fashion that would always prevent the situation that you described from taking place." In light of Interior's vast landholdings, he doubted "that there are enough people or enough money in the Federal Treasury always to protect all the resources."[9]

Hodel later confessed how Bingaman's question had stuck with him, causing him to reflect on the magnitude of the challenge to safeguard America's public lands. Troubled by the vagueness of his congressional testimony, he convened a series of meetings with his agency planners and other public land managers and users to explore ways to improve the federal government's fulfillment of this obligation. Lacking consensus on how to proceed yet driven to demonstrate the administration's responsiveness, he proffered a low-cost educational initiative that would implore citizens to volunteer their services on the front line of public lands stewardship.[10]

Hodel's innocuous proposal, which avoided any need for budgetary or staff expansions, proved attractive to Interior's political appointees and their White House superiors. It eventually evolved to become the Take Pride in America program. Although its modest aspirations and bare-bones assets ensured the program's negligible impact on the management of public lands, Take Pride was welcomed by the administration's public relations staff, who were always eager to parade positive examples in their ongoing efforts to ameliorate Reagan's environmental image. By prioritizing civic over governmental action, the volunteer-oriented initiative eschewed federal regulations and increased expenditures. It played into conservative beliefs that the enlightened self-interest of the private sector offered the ideal approach to public lands stewardship. Hodel was confident that the president would embrace Take Pride's emphasis on voluntarism because Reagan had repeatedly signaled his mistrust of government and his preference for private initiatives, themes memorably encapsulated in his

1981 inaugural address when he asserted "government is not the solution to our problem; government is the problem."[11]

Voluntarism had already become one of Reagan's recurring themes. Speaking before the National Alliance of Business in October 1981, he announced the creation of a Presidential Task Force on Private Sector Initiatives by extolling the virtues of voluntarism, calling it "a means of delivering social services more effectively and of preserving our individual freedoms." Alleging that a reduction in the number of volunteers would be more disruptive than a reduction in the federal budget, he said his administration would work to "elevate voluntary action and private initiative," endeavoring "to increase their influence on our daily lives and their roles in meeting our social needs." As the president explained, "For too long, the American people have been told they are relieved of responsibility for helping their fellow man because government has taken over the job. Now we seek to provide as much support for voluntarism, without federalizing, as possible." In calling for a "spirit of shared sacrifice," Reagan declared that his administration was giving "government back to the people."[12]

In December, the White House heralded the establishment of the President's Volunteer Action Awards, which would "honor outstanding volunteer achievement by individual citizens and their organizations." Recreation and the environment stood as one of seven award categories. "Throughout our history," Reagan told the small gathering, "Americans have always extended their hands to neighbors in assistance. . . . I believe this program of recognition is vital to call attention both to what is being done by American volunteers and to what can be done through voluntary action."[13] In 1984, the White House launched the President's Citation Program for Private Sector Initiatives, with one of the first awards going to the Advertising Council.[14] At a Rose Garden ceremony honoring youth volunteers in April 1985, Reagan intimated his approval of Hodel's plan by praising the "over 10,000 young people" of the new Touch America Project who had worked under the supervision of Forest Service rangers "to improve the public lands by blazing trails, stabilizing streams, and cleaning mudslide damage."[15]

Take Pride in America epitomized Reagan's outward-facing political approach: positive, hopeful, oriented toward individuals and the private sector, and minimizing the role of government. The program demanded little federal accountability; responsibility rested with the public, whose members were being asked to act voluntarily on matters about which they presumably cared deeply.

And the benefits flowed in both directions. This modest government action would not burden business with additional regulations, whereas it allowed the administration to counter its critics by presenting an alternative environmental narrative—a symbolic initiative that elevated the patriotic role of American volunteers, the dignity and valor associated with citizen action, and an abiding faith in the capacity of individuals to make a difference.[16]

With a green light from the White House, Hodel asked the Advertising Council for help in promoting the new program, which the Department of the Interior would orchestrate on behalf of public lands agencies at the federal, state, county, and municipal levels. His September 1985 letter to the council emphasized how the growth in outdoor recreation compounded the difficulty of protecting and caring for America's public lands. Interior was responsible for 510 million acres of the nearly 700 million acres managed by the federal government. Pointing to the diversity of these resources, Hodel explained that "the great public estate includes vast stretches of public domain, the wildlife refuge system, more than 300 national parks and historic sites, a huge national forest system," in addition to state-managed forests, parks, and preserves and municipal parks, playgrounds, and open spaces. As "owners" of these lands, he said, Americans "have a responsibility for their care."[17]

Interior's proposal highlighted the agency's commitment to work with existing national, state, and community organizations to match conservation needs with available volunteers. National parks, it said, were receiving "over 326 million visits per year with another 27 million visits on public domain lands, 25 million visits on wildlife refuges and 50 million on reclamation lands." The preceding decade had witnessed a 43% increase in national park attendance, as well as a spike in the use of motorcycles and off-road vehicles, especially in the deserts of the Southwest. With the swelling numbers of visitors came a surge in litter, vandalism, and harm to natural resources. Interior planned to motivate groups and individuals to care for parks, refuges, and playgrounds through their donated time, goods, and services. Volunteers would also be encouraged to report "vandalism of public facilities, or the theft of prehistoric artifacts or the illegal taking of protected wildlife."[18]

The Ad Council knew that such campaigns must convince people to think differently, that is, "mental handcuffs had to be removed from many minds."[19] When the council agreed to take on the Take Pride in America campaign, the relevant mental handcuffs involved assumptions of who was responsible for public lands stewardship. The challenge was to persuade individual Americans that that job ultimately rested with them, rather than with government agencies.

Following the proposal's quick acceptance, Hodel signed a $400,000, 18-month contract with the Ad Council. He tasked Interior's Office of the Assistant Secretary for Policy, Budget, and Administration with coordinating the agency's initial efforts, including administering the contract, providing internal staff support, and seeding the program with $16,000 from its own operating budget.[20] Interior's main public lands departments—National Park Service, Bureau of Land Management, Bureau of Reclamation, and Fish and Wildlife Service— reprogrammed proportional amounts from their budgeted funds to launch the campaign. Deputy assistant secretary G. R. Riso described what was initially called the "National Education Campaign on the Public Lands," stating that it "will assist the Department in its mission to care and promote the wise use of lands and resources of all kinds."[21]

In October 1985, Interior issued a two-page brochure introducing "Take Pride in America: This Land Is Your Land" as a program encompassing all public lands, "from national parks, recreation areas, seashores, and landmarks; to national forests and wilderness; to wildlife habitat and refuges; to rangeland and deserts; to reservoirs, dams and their recreation areas; to multiple-use lands which produce energy, minerals, and timber." As the brochure stated, "If citizens could think of the public land as *belonging to them* and treat it as if it were *their personal property*, careless activity would diminish."[22]

The campaign's architects had banked on a high-profile unveiling in the president's 1986 State of the Union Address, which was scheduled for 28 January. However, the televised explosion of the space shuttle *Challenger* that morning led Reagan to postpone his speech for a week.[23] Although the president dropped the Take Pride announcement from his revised State of the Union Address, he included it in his "Message to Congress on America's Agenda for the Future" submitted two days later. Asserting the need to "put our trust in people, rather than in the Government, to solve the problems before us," he urged all Americans to "take pride in their outstanding public lands and historic sites that belong to everyone," adding, "we must all work for a renewed awareness that these lands are our lands."[24]

In March, Hodel promoted the new initiative on Capitol Hill by hosting a small congressional breakfast. His follow-up letters stressed the campaign's appeal to various constituent groups sympathetic to the goals of the Sagebrush Rebellion.[25]

Take Pride, he told the congressional members, would recognize and expand existing volunteer activities in such areas as trail maintenance, litter collection, and support of ecological and archaeological research. He proudly enumerated the program's early corporate support: a cruise ship company's $43,000 donation to Alaska's Glacier Bay National Park and Preserve to "help defray the cost of providing NPS naturalists on board the ships"; Honda Motor Company's Team Clean Project providing "a trash compactor, three motorized all-terrain bikes, three double-vault toilets, and 50,000 trash/litter bags with the Team Clean label" to the Bureau of Land Management's Idaho State Office; and an American Motorcycle Association family weekend at the Bureau of Land Management's Johnson Valley Open Area near Barstow, California, where participants removed "an estimated four tons of glass, trash, junk cars, and other debris."[26]

The Outdoor Writers Association of America invited Hodel to deliver the plenary lecture at its annual meeting in June. The Interior secretary spoke at length about Take Pride in America, assuring his audience of scribes that the program rested on the premise "that when people feel a real sense of ownership for and are involved in the care of [public] lands, there are fewer abuses." The goal, he said, was "to heighten awareness on the part of all Americans that these lands are their lands to be protected *for* them, not *from* them." Hodel insisted that Take Pride was not being created as "a massive federal program or to supplement our budgets."[27] What he failed to say, however, was that White House officials expected that modest investments in the volunteer-based initiative would yield rich dividends in image improvement for the Reagan presidency.

Although presented as a nonpartisan, apolitical project, Take Pride's unstated objective was to foster political passivity among the electorate and decrease negative perceptions of the administration. The Executive Office of the President's Council on Environmental Quality (CEQ) confessed that the Take Pride in America name was "unabashedly designed to tap into patriotic feelings to help protect our public lands and natural resources."[28] The council contended that littering and vandalism constituted the two most prevalent problems facing land managers and that they "are also the two problems most likely to be mitigated by a public awareness effort," as neither of them were propelled by monetary incentives. According to the council, "Littering is usually attributed to laziness. Acts of vandalism are nearly as varied as they are common: shooting at signs, carving initials in backcountry cabins, breaking fixtures in public rest rooms, painting graffiti on a wall."[29] In detailing Take Pride's philosophical underpinnings, CEQ reported secretary Hodel's stipulation that the campaign remain "consistent with two of the most prominent themes of the Reagan Presidency, the first being voluntarism. Take Pride in America is not being forced on anyone. Participation is voluntary, from the highest levels on down." The second major theme "is consistency with fiscal restraint. The campaign is being implemented with minimal expenditure of taxpayers' money."[30]

ADVERTISING COUNCIL INVOLVEMENT

Not coincidentally, the Advertising Council shared the Reagan administration's goals of minimizing the role of government, maximizing the responsibility of individuals, and defending corporate and business interests from criticism and attack. To strengthen Take Pride's patriotic appeal, the council's public service announcements focused on the connections between love of country and love of the outdoors, thereby transcending political, religious, and cultural orientations. The advertising industry was well attuned to the post-1950s growth in national voluntary associations, including those with environmental missions, and the council exploited this set of values to shield Take Pride from overt negative assessments.[31]

Celebrity spokespersons, long viewed as invaluable assets within commercial advertising, had been featured in Ad Council campaigns from the very beginning. Even the forest fire prevention campaign, with its renowned pitchman Smokey Bear, had secured endorsements and radio announcements from a star-studded cast that included Louis Armstrong, Vicki Carr, Ray Charles, Ella Fitzgerald, James Mason, Gregory Peck, Norman Rockwell, Rudy Vallee, and John Wayne.[32] The council adopted a similar game plan for Take Pride in America.

The council appointed Philemon N. "Phil" Hoadley, director of advertising and marketing for Citibank, North America, as the campaign's volunteer coordinator and W. B. Doner and Company of Baltimore as the volunteer advertising agency.[33] Developing a pro bono, public service advertising campaign through the Ad Council presented a golden opportunity for practitioners, given the nationwide, multimedia exposure of those campaigns. Because Take Pride was W. B. Doner and Company's first Ad Council project, the firm was highly motivated to showcase its talents.

As savvy marketers, Doner's admen grasped the necessity of crafting messages that would resonate with a wide audience, including adult males who might not normally support environmental causes. Their solution was to use Hollywood "tough-guy" movie actors to convey a sense of caring about, and taking responsibility for, the nation's public lands. Associating macho film stars with Take Pride in America, they reasoned, would serve as a masculine branding of the campaign, heightening its appeal among men otherwise inhibited by "environmental-feminine" stereotypes. Everyone agreed on the need to reach this demographic, as young males were the major perpetrators of vandalism and thefts on public lands. Department of the Interior officials offered to solicit the president's direct assistance in recruiting the desired film stars.[34] Reagan liked to frame his own engagement with wildlands in similar masculine stereotypes, as depicted in Hollywood's classic Westerns. Commenting on the association of masculinity and conservative patriotism, Deborah Bright observed in 1985, "Like Philip Morris' Marlboro Man, today a white-hatted Reagan rides his horse or chops wood for the camera on his Santa Barbara ranch, a rugged individualist drawn up to specs by Central Casting."[35]

In June, secretary Hodel told presidential assistant Al Kingon that the Take Pride ads "will use a series of 'tough, good guy' celebrities to encourage American citizens to help stop abuses of our public lands." Emphasizing the importance of selecting "the right entertainers" to pitch the campaign, Hodel argued that "if the request for participation were to come from the President, we would be assured that the top personalities would volunteer."[36] He recommended sending invitations to Clint Eastwood, Charles Bronson, Carl Weathers, Sylvester Stallone, Louis Gossett Jr., Telly Savales, Arnold Schwarzenegger, James Coburn, Chuck Norris, Ken Norton, and Burt Reynolds. His draft letter for the president's signature read,

> All over the country, abuses and misuses of
> public lands are getting out of hand. Historic sites
> are being looted, parks are being vandalized and
> just about everything from children's playgrounds
> to wildlife refuges bear the savage scars of abuse.
> One cultural resources expert estimates that 80 to
> 90 percent of the prehistoric ruins in the Southwest
> show signs of vandalism or looting. Such abuse
> must be stopped. . . .

But before we can get the public involved, we have to make them concerned. In short, we need to touch a nerve. That is where you come in. The image you have in this country is one of a "good guy" seeking justice. Just as important, you are seen as a leader and as a proud American.

If *you* would speak out against these abuses of our public lands in national public service announcements, I feel that the public would respond positively. Your indignation would become their indignation, and your plea for help would become their cause. I feel that you are one of a handful of people who can get the job done.[37]

The campaign's architects hoped that the president would be supportive, given his friendships with the actors, previous interactions with the Ad Council, and belief in the capacity of celebrity-infused advertising to affect change.[38] The Ad Council's Robert Keim recalled his warm reception in the White House during Reagan's first year in office, explaining that the president not only knew about the council but had "delivered some of the War Advertising Council messages way back, and Nancy Reagan had done television and radio spots for the Peace Corps and Foster Grandparents quite recently."[39] Predictably, Reagan found the new initiative appealing, just as he found the intersection of celebrity and politics natural and desirable.[40]

Ultimately, Clint Eastwood, Charles Bronson, and Lou Gossett Jr. were persuaded to appear in Take Pride public service announcements, which the Ad Council launched in spring 1987 with the theme "Bad Guys abuse public lands. Good Guys save them."[41] By featuring this trio of macho movie stars, the ads drew on the actors' film portrayals of stalwart individuals consumed by causes larger than themselves—characters who pursued justice above all else, serving the good of the community in circumstances where government proved inadequate. All three actors had played self-reliant, idealistic tough-guy characters, and all had cultivated film personae as resolute individuals prone to take matters into their own hands, driven not by selfish motivations but by a sense of justice and a cynical assessment of the capabilities of government agencies and bureaucrats. Their fictional characterizations mirrored the Reagan administration's political conservatism. They also reflected the Ad Council's long-running approach of emphasizing individual responsibility and simple, direct action.[42]

When the creators began considering spokespersons, Clint Eastwood came immediately to mind. Having accepted President Richard Nixon's appointment to serve on the National Council of the Arts, the veteran actor had already demonstrated his willingness to engage with government initiatives compatible with his values. His film persona and broad fan base were what really mattered, of course. Eastwood was renowned for lone-wolf roles in various Westerns when he developed a more contemporary character in *Dirty Harry* (1971), a maverick San Francisco police inspector who packed an outsized .44 Magnum handgun and was unafraid to go above the law to bring down an elusive and psychotic serial killer. Eastwood reprised his portrayal of the antihero "Dirty" Harry Callahan in four sequels, cementing the actor's standing as a libertarian icon.[43]

By choosing Charles Bronson, the campaign capitalized on the established actor's career as a star in Westerns and then a hit vigilante film. In *Death Wish* (1974), Bronson had portrayed a liberal, mild-mannered New York City architect forced to confront the horror of his wife's murder and his daughter's plunge into a vegetative coma following a brutal gang rape. Driven by blinding fury and loss of faith in the criminal justice system, the character devolved into a monstrous avenger. Bronson appeared in four *Death Wish* sequels and found himself cast in similar law-and-order films during the 1970s and 1980s.[44] Both the *Dirty Harry* and *Death Wish* film franchises gained notoriety for graphic cinematic violence and their protagonists' unflinching, righteous vengeance. By the mid-1980s, Bronson and Eastwood had become Hollywood's undisputed poster boys for vigilantism.

Louis Gossett Jr. had enjoyed early theatrical success in New York with more serious dramatic roles, including the 1959 Broadway production of Lorraine Hansberry's *A Raisin in the Sun* and the 1961 film version of the play. Gossett's Emmy Award–winning performance as Fiddler in the epic television miniseries *Roots* (1977) had brought star status, and he then won an Academy Award for his portrayal of a hard-nosed drill sergeant in *An Officer and a Gentleman* (1982). During the 1980s, Gossett landed a series of cinematic roles as tough characters in various action-adventure films, most notably as aging fighter pilot Charles "Chappy" Sinclair in two box office successes, *Iron Eagle* (1986) and *Iron Eagle II* (1988).[45]

Eastwood, Bronson, and Gossett were thus all known for playing movie characters imbued with moral certainty, unbreakable self-sufficiency, and cynical distrust of institutions, often deploying violence in a retributive pursuit of justice.[46] The Ad Council envisioned channeling those film personae to combat the neglect and despoliation of public lands, to make volunteer-based public lands stewardship a moral cause, to sanctify individual action, and to impart a stigma to such careless, neglectful, and abusive behavior as vandalism, historic artifact theft, poaching, and littering.

The first three public service announcements screamed anger and action: "Clint Eastwood Is a Little Upset," "Charles Bronson Isn't Happy," and "Lou Gossett Is Annoyed." The script for the Eastwood spot read,

> EASTWOOD: It seems some misguided individuals out there are abusing our public lands. They're vandalizing our public parks and playgrounds and they're overrunning our wild areas. Real nice guys. Some clowns are even stealing artifacts from historic sites. Now, when I hear about things like that, it really bothers me. I find it unacceptable and I know you do, too. Because these lands are ours—yours and mine.
>
> Now, I know what you're thinking—what can I do? Well, you can either sit there and do nothing or you can start by getting some information on how you can help stop land abuse. As I see it, these people who are abusing our public lands can either clean up their act or get out of town.

The Bronson script upped the ante:

> BRONSON: Sure takes guts to vandalize parks or beat up on trees. But that's what some jerks are doing to our public lands. Only the land can't fight back. But we can—we can save our lands—you and me. Let's face it, someone who gets his kicks punching out flowers shouldn't be too much of a match for us.

FIGURE 17. Take Pride in America ad featuring Charles Bronson. Courtesy of Ad Council Archives, University of Illinois Archive, record series 13/2/215.

The Gossett script did likewise:

> GOSSETT: Hey, y'know we've got some real bad guys in this country—abusing public lands, defacing parks, robbing historic sites. These are our lands— yours and mine—you know, the good guys. Are you going to let a bunch of bad guys run us off our public lands? Or are you going to help save the lands? Let's show these bad guys that the good guys always win.[47]

FIGURE 18. Take Pride in America ad featuring Lou Gossett Jr. Courtesy of Ad Council Archives, University of Illinois Archive, record series 13/2/211.

One magazine ad displayed Charles Bronson's head under the quotation "Are you gonna let a bunch of half-wits turn our public lands into a public disgrace?" The hypermasculine text declared,

> Vandalism of parks and playgrounds. Theft from historic sites. Killing endangered animals for profit. Litter and other thoughtless behavior. This is what's happening to our public lands today. And that's a public disgrace.

Some people, either through ignorance or spite, are abusing our recreation areas, wildlife, and our history. It's more than a shame, it's a crime.

And if we sit back and let it continue, we're not much better than the bad guys. So we have to fight back.

Right now, in your area, there are good guys—individuals and groups—who are dedicated to helping our public lands. And they're tough. A lot tougher than the clowns who get their kicks out of scrawling their names in public areas.

If you write to us, we'll tell you how you can help. Let's keep the public lands something the public can be proud of.[48]

Newspaper advertisements showcasing Lou Gossett Jr. proclaimed, "Some real bad guys are wrecking the public land. Any good guys want to help save it?"[49] Each ad encouraged people to write to the Take Pride in America office to obtain additional information, including a booklet outlining 50 ways to get involved, along with particulars on public lands in the inquirer's home state.[50] The sample print ad sent to the business press in March 1988 featured a close-up of Gossett starring down the camera lens, his raised finger pointing to a quote hovering above his head: "I'd like to stop public land abuse by myself. But the bottom line is that I need your help." Beneath his image, a hopeful reminder that "right now, in your area, there are good guys—businesses and corporations—who are dedicated to saving our public lands."[51]

The tough-guy/good-guy advertising campaign for Take Pride in America played out across the country in print ads and outdoor signage and in public service announcements on radio and television. The Ad Council campaign succeeded in generating a heavy stream of requests for information packets. Promoting a program of volunteer conservation workers was one thing, of course; operating such a program was quite another. Responsibility for actually running Take Pride in America fell to the program's staff within the Department of the Interior.

CHAPTER 6

TAKE PRIDE'S POLITICAL CONSTITUENCIES

Competing visions of appropriate public land management have long complicated government deliberations over natural resources policy, and they eventually roiled the internal politics of the environmental movement. In the twentieth century, groups that had traced their origins to activities like nature hikes and birdwatching now had to contend with mechanized technology in the backcountry. The rising popularity of motorized recreational equipment intensified simmering conflicts, especially when some organizations and communities began to adamantly oppose operation of motorcycles, snowmobiles, jet skis, powerboats, dune buggies, and other off-road vehicles in state and federal wildlands. Conservationists and traditional outdoor sportspersons found themselves increasingly at odds with machine-oriented recreationalists who vigorously pressed for unhampered use of public lands.[1]

The Take Pride in America initiative emerged at a time of soaring protests among off-road vehicle (ORV) owners upset about a series of earlier presidential directives that had limited their access to certain federal lands. The explosive growth of ORV use in the 1960s had caused significant environmental damage (including soil compaction and erosion, degradation of air and water quality, fragmentation of wildlife habitat, and elevated noise levels) wherever motorcycle, dune buggy, four-wheel drive vehicle, and snowmobile activity was concentrated. Ironically, the "off-roading" craze coincided with the nationwide surge of people seeking quieter, more passive forms of outdoor recreation, such as backpacking, cross-country skiing, nature photography, fly-fishing, river running, and mountain climbing. The incompatibility of motorized and nonmotorized recreational activities exacerbated the challenges of public land management. President Nixon responded in 1972 by partially limiting ORV use on public lands. Five years later, President Carter strengthened those restrictions by closing federal lands to ORVs wherever their operation threatened environmental and cultural resources.[2] The backlash generated by these executive orders continued to burn hot into the 1980s as Reagan took office. In addition to lobbying their state- and federal-level elected officials for expanded rights to use public lands, ORV organizations welcomed the Department of the Interior's new Take Pride in America program, which offered them an opportunity to counter their critics by demonstrating their civic responsibility via voluntary service activities. By endorsing the demands of ORV operators, who tended to be politically conservative, the Reagan White House employed them as a wedge against environmental opponents of the administration.[3]

Many of the first groups to endorse Take Pride in America were less concerned with promoting voluntarism on public lands than they were in expressing political support of Donald Hodel, who had earned their loyalty well before his installment as the 45th secretary of the Interior. Perceiving him as a potential advocate for their cause, several representatives of motorized outdoor recreational and commercial tourism interests testified on behalf of and/or submitted written statements in support of Hodel's 1985 nomination to head Interior.[4] The most enthusiastic champion of Hodel's nomination—and, later, of Take Pride in America—was Derrick A. Crandall, president of the American Recreation Coalition, "a federation of some 100 organizations active in the recreation field." The American Recreation Coalition's endorsement of Hodel, Crandall said, was based on the recreation leaders' "considerable contacts" with the nominee during his terms as under secretary of Interior and secretary of Energy, when he consistently "demonstrated an appreciation for the importance of recreation in the American lifestyle and in our Nation's economy." In what came to serve as a foundation for the Take Pride initiative, Crandall said that Hodel "helped nurture an attitude of partnership between Government land management agencies and private interests ranging from park concessioners to enthusiast member organizations seeking to volunteer their services on Federal lands."[5]

The Take Pride in America initiative unfolded within this contested arena, where outdoor recreationalists with different proclivities often parted ways. The controversy over limiting snowmobile access in Yellowstone National Park, which attracted national media attention in the 1990s when it erupted in the courts, exemplified the enduring schisms among public land enthusiasts, the divisions between those who perceived national parks and wildlands as refuges for solace and appreciation of nature and those who regarded them as destinations for exhilarating, machine-enhanced pastimes.[6]

Although all types of outdoor recreationalists cherished public lands as sites for their leisure quests, they could differ dramatically in their equipment preferences (e.g., skis versus snowmobiles) and their political attitudes toward land use, conservation, and wildlife.[7] Some recreationalists placed a premium on protecting plant and animal life and ecological values so that they might treasure and learn from nature, to observe or photograph the nonhuman world. Others prized wide-open spaces in which to ride their off-road vehicles or motorboats, deriving special pleasure in pursuing this hobby as a family unit, taking their kids away from cities and suburbs and "bad" influences to appreciate natural landscapes and have fun with like-minded enthusiasts. Both groups were highly passionate and sincere. Passive recreationalists sought serenity and tranquility, engaging with nature for its own sake, whereas motorized recreationalists sought social comradery and competition centered on muscular, loud machines, with public lands serving as a scenic playground. Although they espoused opposing interpretations of public lands, they were linked by the attraction of spending time under an open sky, which engenders a sense of freedom and escape—a renewal of spirit. Such contrasting perspectives posed an understandable managerial challenge, especially when some land uses were incompatible with others.[8]

Even though many individuals considered themselves members of both camps, some matters generated constant friction, particularly in designated wilderness areas and among groups engaged in antithetical activities. In his classic text on outdoor recreation, Robert Manning analyzes the disagreements among such diverse outdoor recreationalists as "canoeists and motorboaters, hikers and motorcyclists, hikers and mountain bikers, cross-country skiers and snowmobilers, hikers and stock users/horseback riders, fishers and water skiers, hunters and non-hunters, and skiers and snowboarders."[9] He found that public land managers commonly (and, in Manning's opinion, sensibly) addressed these incongruities by instituting zoning restrictions to segregate activities—ORV use allowed in this section but prohibited on that section.[10]

Exceptions abound, but it has not been uncommon for differences in outdoor recreational preferences to be associated with differences in political orientation. Although more correlation than causation, some activities attracted adherents who strongly sided with environmental organizations, whereas other activities attracted adherents who loathed environmental organizations. Less discernable a generation or two earlier, these political divisions began to harden in the 1970s, with environmentalists increasingly trending liberal and motorized sports enthusiasts increasingly conservative. Contrasting political philosophies regarding public land management helped widen the divide between these groups. Off-road vehicle devotees, for example, generally opposed "locking up" federal lands through wilderness designation because that severely restricted permissible activities within the boundaries.

Motorized recreational groups worked harder to capture Take Pride in America than did most other organizations, often engaging with the program as part of their broader effort to shape public opinion. Their involvement helped to move the work of citizen volunteers away from conservation toward recreation. Indeed, reactions to Take Pride tracked closely with how individuals and organizations viewed environmentalism, public lands (and the federal agencies that oversaw them), and the Reagan administration in general. Mainline conservationists remained skeptical. Other groups of outdoor enthusiasts—especially those that did not self-identify as environmentalists—tended to be more supportive. This situation enabled Take Pride to bring into the fold outdoor-oriented organizations not normally allied with environmental causes. The American Horse Council, for example, whose members consisted of recreational riders and industry representatives advocating the development of and access to trails on public lands, wholeheartedly endorsed the Take Pride message. So, too, did recreational ORV users, a constituency the Reagan administration warmly welcomed.[11]

The United Mobile Sportfishermen also embraced Take Pride. This coalition consisted of 18 East Coast mobile sportfishing organizations, several of them self-proclaimed beach buggy associations. Their members were anglers who drove their vehicles upon coastal beaches to prime locations for surf casting. They formed an interest group enraptured by the broad expanses of public beaches, especially along barrier islands. Because they drove upon those very shorelines, parking their vehicles on the sand, they often found themselves in conflict with traditional fishers and beachgoers.

In a December 1985 letter to secretary Hodel, United Mobile Sportfishermen executive director William Miller praised the newly announced Take Pride campaign and asked for stronger recognition of his constituents' conservation work. He pointed to the voluntary efforts his organization's members had made to the upkeep of public seashores, including "beach grass planting, black pine planting, beach cleanup, snow fence installation, and assistance to agencies in preparation of educational slide presentations for indoctrinating ORV users in respectful beach use prior to issuance of their permits." Mobile sportfishermen had been engaged in such projects for more than 25 years, Miller said, and thus represented "*the* major source of volunteer labor at most coastal areas." As users of these lands, "they wanted to return something for the enjoyment they received and to protect for their children what they have come to love." He observed that "the critics of mobile sportfishing access at Cape Cod and everywhere else are always notably absent when conservation projects need doing. It seems their only commitment to the environment is by mouth, pen and lawsuit."[12]

Take Pride in America held its first big event in the summer of 1986 within the C&O Canal National Historical Park. The previous November, Hurricane Juan had inflicted heavy flood damage to the upper reaches of the Potomac River, destroying more than 16,000 homes in Pennsylvania, West Virginia, Maryland, and Virginia and inundating long stretches of the historic, 185-mile canal, which hugs the Potomac on its run from Cumberland, Maryland, to Washington, D.C. Besides seriously eroding the towpath, the deluge clogged the canal and its locks and culverts with tons of silt, debris, and uprooted trees. Floodwaters damaged campgrounds, footbridges, and lockhouses and forced the closure of nearly 70% of the park, which faced estimated cleanup and repair costs of more than $9 million. With the National Park Service absorbing a 30% cut in its annual funding and Congress appropriating only $2 million in supplemental emergency funds in 1986, fully reopening the popular park without additional help would take up to seven years. Although skilled artisans were required to make infrastructure and building repairs, the massive debris cleanup depended more upon muscle than upon expertise, making it a task well suited for volunteer labor. Recognizing how this need for donated assistance matched the aspirations of Interior's Take Pride in America program, Park Superintendent Richard Stanton and his staff worked with Boy Scout and Girl Scout officials in organizing a gathering to speed the project along.[13]

The National Park Service promoted the "Clean-up Camporee" with the tagline "The Canal Needs You," directing its appeal to scout troops in Maryland, Virginia, West Virginia, Pennsylvania, and the District of Columbia. As a local newspaper reporter described the early planning, "Scouts under the supervision of their troop leaders and park staff will work on clearing the towpath, cleaning up campsites and other projects as the need arises." Noting that "nobody goes through firewood" like troops of Scouts, Stanton planned to provide the youthful volunteers with all the logs and timber they cared to burn—all of it flood-salvaged detritus.[14]

Hodel kicked off the summer-long event on 1 June 1986 at the Potomac Fish and Game Club near Williamsport, Maryland, site of one of the five camps set up to accommodate the Scouts. Special red, white, and blue banners proclaiming "C&O Canal Cleanup Camporee—Take Pride in America" flew over each campsite. Ultimately, more than 7,000 Scouts participated, most of them cutting brush, carting debris pulled from the canal bed, lugging tree limbs and logs sawed by Park Service maintenance workers, and piling everything up to be trucked away.[15] Hodel praised the volunteer efforts in his invited address before the Outdoor Writers Association of America. Describing how "thousands of boy and girl scouts, 4-H-ers, and other volunteers from all over the Eastern Seaboard are coming together for the C&O Canal Cleanup Camporee," he predicted that the personal involvement of these young people in restoring the historic canal would mean "they will 'own' it when they are through. I pity any future Interior Secretary who fails to pay adequate attention to 'their Canal.' They will carry with them an attitude that assuredly will affect their reactions to similar areas wherever their futures take them."[16]

Park Superintendent Stanton summarized the camporee in a widely distributed guidebook publicizing the event:

> Most of the park is closed to visitors above Seneca, Maryland.
> Debris is scattered everywhere. The park is a mess.
> We don't have enough money to clean up. We need you.
> Come for a day, a week or as long as you can during June, July, and August.
> We will have several large working camps set up, mostly "upriver".
> Individuals or groups will be assigned to a working camp near the Canal.
> Primitive camping! You'll love it. All we furnish is potable water, sanitary facilities and work . . . . . . so:

FIGURE 19. Pages from Jack Elrod's 1987 coloring book, *Take Pride in America with Mark Trail*, which promoted voluntary stewardship of public lands among the nation's youth. Courtesy of Department of the Interior.

> Come fully self-contained. Food stores are not unreasonable distances away.
>
> Please, minimum of four hours of hard work, per person, per day.
>
> The Canal is mostly closed but hiking and biking are nearby.
>
> Bring your canoes. The Potomac is runnable in most sections in Summer.
>
> Volunteer hat and special pin for each volunteer.[17]

The camporee proved a boon for the C&O Canal cleanup, yet it failed to shield the Take Pride program from congressional scrutiny in spring 1987. Following his budget testimony before the House Appropriations Subcommittee on Interior and Related Agencies, Hodel wrote to the chair of the Subcommittee on Interior and Related Agencies of the Senate Committee on Appropriations, Robert C. Byrd (D-WV), to elaborate on the points he had raised in the other chamber. Take Pride was not a new departure for Interior, he said, but "a natural extension" of its programmatic responsibilities as a land management agency. Beyond the high costs inflicted by vandalism, littering, and misuse of public lands, he noted "it is even more critical that the enjoyment of our parks, recreation areas, and the like is diminished for every visitor who comes behind the vandal until we have repaired the damage." The voluntary nature of the Ad Council's public service advertising campaign limited the federal government's financial responsibilities to direct costs, he said, adding that Interior has been "fortunate to obtain the services of Clint Eastwood, Charles Bronson, and Lou Gossett, Jr., to serve as celebrity spokesmen for the Take Pride public service campaign. I have been told that were these celebrities available for commercial advertising, they would probably charge around $1 million each for their endorsement. The Advertising Council estimates that the free public service air time and TV and radio and the print public service ads in newspapers and consumer magazines, if purchased, would cost between $20 to $50 million."[18]

Sidney R. Yates (D-IL), who chaired the Subcommittee on Interior and Related Agencies of the House Committee on Appropriations, asked Hodel about the Take Pride campaign in May 1987. Yates acknowledged the program's value but had questions about its written description. Specifically, he "wondered where funds for the campaign were coming from inasmuch as the budgets before us make no request for it. Are all agencies in the Department being assessed for the campaign?" As Congress finalized the next fiscal year's appropriation, he said, "it would be useful for us to know what your plans for the program in fiscal year 1988 are, so that, if appropriate, we can identify funding for the program. If we have a clearer picture of what you are trying to do in this regard, we can give the proposal every consideration."[19] Hodel replied that Interior remained "fully prepared to continue funding Take Pride in 1988 using normal reimbursable procedures of pooling resources to accomplish our objectives in the most efficient manner consistent with provisions of the Economy Act." He estimated that the program's costs would remain unchanged: roughly $500,000, excluding salaries. Interior, he said, "will continue the public response mechanisms and that contract, and therefore, will continue production of the printed materials necessary for the response mailings. We also will be continuing the awards program, an integral part of the Take Pride initiative, and expending funds to support that aspect of the campaign."[20]

FIGURE 20. President Reagan addressing Take Pride in America award winners at a 21 July 1987 White House Rose Garden event, along with campaign spokespersons Clint Eastwood (center) and Louis Gossett Jr. (left). Courtesy of Reagan Presidential Library.

THE NATIONAL AWARDS PROGRAM

Although the Ad Council orchestrated the media promotional efforts, the Department of the Interior developed the annual Take Pride in America awards program, which became both a means of public encouragement and a platform for reinforcing political support. The awards recognized outstanding examples of volunteer land stewardship among various categories, such as individuals, youth groups, businesses and corporations, civic and citizen groups, public and private partnerships, state and local government agencies, and nongovernmental organizations. The first ceremony took place in July 1987 at the National Arboretum, a U.S. Department of Agriculture research and public education facility overlooking the Anacostia River in northeast Washington, D.C.[21] The 127 finalists—from 39 states and selected from more than 525 nominations—were all invited to participate in the ceremony.[22] Seeking to maximize news coverage, Interior issued a press release under the headline "Celebrities to receive awards for serving as spokesmen for the Take Pride in America campaign," stating that Vice President George Bush would be honoring Clint Eastwood and Louis Gossett Jr. for their civic contributions.[23]

Following the morning program on the arboretum's resplendent grounds, where more than a thousand people gathered, Reagan presided over a smaller, winners-only ceremony in the White House Rose Garden. Three cabinet secretaries—Donald Hodel of Interior, William Bennett of Education, and Richard Lyng of Agriculture—joined the president that afternoon. Contextualizing the initiative's emphasis on volunteering while attempting to give it a bipartisan ring and political legitimization, Reagan linked Take Pride with Lady Bird Johnson's efforts in the 1960s to encourage community voluntarism on behalf of beautifying America. He both praised the award winners and trumpeted his administration's oversight of the nation's public lands and natural resources. Stating that "some of America's greatest assets are, of course, the parks, national forests, and other public lands that have been set aside for the benefit and enjoyment of our people and for future generations," the president commended those individuals who had taken the time to care for the citizenry's landed inheritance. He added,

> When Secretary Hodel came to me with the idea of a Take Pride in America campaign, I thought it was terrific. If we really rely—or totally rely on government, whether in conserving our public lands or in any other worthy endeavors, the job is not going to get done. Public land managers have a tough assignment, and they take their responsibility seriously, yet I'm certain they will verify that there can be no greater boon to the conservation and preservation of America's national treasures than the active involvement of the American people. This is what the Take Pride in America campaign is all about.[24]

The awards ceremony was just the type of upbeat event that Reagan enjoyed. He lent his support the following year by designating May 1988 "Take Pride in America Month" and by again hosting the July awards program on the White House grounds.[25] As the president congratulated that year's 94 award winners, he repeated his praise of the Take Pride in America mission in overtly political and cultural terms, criticizing people who mistreat public lands as "stealing from others, from their fellow citizens and from future generations." He insisted "there's no reason for us to tolerate that. Ask Lou Gossett, Clint Eastwood, or Charles Bronson if they get angry when people abuse our public lands. As these Take Pride spokesmen symbolize, there's a code of conduct, a code of honor, that separates right from wrong; and part of that code guides how we care for our national parks and public lands."[26]

Although the Interior Department ran the Take Pride program, working to ensure its long-run political support and providing interested individuals with information about volunteer opportunities on public lands in their home states, the Ad Council refined its public service advertising campaign in an attempt to expand the appeal to younger audiences. In May 1988, the council's Campaigns Review Committee approved Doner's recommendation to recruit Pee-wee Herman, host of a Saturday morning program on CBS that was "watched by 9.3 million people—6.4 million from 2–17 years old and 2.9 million people 18 and older."[27] Despite the committee's enthusiasm for the creation of a Pee-wee Herman Take Pride in America Club, Herman's schedule fatally delayed negotiations.

Revisiting the portrayal of Take Pride in America made sense in light of Reagan's pending departure from the White House in January 1989. Hodel, too, would be retiring from government service. The task of determining Take Pride's future would be left to the next president and Interior secretary.[28]

CHAPTER 7

GEORGE H. W. BUSH AND A THOUSAND POINTS OF LIGHT

In his bid for the White House, George H. W. Bush wrestled with the need to reconcile the advantages and disadvantages accrued from his eight-year stint as vice president. His goal, of course, was to align himself with those elements of Reagan's presidency that had engendered the broadest public appeal while distancing himself from the political taint created by the most divisive aspects. This textbook strategy of political pragmatism strengthened Bush's campaign platform and projected his capacity for independent leadership. He embraced Reagan's support of voluntarism, for example, yet pledged to be a Teddy Roosevelt Republican, an "environmental president." To lend symbolic credence to that claim, Bush fiercely attacked his Democratic opponent, Massachusetts Governor Michael Dukakis, for the repeated failures to clean up Boston Harbor, then among the country's most polluted water bodies. Speaking to a choreographed assemblage of reporters aboard a Boston Harbor sightseeing ferry on 1 September 1988, Bush blamed Dukakis for the relentless torrent of filth contaminating the governor's home port: "Half a billion gallons of barely treated sewage a day—into the harbor. Seventy tons of sewage sludge per day—into the harbor. PCBs—into the harbor." All this, Bush railed, because Dukakis had delayed construction of a desperately needed sewage treatment system until a federal court ordered him to proceed.[1]

The vice president's campaign managers strove to balance the expediency of such hardball tactics against their candidate's carefully cultivated persona of a public servant committed to gentlemanly, principled, statesmanlike behavior.

This political calculus succeeded, in part because Bush represented the moderate faction of the Republican Party, one anxious about the erosion of its influence to more extreme partisanship. In this respect, Bush's campaign rhetoric calmed latent anxieties among many voters that the former Texas oil company executive might harbor deep-seated anti-environmental sentiments. Mainstream environmental organizations, however, remained keenly aware of Bush's role in weakening environmental regulations as chair of President Reagan's Task Force on Regulatory Relief.[2]

Bush's aggressiveness proved effective. His substantial winning margin made him the first incumbent vice president to be elected president since 1836, when Martin Van Buren channeled the popularity of President Andrew Jackson. Once in office, Bush held true to his centrist stance, drawing attention to serious environmental problems, making sympathetic appointments to key agencies, and generally avoiding political backlash. Although he never made environmental quality a priority, Bush initially backed up his words with actions: working to curb acid rain and ocean dumping, setting aside designated wilderness areas, boosting the Environmental Protection Agency's enforcement efforts, and planting millions of trees on public lands. Nevertheless, it was always clear that he would toe the conservative line, favoring economic over environmental goals while insisting that the nation could have both a clean environment *and* a healthy economy. Ever the pragmatist, Bush assured Americans that, if ever faced with a conflict between the environment and the economy, he would always side with the latter.[3]

Such an approach reflected Bush's old-school Republican values rather than any notable shifts in his party's political landscape. Prior to the 1980s, federal environmental legislation had routinely attracted bipartisan support, with congressional voting patterns often influenced more strongly by regional factors than by party affiliation.[4] As questions associated with natural resources and the environment became increasingly partisan during the Reagan administration, Bush had to contend with churning crosscurrents within the GOP. As a candidate, Bush may have pleaded the case for responsible stewardship and environmental quality, but his overarching goals as president varied little from Reagan's. In this respect (and as environmentalists suspected), Bush drew from his vice-presidential experiences chairing the Presidential Task Force on Regulatory Relief, an initiative to reduce the economic burden of federal regulations on American businesses. Animated by that anti-regulatory bias, Bush took a page from his predecessor's playbook by appointing his own vice president, Dan Quayle, to chair the new Council on Competitiveness, an office established to ensure that business considerations remained paramount in deliberations concerning regulatory policies.[5]

Despite everything, Bush's economic conservatism did not express itself in rigid, anti-environmentalism. And nothing exemplified his temperate approach more clearly than his selection of a well-respected conservation leader, William K. Reilly, to head the Environmental Protection Agency (EPA). Before rising to the presidencies of the Conservation Foundation and World Wildlife Fund, Reilly had served as a senior staff member with President Nixon's Council on Environmental Quality, which Russell Train had overseen prior to becoming EPA's second administrator in 1972. Reilly was a political centrist who embraced Bush's conception of voluntary action as a preferred alternative to regulation, believing that cooperation among government, industry, and environmental organizations could achieve mutually desirable results outside a regulatory framework.[6] Speaking at Reilly's swearing-in ceremony, Bush emphasized his commitment to uphold EPA's mission by "finding ways to clean up the environment without stifling the economy." He expressed his confidence in Reilly's ability to find common ground and transcend the confrontations dividing the country.[7]

Perhaps as much for symbolic posturing as for any honest faith in its political feasibility, Bush proposed creating a cabinet-level department of the environment that would absorb EPA and the major agencies responsible for public lands.[8] The impulse to rationalize the federal government's administration of natural resources was nothing new. From Herbert Hoover and Franklin Delano Roosevelt to Richard Nixon and Jimmy Carter, presidents had periodically advocated grand reorganizations, and all of these efforts had fizzled. The reshuffling of agency authorities so threatened the intricate and engrained complex of vested interests, lines of influence, and congressional jurisdictions that the political costs had been insurmountable.[9]

Bush outlined a pair of more easily achievable environmental initiatives in his 1990 State of the Union address. The first entailed expanding the national parks, forests, and wildlife refuges through an "America the Beautiful" program, with the aim of improving "recreational facilities on public lands." The second called for planting "a billion trees a year" through a collective effort that would "keep this country clean from our forestland to the inner cities and keep America beautiful for generations to come."[10]

These colorful—but ultimately insubstantial—objectives, along with his proposed department of the environment, attracted little media coverage, despite Bush's frequent references to them in subsequent public addresses. Anticipating the likely attention to be lavished on the twentieth anniversary of Earth Day in April 1990, the president used the White House grounds in March for a tree-planting ceremony and the unveiling of the National Tree Trust Act of 1990, his ambitious, nationwide program to blend public-private partnerships and volunteer efforts to plant one billion trees annually for ten years. Like Johnny Appleseed on steroids, this arboreal initiative sought to encompass rural and urban areas in all fifty states. The administration's budget request included $175 million for the tree-planting endeavor, which would be facilitated by a private nonprofit foundation empowered to raise funds, recruit volunteers, and forge alliances among individuals, businesses, governments, and community organizations. The foundation would call "for each American to become a volunteer for the environment" and would use "state forestry agencies and private tree-planting organizations—volunteers helping thousands of new volunteers to learn not only how and where to plant trees but how to care for them, why we need them, and how they help the environment."[11]

RELAUNCHING THE TAKE PRIDE CAMPAIGN

Bush's signature domestic program became what he called the "thousand points of light," a multipronged initiative to promote volunteerism in addressing such social problems as drug abuse, illiteracy, homelessness, hunger, and environmental decay. In his 1989 inaugural address, the president declared, "The old solution, the old way, was to think that public money alone could end these problems. But we have learned that that is not so. And in any case, our funds are low. We have a deficit to bring down. We have more will than wallet, but will is what we need." The nation's greatest resource, he said, remained "the goodness and the courage of the American people," and with that, he turned to his volunteer-based idea: "I have spoken of a Thousand Points of Light, of all the community organizations that are spread like stars throughout the Nation, doing good. We will work hand in hand, encouraging, sometimes leading, sometimes being led, rewarding." Reaching to inspire his fellow Americans, he insisted, "The old ideas are new again because they're not old, they are timeless: duty, sacrifice, commitment, and a patriotism that finds its expression in taking part and pitching in."[12] As a vehicle to implement his political goal, the White House established the nonprofit Points of Light Foundation.[13]

Even though the more sharply focused Take Pride in America initiative fitted well philosophically with Bush's vision of volunteerism, the president did not make the public lands stewardship program an explicit element of the Thousand Points of Light campaign. Nor did he mention Take Pride in his frequent Points of Light speeches. Nevertheless, Take Pride in America found an enthusiastic advocate in the new secretary of the Interior, allowing it to continue during the Bush administration as a separate—albeit lower-profile—program.

Since the Kennedy and Johnson administrations, Westerners had headed the Department of the Interior. Bush held with tradition by selecting Manuel Lujan Jr. of New Mexico. Having served in the House of Representatives from 1969 to 1988, Lujan was a seasoned politician with a long record of engaging in issues of concern to the Department of the Interior, notably in his role as the ranking minority member of the House Committee on Interior and Insular Affairs from 1981 to 1985, followed by three years as ranking minority member of the House Committee on Science and Technology. Lujan's principal legislative interests had centered on Indian affairs, the expansion of nuclear power, and opening federal lands to commerce and recreation. In contrast to EPA Administrator William Reilly, who enjoyed the respect of environmental leaders, Lujan's reputation among conservationists bordered on the dismal. He had unfailingly supported Interior secretary James Watt, and his voting record in the House had consistently placed him among the League of Conservation Voters' lowest-rated congressional members. Unlike the pugnacious Watt, however, the mild-mannered Lujan was generally viewed as a nice guy, someone devoted to constituent service. Indeed, he had made several friends within New Mexico's environmental community, more often than not supporting their local causes. On a personal level, Lujan and Bush had bonded when they served together as Republican freshman members of the House between 1969 and 1971. It also helped that Lujan shared Bush's prioritization of pollution abatement over resource conservation.[14]

Take Pride in America captured Lujan's attention from the outset. As he saw it, the public lands stewardship program offered an innocuous way to highlight Bush's environmental and conservation goals and was an approach unlikely to offend anyone from steadfast environmentalists to natural resources exploiters.[15]

Soon after the announcement of Lujan's selection, Frank Boren, president of The Nature Conservancy, wrote to the secretary-designate about the organization's past successes in harnessing volunteer efforts, which he commended as a model for the Department of the Interior. Boren alerted Lujan to "the unbelievable amount of free labor that is available to conservation from the citizens of this country." The wise use of volunteers, he emphasized, could significantly reduce the high costs of restoring public lands. "They are fantastic people," he said. "I realize that you are swamped and don't need a lot of free advice. However, I wanted you to be aware of this resource that is out there now and is doing good work now."[16] Lujan responded enthusiastically, telling Boren "President Bush and I have agreed to a 10-point agenda to direct the administration of the Department of the Interior, and the promotion of volunteerism on public lands is a key part of that agenda. This is a reflection of the President's vision of a 'thousand points of light,' the citizens of this great country of ours being actively involved at all levels of American life and American government." He added,

> The continuation of the Take Pride in America campaign, with its focus on the development of a national public lands stewardship ethic through education and volunteerism, is a prime example of our commitment to the involvement of citizens with their public lands. It is my understanding that during the last two years, a number of Nature Conservancy projects have been nominated to the Take Pride awards program. This undoubtedly is a result of the many years of fine leadership which The National Conservancy has provided in the area of conservation and public education.[17]

Lujan became the 46th secretary of the Interior on 8 February 1989. At the swearing-in ceremony, Bush emphasized the "great contribution being made by volunteers who participate in the many programs to keep America beautiful and to make it possible for more Americans to use and enjoy the outdoors."[18] Although the president's emphasis on nationwide community service extended beyond Interior's portfolio, Lujan appreciated just how well Take Pride imbued the spirit and goals of the Points of Light initiative and how advancing one would

GREEN PERSUASION

advance the other. Lujan instinctively grasped the support he could generate for the Interior-led program through allegiance with the Thousand Points of Light campaign, as well as the favor to be gained by heralding the White House initiative via his agency's Take Pride public announcements. Thus, with Lujan's commitment and Bush's blessing, Take Pride in America retained its foothold within the executive branch.[19]

Ever the politician, Lujan was not beneath exploiting his rapport with the president. He invited First Lady Barbara Bush to serve as honorary chair of the Blue Ribbon Panel of Judges for the Take Pride awards. Flattered by the Interior secretary's compliments of her leadership abilities and "personal commitment to education," Barbara Bush accepted—reassured by Lujan that "this very exciting program embodies so much of what the Bush Administration stands for—education, volunteerism, community spirit, protection of our natural and cultural treasures, and a deep love and devotion to the United States of America."[20]

Lujan also understood the importance of the campaign's celebrity spokespersons, and in May he invited Clint Eastwood to continue his involvement. Noting that "President George Bush has claimed volunteerism and education as two of his special emphases under his 'thousand points of light' program," Lujan stressed his intent "to support the President in these efforts particularly through the Take Pride campaign, with its focus on public awareness and education, and the development of a stewardship ethic—which I believe can have a positive effect on all aspects of our society."[21]

President Bush spoke publicly about the Take Pride program in his June 1989 address to the Family Motor Coach Association at the Virginia state fairgrounds in Richmond. Pointing to the wanderlust that compelled recreational vehicle owners to forgo "real estate for wheel estates," Bush commented, "When this organization was founded by a handful of families in 1963, no one could have predicted that 26 years later you'd be 65,000 strong and still growing."[22] Playing to the group's love of sightseeing and the open road, he touted his administration's efforts to safeguard the national parks and expand scenic byways under Bureau of Land Management and Forest Service jurisdiction. It was a pleasure, he said, "to hear that so many of you are reaffirming the ethic of conservation by getting involved in the Take Pride in America program, promoting the careful stewardship of our public lands and resources."[23]

Lujan's tenure in the House of Representatives had sharpened his skills with constituents and led him to expand the size and diversity of the Blue

Ribbon Panel of Judges.[24] The new panel charged with selecting Take Pride in America award winners included congressional members, governors and state legislators, federal and state agency heads, corporate and education leaders, celebrities, and representatives from conservation, hunting, youth, and outdoor recreation organizations. Environmental groups had a place at the table, but little more.[25]

The president and First Lady presided over the third annual Take Pride in America National Awards Ceremony, which took place on the South Lawn of the White House in July 1989. Country music entertainers Lee Greenwood and the Moody Brothers warmed up the crowd, with Greenwood serving as master of ceremonies. Lujan told the 3,000-person audience that the Take Pride award winners represented "104 points of light in America's bright sky of volunteerism."[26] President Bush's impromptu remarks epitomized his clipped speech pattern: "And now, as you may know, I, too, love the outdoors—always have. Love to hunt and hike and go fishing in the Keys or out West." He then turned to his formal address:

> Last month we celebrated the volunteer spirit,
> which is as timeless as America and as timely
> as today. For by launching the Points of Light
> Initiative, we sounded a nationwide call for each
> American to engage in community service. Well,
> this afternoon we renew that call in the cause of
> conserving our national and cultural resources and
> of enshrining our parks, forests, wildlife, waters,
> and monuments. For the great outdoors is precious,
> but fragile. To preserve it, we must protect it.[27]

In September 1989, Lujan wrote to Department of Labor secretary Elizabeth Dole and Department of Housing and Urban Development secretary Jack Kemp urging them to participate more actively in the Take Pride campaign.[28] He later asked the same of the heads of the Tennessee Valley Authority; EPA; the Departments of Commerce, Agriculture, Education, and Transportation; and the Army Corps of Engineers, pointing to the initiative's continued growth, which had recently added two new federal agency partners—the Department of Veterans Affairs and the Peace Corps—to join with the 48 partner states. Telling them the "program has the full support of The White House as part of the President's 'thousand points of light' initiative" and that it "embraces all the values of President Bush's emphasis on national service," he concluded by soliciting their "active participation."[29]

THE ADVERTISING COUNCIL

In developing the Take Pride in America campaign, the Ad Council strove to build a broad coalition of sympathizers by targeting organizations committed to voluntary action in outdoor settings (such as scout troops and gardening clubs) but unaligned with environmental groups critical of White House policies and actions. It also began to expand the program's demographic reach. In May 1989, the Ad Council's campaign coordinator, Harold Handley, pitched a youth-oriented series featuring the television character ALF (aka "Alien Life Form"), the gruff, wild-eyed, furry extraterrestrial title character of a popular NBC sitcom. In the campaign's effort to target younger audiences, Handley said, "We have been fortunate again to obtain the services of a celebrity recognized by young and old as our new spokesman—or perhaps I should refer to him as our 'spokesalien' ALF. He is encouraging us to care for our planet. He says he doesn't want to have to look for a new one."[30] In the public service announcements, the puppet ALF pled the case for Planet Earth:

> Yo, Alf here.
> I'd like to talk to you about your planet. I like it and you should too.
> A lot of people aren't taking very good care of it. For starters: they're abusing our public lands, they're littering the beaches, vandalizing the parks, trashing the playgrounds, and basically treating the planet like rental property.
> Frankly, I don't understand it. People like that are running loose and I'm the one who has to hide in the kitchen.
> Look, folks, public lands are not like pizzas— you just can't pick up the phone and order more.

I should know, my planet was really abused. The next thing we knew, it was gone.

Public land is our friend. If we don't take care of it, it'll be destroyed.

If you want to help me take care of our public lands, call me.

I'll send you all kinds of neat stuff. Even a recent photo of myself.

Please let's save the planet. I don't want to have to look for another one.[31]

In summer 1989, Eisaman, Johns & Laws replaced W. B. Doner and Company as the volunteer advertising agency in charge of the Take Pride account. By then, Doner's ALF idea had already paid off. During the first two months, ALF public service ads had generated more than 100,000 telephone inquiries.[32] Eisaman, Johns & Laws, however, proposed an important redirection of the campaign, seeking to motivate action rather than awareness. The new target groups included college-educated, 25- to 54-year-olds making more than $30,000 annually, promoting volunteerism along with a message that "an individual can make a difference." The goal was to "give people something to do as opposed to what not to do."[33] The Ad Council approved the revised strategic plan and, in January 1990, considered creative concepts for a new television campaign featuring Linda Evans, the television actor best known for her central role in the ABC prime-time soap opera *Dynasty*, which aired from 1981 to 1989.[34]

That season, the Ad Council concluded its Take Pride in America campaign, claiming that it had "successfully met its goals and is in the process of being completed."[35] Such termination was not unusual. Indeed, the majority of the council's advertising campaigns lasted only a few years. Rather than continue with Take Pride, the council teamed with the White House to launch an alternative series of public service announcements that hewed closer to President Bush's priorities: the Points of Light volunteer initiative. The new campaign, which was sponsored by the Points of Light Foundation rather than the federal government, sought to steer "people to community service," a goal that inspired the tagline "Do something good. Feel something real."[36]

The loss of Ad Council involvement did not, however, spell the end of Take Pride. It merely shifted responsibility for promoting the public lands stewardship effort to the Interior Department's staff. Although reduced in scale, Take

Protect Your Public Lands/Youth Campaign
for Take Pride in America, U.S. Department of the Interior [CC]
Please discontinue use: February 1, 1990.

Public Service Announcements

Available in :60, :30 versions

"Take Pride/Youth"

(MUSIC UNDER)
ALF: Yo, Alf here.

I'd like to talk to you about your planet.
I like it and you should too.

A lot of people aren't taking very good
care of it. For starters: they're abusing
our public lands,

they're littering the beaches, vandalizing
the parks, trashing the playgrounds,

and basically treating the planet like
rental property.

Frankly, I don't understand it. People like
that are running loose and I'm the one
who has to hide in the kitchen.

Look folks, public lands are not like
pizzas—you just can't pick up the phone
and order more.

I should know, my planet was really
abused. The next thing we knew, it was
gone.

Public land is our friend; if we don't take
care of it, it'll be destroyed.

If you want to help me take care of our
public lands, call me.

I'll send you all kinds of neat stuff. Even
a recent photo of myself. 1-800-446-4ALF

Please, let's save the planet. I don't want
to have to look for another one.

A Public Service Campaign of the Advertising Council [Ad Council]

CNPL-8160/8130
189

Volunteer Advertising Agency: W.B. Doner & Company Advertising, Baltimore
Volunteer Coordinator: Harold J. Handley, Vice President, Sales & Marketing, McCormick & Co., Inc.

FIGURE 21. Television storyboard for a 1990 Take Pride in America ad featuring the puppet ALF. Courtesy of Ad Council Archives, University of Illinois Archives, record series 13/2/207.

Pride endured throughout the Bush administration, operating side by side with the Points of Light initiative, each reinforcing the other in spirit, but working independently to address different objectives.[37]

Anticipating the eventual termination of the Ad Council's assistance, Interior's internal Take Pride in America Task Force published a special issue of its newsletter, *National Campaign News*, offering practical media advice to agency staff. For example, the newsletter stated that "articles or editorials in your local newspaper or on your local radio or television stations in support of Take Pride in America Month are among the most effective tools you can use to get attention and support for stewardship activities in your community. An editorial carried by a newspaper or broadcast by a television or radio station gives stewardship and volunteerism an important third-party endorsement."[38] As far as next steps, it added, "Once you have identified your strongest media contact(s), call or sit down with that individual to discuss an angle on stewardship activities in your area. Use Take Pride Month as the 'hook' and identify activities that have taken place in your area or your State. Be prepared to identify some activities which will take place during Take Pride Month and bring them up-to-date on the public service campaigns featuring the 'tough, good guys' (Clint Eastwood, Charles Bronson, and Louis Gossett, Jr.)."[39]

Lujan drew on his legislative experience and personal networks to secure bi-partisan passage of the Take Pride in America Act, which President Bush signed into law on 28 November 1990.[40] Senator Steve Symms (R-ID), who introduced the bill, said that Take Pride represents "a great example of how government can help, not by imposing burdensome regulations, but by recognizing those tireless individuals and groups who take it upon themselves to identify and solve problems." Appealing to the conservative agenda of curtailing domestic federal expenditures, Symms asserted that "giving people the recognition they deserve is a simple act and one that makes government a partner with the governed instead of an adversary."[41]

The statute made Take Pride in America a permanent office within the Department of the Interior, allowing for the direct allocation of federal funds to support it, largely in the form of facilities and administrative services. It also authorized Take Pride to raise private funds, accept gifts, and recruit volunteers. The program's formalized mission changed little from its original conception to conduct a public awareness campaign, run a national awards program, and encourage public appreciation of the nation's lands and resources, but the act increased the program's perception of legitimacy and its chance for longevity by not having to rely on the pleasure of the White House for its existence. Such legislative authority made it more difficult for any future administration to eliminate the program.[42]

In spring 1991, Lujan impaneled the Take Pride in America Advisory Board, assembling a diverse, nationwide membership to help publicly validate the program, increase its visibility, strengthen its regional backing, and provide programmatic guidance. The board's charter called for an annual operating budget of $100,000 and a two-year life span, unless "renewed by the Secretary of the Interior in accordance with the Federal Advisory Committee Act."[43] Lujan used the board to bring new participants—or at least new supporters—into the fold. His appointment authority served as a subtle, if token, display of his ability to bestow public recognition, and he continued to favor representatives of the private (for profit) sector over those from environmental and conservation organizations. Befitting that strategy, he selected American Recreation Coalition president Derrick Crandall to chair the board.

Despite Take Pride's espousal of personal sacrifice, volunteerism, and love of country, the program's operation never acquired immunity from politics and patronage. In fall 1991, when Lujan needed to fill the unexpired term of a member who had resigned from the Take Pride in America Advisory Board, he turned to a public affairs specialist with deep Republican ties and extensive experience in Washington, D.C., and New Mexico, including as director of congressional and media affairs in the White House Office of Telecommunications, political and fundraising consultant to the National Republican Congressional Committee, and political campaign director for a U.S. congressional campaign.[44] In her December 1992 transmittal memorandum to the Interior secretary, Take Pride in America Director Anne House Quinn emphasized the program's great potential and strong presidential backing. It had 14 federal agency partners and the support of "numerous private sector organizations," she said, and—in 1991—8 million Americans across all 50 states contributed more than 12 million hours of service through the program, while Take Pride's seven full-time employees worked with a budget of $1.6 million.[45]

GREEN WASHING TAKE PRIDE

Thanks to Interior secretary Lujan's administrative astuteness, Take Pride survived as an innocuous and symbolically compatible component of President Bush's nationwide volunteer effort. From the White House's perspective, the political calculus was simple: Take Pride gave the administration the appearance of being committed to environmental values without relying on regulations or the reorientation of natural resource policies—or without fully funding federal land management agencies. It also offered a "green washing" opportunity to participating organizations. Entities vilified by environmentalists (such as the

American Petroleum Institute) could assist the Take Pride program in the hope of earning recognition for their responsible treatment of public lands.[46]

To his credit, Lujan knew when to take advantage of an easy way to ingratiate himself with the White House and how to do so without stepping on anyone's toes. Promoting the Take Pride program allowed him to distribute a few favors—as minor as they might have been—among a wide group of individuals and organizations. It also cast Lujan in the role of heading an effort extending beyond his agency, to the extent that Take Pride represented a coalition of federal, state, and private entities.

Whereas President Reagan had issued a formal proclamation designating May 1988 Take Pride in America Month, Lujan took it upon himself to declare May as the perpetual Take Pride in America Month.[47] In sending this news release to the nation's governors, Lujan expressed his hope that they would issue similar state-based proclamations, adding, "Your recognition will provide a great boost to the many individuals and organizations conducting volunteer stewardship activities in your State."[48] The Interior secretary encouraged his staff to participate in the various volunteer projects scheduled for May 1989, explaining that he and the president "share a commitment to the responsible stewardship of our natural, historic and cultural resources, and the development of a strong outdoor ethic among all Americans."[49] One of those May events would take place in Rawlins Park, which was situated just to the north of the Interior Department's Washington, D.C., headquarters. In describing the "jamboree celebration" to the director of the Office of Personnel Management, whose headquarters building bordered the opposite side of the park, Lujan invited the agency's staff to attend the event, noting "we will be entertained by The Moody Brothers, a country/western group which has been very supportive of the Take Pride campaign."[50] Lujan also asked Interior's bureau directors to urge their staffs to join the outdoor festivities and to view the Take Pride in America exhibit and video installed in Interior's famed art deco, mural-adorned cafeteria.[51]

In February 1990, Lujan reported to Ben Love, chief scout executive of the Boy Scouts of America, "on the joint scouting activities within the Department of the Interior," especially those that would enable Scouts to fulfill their public service obligations.[52] Lujan attached material from the National Park Service, which set forth the requirements for securing the Scouts' new Take Pride in America patch by completing Park Service–managed projects.[53] The Boy Scouts of America and Interior's Take Pride campaign office jointly developed guidelines for earning the patch. As Take Pride's *National Campaign News* explained, "Take Pride projects must be educational, worthwhile and memorable, and also benefit the public lands. Each Scout may earn one Take Pride patch and an unlimited number of federal agency bars (one for each project completed). Take Pride patches and bars may be earned in conjunction with merit badges and in fulfillment of requirements for Star, Life and Eagle ranks."[54]

The theme "We can make a world of difference" graced Lujan's self-proclaimed Take Pride in America month in 1990. The big event was capped on 31 May with an Oak Ridge Boys concert, to which news reporters were cordially invited.[55] Although Clint Eastwood, Charles Bronson, and Louis Gossett Jr. were no longer participating in Take Pride, Lujan proudly stated that the campaign was "presently in the process of producing advertising featuring actress Linda Evans."[56] The Take Pride office issued a news release summarizing the initiative's "public service awareness campaign using radio, TV and print media" and noting that Evans would be delivering "the message that there is something that everyone can do to Take Pride in America and help to protect our environment."[57] With the Evans public service announcements ready for distribution in July, Lujan explained to television public service directors that "Ms. Evans calls on all of us to take action on behalf of our environment. 'After all, some pretty important people are moving in,' she says, as giggling children surround her."[58]

The nationally syndicated television program *Entertainment Tonight* ran a short interview with Evans in June 1990. Reporter Leeza Gibbons asked the star of ABC's prime-time soap opera *Dynasty* about her role with the revamped public lands stewardship program. Setting up the piece, Gibbons stated that "Linda Evans has made headlines in her home state of Washington for speaking out on environmental issues, now she's added her clout to the Take Pride in America campaign adding her name to an impressive line-up of stars." Gibbons elaborated that the new Take Pride spokesperson "is spreading the word about the environment. Of all the roles she's been asked to play over the years, she says none has made her prouder than this one." The camera then focused on Evans, who said, "I was pleased they chose me because I was someone who cared. I've been working in environmental causes for a few years and this gave me an opportunity to tell an awful lot of people something I think is very important." She emphasized that "everybody has to do something and everybody can do something, and that's what we're trying to say to them."[59]

Take Pride's new Linda Evans–endorsed ads gained little traction for the program—or for the president's credibility. From the moment he entered the White House, George H. W. Bush pursued an environmental policy that was more sympathetic and activist than Reagan's, yet it fell short of what many environmental organizations desired.[60] Failing to garner the support he thought he had earned, Bush tempered the attention he paid to environmental matters, a shift that reflected the environmentally unsympathetic stance of the president's senior staff, notably Vice President Dan Quayle, Chief of Staff John Sununu Jr., and Office of Management and Budget Director Richard Darman. Like Reagan, Bush remained committed to encouraging citizen volunteerism and promoting partnerships between the public and private sectors, rather than fully funding government initiatives. Toward that end, in December 1990 he signed an executive order establishing the President's Commission on Environmental Quality, with the charge of advancing conservation, education, international cooperation, and pollution prevention through public-private partnerships. To encourage voluntary activities, he launched a program of presidential awards in conservation and environmental affairs.[61] Despite these efforts, voluntary stewardship of the nation's natural resources faded from Bush's agenda as he prepared for his reelection bid.

CHAPTER 8

GEORGE W. BUSH AND TAKE PRIDE'S REVIVAL

George H. W. Bush vigorously defended his environmental record during his reelection campaign but did so without listing Take Pride in America among his administration's accomplishments.[1] Advised by political strategists that the volunteer-based, public lands stewardship program lacked salience, Bush focused on what his team perceived as more substantive achievements. At his October 1992 campaign stop in Paducah, Kentucky, for example, he touted the signing of the Clean Air Act and his administration's programs on wetlands protection, reforestation, and ocean dumping restrictions. He also attempted to portray his Democratic opponents (especially presidential candidate Bill Clinton's running mate, Al Gore) as environmental extremists. Bush stressed the need for *balance*, quipping, "You've got a guy coming over here in Ozone Man, Gore, and he'll shut down this country, I'll tell you." Pointing to Gore's championing of the endangered spotted owl in Oregon and his advocacy of raising automotive fuel efficiency standards, Bush warned that "it is too much when you go and say that the owl is so important that you're going to throw 30,000 people in the timber business out of work; or go up, as Mr. Gore's book says, and say you want 40- to 45-miles-per-gallon standards, fuel efficiency standards. You've got some auto stuff in this State, and you're going to throw those workers needlessly out of work by setting these strange and too far-out standards."[2]

Thanks to lingering concerns over the 1990–1991 recession, however, political topics like environmental regulation found less traction. The economy dominated the 1992 presidential election. Unable to rally support from environmental organizations and forced to shield himself from the harsh barbs launched by ultraconservative critics, Bush largely abandoned the environmental priorities that had animated the early months of his administration.[3] The ecological calamity of the 1989 *Exxon Valdez* oil spill in Alaska's Prince William Sound, combined with the administration's efforts to open the Arctic National Wildlife Refuge to oil drilling, further strained Bush's standing among the conservation community and led the Clinton campaign to feel secure that voters with strong environmental leanings would remain solidly committed to the Democratic ticket. This confidence intensified Clinton's focus on economic matters, a strategy that ultimately proved successful and influenced the new administration's agenda. Even if environmental matters had not registered at the top of the electorate's priority list, Clinton's transition team was well aware that membership in environmental and conservation associations remained high. Those numbers—combined with the passion felt toward their causes—would make environmental supporters a potent political voice, with implications for programs like Take Pride in America.[4]

BRUCE BABBITT AT INTERIOR

Following Bush's reelection defeat, Interior secretary Manuel Lujan angled to ensure the programmatic longevity of Take Pride in America by burnishing its apolitical nature. On the eve of his departure, Lujan sent secretary-designate Bruce Babbitt the Take Pride Advisory Board's recently prepared recommendations, stating that when he had begun his tenure at the Department of the Interior, "Take Pride in America was a rising initiative started by my predecessor Don Hodel. His idea was to educate all Americans that they own our public lands and urge them to volunteer to take care of our lands." Lujan said he was impressed by the citizen involvement in all 50 states, which had prompted him "to expand the Take Pride effort into a broad-based, environmental program." Soliciting Babbitt's support, he emphasized that Take Pride "can never be measured by the tons of trash its volunteers remove from our lands or the millions of dollars it saves a state. It can, however, stand tall when it comes to bringing the citizens of our great nation together for the good of our country."[5]

Babbitt, who had served as Arizona's attorney general (1975–1978) and governor (1978–1987) and unsuccessfully sought nomination as the Democratic presidential candidate in 1988, had other ideas. Because Take Pride had taken root during the notoriously anti-environmentalist Reagan presidency, it remained suspect among many people sympathetic to conservation ideals. Once in office, Babbitt asked Interior's legal counsel whether the program could be discontinued. Acting solicitor Timothy Elliott submitted his findings in March 1993. He concluded that the Interior secretary had the requisite authority to terminate Take Pride, either ceasing it outright or reducing its operations, "despite the fact that the program is created by statute." Moreover, the secretary could determine that "very little or none of the administrative services" for Take Pride are "necessary and appropriate." Elliott then outlined the bureaucratic processes for shutting it down.[6]

In April, Babbitt ordered the immediate "cessation of the activity of the Take Pride in America Program."[7] Two months later, he asked the congressional appropriations committees to approve the reallocation of $400,000 in Take Pride funds to support President Clinton's newly established Council on Sustainable Development. As the Interior Department told House subcommittee chairman Sydney Yates, "The President is committed to a national strategy that uses our natural resources to meet the needs of the present without compromising the future. To this end, the Council will develop and recommend an action strategy on sustainable development that will encourage economic growth, job creation, environmental protection, and the effective use of our natural and cultural resources." Moreover, the agency assured Yates that the council "will encourage stewardship and promote public participation in a conservation ethic."[8]

To signal his respect for the values and accomplishments of Take Pride in America, Babbitt explained his "difficult decision" in letters directed to more than 200 of the initiative's principal supporters. Aiming to appease the program's politically conservative backers, he argued that "Take Pride in America is a responsibility that can likely be shifted to the private sector." Babbitt assured them that the Clinton administration remained "solidly committed to increasing volunteerism and national service" and would make every effort to foster activities "at the local level" rather than directing funding toward "a huge national program." He pointedly emphasized that the White House was not abandoning support of volunteerism on public lands; it had "simply chosen a different vehicle."[9]

Rather than scrubbing Take Pride from the books, Babbitt simply mothballed it, leaving it dormant and defunded. With the national program in abeyance, some state groups continued with their own recognitions of volunteers working on public lands, but coordination among the state-run efforts slumped with Babbitt's disbandment of the Take Pride in America Advisory Board, an action he took in accordance with the administration's effort to reduce the number of nonmandated federal advisory committees.[10] Derrick Crandall, president of the American Recreation Coalition and chair of the Take Pride in America National Advisory Board during George H. W. Bush's presidency, argued in vain for the program's resurrection. The Interior Department even denied the coalition's request to use the Take Pride slogan and logo.[11]

The Clinton administration conveyed its espousal of voluntarism in several ways, including through its support of the nonpartisan Points of Light Foundation. Ed Segal, who headed the White House Office of National Service, worked with the foundation to advance Clinton's own ambitious national service initiative, AmeriCorps. Indeed, the president's proposed 1994 federal budget earmarked $5 million for the Points of Light Foundation, the same amount allocated to it during the final year of Bush's presidency.[12]

There was no denying the value Clinton placed upon voluntarism and the role of citizens in public lands stewardship. He merely chose a different mechanism to implement those goals. In 1993, the White House introduced the AmeriCorps National Civilian Community Corps (NCCC), which was modeled on the Civilian Conservation Corps, the New Deal organization founded 60 years earlier. The NCCC was a nationwide program aimed at young adults, providing 10-month terms of service, sending teams of 8 to 12 people to assist with conservation projects, infrastructure improvement, urban and rural development, and disaster relief.[13]

GALE A. NORTON'S SECRETARYSHIP

Different occupants of the White House have stressed different aspects of volunteer service, but by the dawn of the twenty-first century, there was little doubt that voluntarism remained a valuable political tool for American presidents. After barely defeating Vice President Al Gore in the disputed November 2000 election, George W. Bush revived his father's rhetoric promoting voluntarism as a way to lessen (symbolically, if not literally) the role of the federal government in addressing social problems and needs. Rather than building upon Bush 41's Thousand Points of Light program, Bush 43—like Clinton before him—established something new. The nature and timing of that creation were influenced by the coordinated terrorist attacks of 11 September 2001. President Bush harnessed the resulting surge in patriotism by urging Americans to serve their country as volunteers through the USA Freedom Corps, which incorporated the Clinton administration's AmeriCorps program.[14]

Because Bush's stance on environmental and natural resources policy aligned closely with the positions staked out by Ronald Reagan, it came as no surprise when Bush selected James Watt's protégé Gale A. Norton to head the Department of the Interior.[15] Norton was born in Wichita, Kansas, but moved to Colorado, earning both bachelor's (1975) and juris doctor (1978) degrees from the University of Denver. After she finished law school, Watt hired her as a staff attorney at the Denver-based Mountain States Legal Foundation. When Watt later became Reagan's Interior secretary, he recruited Norton to join the agency as an associate solicitor, a job she held until 1990. From 1991 to 1999, she served as attorney general of Colorado, where she solidified her reputation as a critic of federal regulations affecting public lands.[16]

Law professor Richard Lazarus has explained how Norton resolutely sought to redirect the Department of the Interior away from Clinton era values. Besides advancing Bush's goal of allowing oil exploration and development in the Arctic National Wildlife Refuge, Norton eliminated "environmental regulations and bonding requirements applicable to mining on public lands; authorized oil drilling near national parks; barred the reintroduction of grizzly bears to the Northwest; reversed the Clinton administration policy to now reopen Yellowstone National Park to snowmobiling; and reduced a Clinton administration two-year mining moratorium on 1 million acres under consideration for national monument designation to a ban of new mining on only 117,000 acres of the land."[17] Just as Watt had done during Reagan's first term, Norton's emphasis on opening public lands to resource extraction ignited fiery opposition within environmental and conservation communities.[18]

Norton's goals may have mirrored Watt's, but her style was more in line with Donald Hodel's. That low-key approach made Norton receptive to the idea of resurrecting Take Pride in America. Reactivating the public relations program, her senior advisors counseled, offered one way to shield the Bush administration from the anticipated criticism. It would also underscore the president's emphasis on personal responsibility and voluntary land stewardship.[19] Norton heard from other interests as well. Derrick Crandall, the former Take Pride advisory board chair who had lobbied the Clinton administration to keep the program functioning, headed an effort to reinstate Take Pride. He was quick off the blocks, submitting written recommendations to the Bush 43 transition team in December 2000. Meeting face-to-face with White House and Interior staff in March 2001, Crandall emphasized how volunteerism could expand the productivity of federal public lands agencies and "address a troublesome decline in youth participation in traditional outdoor recreation activities."[20] Two weeks after the 11 September terrorist attacks, he implored Norton to consider the healing power "of outdoor activities on America's public lands in helping the nation deal with the stresses of life." The outdoor recreation lobbyist also pushed for a relaunching of "Take Pride in America and a high visibility campaign to encourage volunteerism on federal lands—an effort designed to capitalize on current patriotic fervor and the predicted steady increase in time by Baby Boomers, a generation of Americans with a special passion for the outdoors."[21]

After consulting with her inner circle at Interior, Norton agreed to explore these matters.[22] In October 2001, she summoned leaders of the recreation industry to a meeting, where she listened to their pleas for prioritizing the recreational use of the public lands. To temper the widespread anxiety triggered by the 11 September attacks, they advised heightening security measures on the agency's domains. They also recommended a new effort to introduce children to the fun of outdoor activities on public lands. Norton's own staff urged her to focus on three groups: "today's seniors; retiring boomers; high schoolers with service requirements for graduation."[23]

By fall 2002, the White House and Department of the Interior agreed to reinstate the Take Pride in America program, folding it into President Bush's USA Freedom Corps initiative, which, they reasoned, would offer an appealing option for those wanting to direct their patriotic efforts toward the enhancement of the nation's public lands. Explaining that the president would announce the move in early 2003, Interior's Office of External and Intergovernmental Affairs informed the agency's bureau and office heads that a revitalized Take Pride would allow Interior "to fulfill the President's call to service in the public lands arena." The program's volunteer initiatives would be designed to "promote stewardship and conservation, while encouraging citizens to use and enjoy the great outdoors."[24]

Lynn Scarlett, Interior's assistant secretary for policy, management, and budget, teamed with Kit Kimball, Interior's director of external and intergovernmental affairs, to coordinate the relaunching of Take Pride in America. Their briefing memo to Norton highlighted the program's three main objectives: "Promote and recognize volunteer programs focused on restoration and stewardship efforts on public lands; Increase citizen awareness of the importance of wise use of public lands and natural and cultural resources; Encourage an attitude of stewardship and responsibility toward public lands and resources." Rather than creating a new set of volunteer activities, the program would build upon existing restoration, recreation, and stewardship projects. Scarlett and Kimball told the secretary that, during the 1980s, Take Pride had "provided a framework that appealed to the traditional public land base, urban residents and moderate environmentalists." A renewed program, they said, would have the added attraction of providing conservation-oriented volunteer opportunities for people wishing to fulfill "the President's call for service."[25]

In January 2003, Scarlett and Kimball briefed USA Freedom Corps Director John Bridgeland and Council on Environmental Quality Director James Connaughton. They outlined the background of Take Pride and the newly added elements that would help expand the USA Freedom Corps through volunteer opportunities on public lands. They also urged that the president announce Take Pride's revival in his State of the Union address. Special care would be taken, they said, to stress the benefits volunteers would bring to the nation as a whole, adding that "the New Take Pride will emphasize—and highlight—the President's call to service and volunteers through new commitments and the integration of many projects and activities not in existence in the late 1980s."[26]

Take Pride's initial mission of curbing public lands abuses—such as theft, vandalism, and littering—was to be paired with the new goal of public lands *restoration*. Scarlett and Kimball said that the enlarged pool of volunteer labor would be especially helpful to underfunded state and local agencies. Take Pride would also be adding a "Master Volunteers" category. Highly specialized professionals, such as engineers, landscape architects, biologists, carpenters, and hydrologists, would "bring extraordinary talent and high-level skill to the public lands arena" and would mentor younger volunteers. Many of these master volunteers would come from the ranks of retired government employees. Scarlett and Kimball pointed to Take Pride's intent to expand its outreach to Hispanics and African Americans, as well as to unions and faith-based organizations.

Greater emphasis would be placed "on inner city and urban sites such as parks, trails, historical monuments, refuse sites, and playgrounds." Moreover, the annual awards program would be revamped by adding categories that recognized individual volunteers on the basis of their accumulated hours of service: the Presidential Level Volunteer would require at least 4,000 hours; the Secretary Level Volunteer, 3,000 hours; and TPIA Level Volunteer, 2,000 hours.[27]

News of the pending rebirth of Take Pride in America prompted the Eastern Lands and Resources Council—a coalition of state offices of conservation, natural resources, and public lands—to pledge their endorsement. Noting that "many States are considering layoffs and budget reductions in natural resource management programs," council president Ralph Knoll told secretary Norton that Take Pride would "provide some of the tools to assist management efforts within the natural resource agencies." He assured her that the council "will do anything it can to make this initiative a success."[28]

American Recreation Coalition (ARC) president Derrick Crandall reiterated his organization's interest in participating, and he pressed Interior to grant ARC an instrumental role in Take Pride's operation. As he explained to the agency's deputy secretary, ARC was not proposing to serve "as a vendor seeking payments from the Department but as a partner willing to contribute our own time and resources." Crandall's support of the Take Pride program during the Reagan and Bush 41 administrations enhanced his and the ARC's political visibility (allowing them to deal directly with federal land agency heads and members of Congress on matters of public interest) and giving them the opportunity to advance causes on public lands that benefited the outdoor recreation industry.[29]

TAKE PRIDE REDUX

Norton formally reinstituted Take Pride on 16 April 2003. Speaking before an audience of reporters at the National Press Club's Newsmaker Luncheon, she said, "By working with volunteers, young and old, we lend our hands to heal our land, one acre at a time. And in so doing, we are celebrating the start of the national, grassroots, bipartisan Take Pride in America program." Her failure to pay tribute to the earlier Take Pride initiative made it sound as if it was a new undertaking. During a media event later that afternoon, she joined Washington Mayor Anthony Williams and actor Rick Schroder to pose with a group of

**TAKE PRIDE
IN AMERICA**

Take Pride in America Campaign Coordinated by the Department of the Interior

FIGURE 22. Take Pride in America bumper sticker sporting the campaign's stylized insignia. Courtesy of Smithsonian Institution Archives.

student volunteers cleaning up debris and planting trees along the shores of Watts Branch, a tributary of the city's long-neglected Anacostia River.[30]

On 28 April 2003, Norton and Crandall signed a memorandum of understanding that established the ground rules for the ARC to assist Interior in carrying out Take Pride–related events and activities.[31] Explaining that the coalition's membership included "the Recreational Vehicle Industry Association, Recreational Vehicle Dealers Association and the National Association of RV Parks and Campgrounds," the trade journal *RV Business* reported that ARC would "coordinate voluntary fundraising for Take Pride."[32]

The Marina Operators Association of America also joined the endeavor, as did the Family Motor Coach Association, Recreation Vehicle Industry Association, Recreation Vehicle Dealers Association, Motorcycle Industry Council, United Four Wheel Drive Associations, Good Sam Club, America Outdoors, Bass Pro Shops, and many others.[33] Such a broad alliance reflected the strong interest among outdoor recreational industries reliant upon the use of public lands and waters. This economic sector was primarily concerned about the enhancement of visitor amenities, as opposed to land and biodiversity stewardship.[34] Michael Molino, president of the National RV Dealers Association, emphasized that his organization was "a strong supporter of responsible recreational use of America's Great Outdoors and the expansion of volunteerism on our public lands." Anticipating Norton's support, Molino said that his staff was preparing to distribute "Take Pride in America decals and posters to our members, with the goal of placing the Take Pride logo on thousands of RVs by this time next year."[35]

Norton named Martha Phillips "Marti" Allbright executive director of Take Pride in America in June 2003. Allbright had worked closely with Norton on two previous occasions: as chief deputy attorney general of Colorado from 1997 to 1998 and as transition chief of staff at the Department of the Interior from January to April 2001. At the time of her Take Pride appointment, Allbright served as senior counsel at Brownstein, Hyatt and Farber in Denver.[36] To publicize the relaunched program, Norton mandated that all the newly printed letterhead of the Department of the Interior and its constituent bureaus include the Take Pride in America logo on the top right corner, with the department or bureau logo appearing on the top left.[37]

Without Advertising Council assistance, the Department of the Interior had to create and implement the Take Pride media campaign on its own, and it met with some initial success. Norton and her staff pulled off a public relations coup by persuading Clint Eastwood to reprise his role as the program's national spokesperson. The movie star's willingness to promote Take Pride sprang from his personal commitment to the cause, which was exemplified by his unpaid, state-level position as a California State Parks Commissioner. The Interior Department produced a set of widely distributed video clips of Norton and Eastwood in Carmel River State Park planting trees with student volunteers from the nearby Carmel River School.[38]

Interior's promotional materials benefited from Eastwood's celebrity endorsement but lacked the polish, saturation distribution, and national impact of the Ad Council's initial Take Pride public service announcements. Recognizing the department's inability to generate an advertising campaign on par with those produced by marketing professionals, Interior officials decided to hitch the program to events guaranteed to attract their own widespread media coverage. Such an opportunity opened in September 2003 when the National Football League (NFL) held an oversized, four-day event on the National Mall before the season-opening game between the Washington Redskins and the New York Jets. In addition to Pepsi Vanilla and the NFL, the festivities were cosponsored by Coors Light, Reebok, Verizon Wireless, AOL, and the Department of the Interior/Take Pride in America. Televised coverage of the game itself played on jumbotron screens erected along the Mall. The open-air festival, advertised as the "NFL Kickoff Football Festival Presented by Pepsi Vanilla," concluded with a postgame concert offered free to members of the military and their families.[39]

Four days prior to the game, Darrell Green and Mark Moseley of the Washington Redskins and Steve Young of the San Francisco 49ers joined Norton and representatives of the Take Pride staff, Home Depot, the nonprofit organization KABOOM!, and local community members to build a football-

FIGURE 23. The National Football League joined with five corporate sponsors and Take Pride in America in promoting the start of its 2003 season with the four-day "NFL Kickoff Football Festival Presented by Pepsi Vanilla" on the National Mall in Washington, D.C. Courtesy of Smithsonian Institution Archives.

themed playground in an underserved neighborhood in southeast Washington. Interior aggressively publicized the attention-grabbing construction, boasting that the volunteer-built "Playground of Hope will be a lasting legacy of the NFL's week-long 2003 season kickoff activities in Washington, D.C."[40]

The festival's main events took place on a 10-block-long stretch of the National Mall, midway between the Capitol and the Washington Monument, a viewscape flanked by Smithsonian museums. Corporate logos decorated the temporary structures, while a lone booth festooned with Take Pride in America banners offered festival information, along with sign-up sheets for volunteer work on public lands.[41] Following the season-opening kickoff, public service announcements for Take Pride in America—narrated by football stars LaVar Arrington, Laveranues Coles, and Patrick Ramsey—played on jumbotrons and during broadcasts of the game on ABC television and CBS radio.[42]

Posters in Washington's Metro subway cars publicized the festival, but there was no papering over the controversy generated by the flagrant commercialization of the Mall, America's most renowned urban national park. On the eve of the game, the *Washington Post* devoted its lead editorial to a condemnation of this "marketing" of the National Mall.[43] The Department of the Interior, as a cosponsor of the event, had a clear conflict of interest. Interior had originally ruled that the jumbotron screens could present the ABC broadcast only if all of the commercials were replaced by public service announcements. But as game day approached, agency officials reversed their decision, giving their approval for those assembled on the Mall to watch the same football coverage and the same commercials seen by television audiences. Drawing on her interviews with National Park Service representatives, *Washington Post* reporter Karlyn Barker explained that "rules prohibiting commercial marketing on the Mall do not apply to this week's NFL extravaganza because the promotional aspects constitute 'sponsor recognition' and not advertising." Agency officials admitted to Barker that this hairsplitting to allow such commercials on the Mall was unprecedented, although they contended that "relaxing the rules is justified by the unique nature of the NFL program." Seeking refuge under the aegis of patriotism, Interior spokesperson Mark Pfeifle told Barker that the festivities "will pay tribute to our fighting men and women who are securing our freedom at home and overseas, especially coming up on the second anniversary of the horrendous attacks of September 11. The event also pays tribute to tens of thousands of people who donate their time to preserve and protect public lands."[44]

In her scrutiny of the relationship between professional sports and the military following the 11 September terrorist attacks, Samantha King observed that the NFL had chosen Times Square as the backdrop for its first season-opening kickoff festival in September 2002. Commenting on the second kickoff festival a year later, she wrote,

> This time the Kickoff took place on the National Mall in Washington D.C. and included performances by Britney Spears, Aerosmith, Mary J. Blige, and Aretha Franklin, who sang the national anthem. The 300,000-strong crowd included 25,000 troops and their families shipped in for the event by the Department of Defense with the promise of a free t-shirt and prime concert viewing. Publicity materials noted that the purpose of this "new tradition" was to "celebrate the resilient and indomitable spirit of America" through a focus on veterans of the "Global War on Terrorism." Although the Pentagon is officially prohibited from participating in corporate promotions, by folding the Kickoff into the Tribute to Freedom program, it was able to promote the event quite freely on its Web site and in communications with service personnel.[45]

King described Take Pride as an initiative that "encourages volunteerism on the nation's rapidly diminishing public lands in lieu of the paid labor force and environmental regulations that have been so dramatically rolled back under the current administration." She also decried the blatant linking of a public service program to commercial objectives.[46]

The appeal of associating Take Pride with the televised NFL event on the National Mall had been irresistible. The potential payoff—measured in viewer exposure—seemed substantial because professional football was then television's most watched sport. Situating that event at the heart of Washington's monumental core also added an air of patriotism. The images evoked messages of strength and masculinity, harkening back to those first Take Pride announcements by Eastwood, Bronson, and Gossett. And association of Take Pride with the event's commercial sponsors fitted with secretary Norton's goal of expanding Interior's partnerships with major corporations.[47]

SADDLING UP FOR THE ROSE PARADE

From the beginning, despite its themes and images celebrating the natural world, the Take Pride program had attracted little participation from environmental and conservation organizations. Outdoor recreational groups and businesses had comprised the major boosters. Typical of these supporters was the American Horse Council, which urged its members to contact their state's Take Pride coordinator "as soon as possible to increase the profile of the equine community" because the program presented a prime "opportunity for AHC members and recreational riders to take part in a worth-while federal initiative that offer[s] benefits to the industry too." Recreational riders could "show our federal officials, who make decisions about access to trails for riders, and the public how large the industry is, how active it is in volunteering and what we do to improve recreational opportunities."[48]

Such enthusiasm from its members led the American Recreation Coalition to sponsor an equestrian entry for the 2004 Tournament of Roses Parade in Pasadena, California. This horseback troop, jointly sponsored by the City of Los Angeles and the Walt Disney Company, celebrated a Los Angeles–based, inner city program called WOW (Wonderful Outdoor World; "an urban camping program designed to bring the great outdoors to children in their neighborhood parks") and focused attention on the importance of outdoor experiences for America's youth. The entry's organizers invited secretary Norton and Take Pride executive director Allbright to ride in the nationally televised parade, accompanied by "eight young Los Angelinos who were first introduced to healthy fun outdoors through our overnight urban camping adventure—and then accepted an invitation to explore the High Sierras as part of our WOW II program."[49]

According to Interior's press release, Norton's participation in the Tournament of Roses Parade was intended "to highlight the nearly 400,000 volunteer hours pledged to work on public lands devastated by this year's forest fires in California." Responding to the 730,000 acres consumed by wildfires, Take Pride in America worked with several California-based organizations to recruit volunteers to "help plant trees, clean up recreation sites, restore trails and perform other tasks needed to rehabilitate damaged land." The goal was to obtain the 730,000 hours of promised volunteer time—one hour for every acre burned in the Southern California wildfires.[50]

To enhance the publicity, Norton wanted to coordinate her parade appearance with an announcement of hours pledged to the restoration effort and enlisted John Stewart, director of environmental affairs at the United Four Wheel Drive Associations, to assist. Stewart set out to measure the unreported hours already donated and to offer a commitment in an equal amount from "a variety of recreation interests from motorized to mechanized (mountain bikes) to non-motorized (equestrian)." On behalf of 15 recreation organizations, Stewart then presented Norton with a promise of 150,000 volunteer hours, bringing Norton's total to 450,000 pledged hours on the eve of the parade.[51] The Good Sam Club, another charter partner of the relaunched Take Pride program, vowed to provide an additional 100,000 volunteer hours to assist in the restoration of Southern California's burned-over public lands.[52]

By then, the revived Take Pride program was gaining energy and new political support. J. Steven Griles, who had worked as a coal industry lobbyist before being tapped by the Bush administration to serve as deputy secretary of the Interior and who became Interior's main representative to Vice President Dick Cheney's energy task force, facilitated Clint Eastwood's return as Take Pride in America's spokesperson. In February 2004, Griles reminded Eastwood's representative Anthony Lombardo of the personal connection: "As you know, during my recent golf game with Clint Eastwood, we discussed Take Pride in America and his possible [reprised] participation as spokesman for this volunteer stewardship initiative." Griles emphasized that "Eastwood has served as a superb role model for stewardship and service, especially with his service as a state parks commissioner, and is still remembered for his trademark 'make my day' PSA's [sic] for Take Pride in the 1980's. Take Pride would be very grateful for his participation and support with the current effort."[53]

Eastwood agreed to stand as the program's sole celebrity spokesperson, and Marti Allbright arranged a photo op and press release announcing his involvement. The 73-year-old filmmaker engaged briefly with a group of 30 fifth graders volunteering on a trail maintenance project and the rehabilitation of picnic tables and benches in the Santa Monica Mountains National Recreation Area, a 20-minute drive from Beverly Hills, and delivered prepared remarks.[54]

In an effort to expand the program's base of supporters and participants, the Take Pride website proclaimed that it "will work to dramatically increase the number of volunteers by expanding participation among youth, senior citizen, Hispanic- and African-American, faith-based and union organizations. Take Pride will also emphasize service to inner city and urban sites, such as parks, trails, historic monuments and playgrounds."[55] Norton spoke to that municipal orientation in her address to the U.S. Conference of Mayors by announcing Interior's "Take Pride in America Cities" program. Communities hosting or sponsoring two or more annual events—such as a cleanup or tree-planting or awards ceremony—could designate themselves Take Pride in America Cities and "use the Take Pride in America logo and service marks at their events."[56]

The American Sand Association (ASA), a California-based organization of off-road motorsports enthusiasts with a special interest in riding on sand dunes clustered in desert, beach, and mountainous settings, represented another interest group seeking to influence public lands policy through the Take Pride program. American Sand Association members referred to themselves as "duners" and named their newsletter *In the Dunes*. On multiday outings, they typically engaged in motor home camping at or near their riding sites. Because the majority of large, dune-dominated ecosystems lie within state or federally owned lands, ASA focused its political efforts on advocating for open access to public lands, which often put them at odds with enforcement of the Endangered Species Act.[57] Although ASA was not a charter member of the relaunched Take Pride in America program, in 2006 it began encouraging its members to participate.[58] The goal was to demonstrate care and concern for public lands and to emphasize self-regulation, attempting to portray motorized recreationalists as part of the solution to—rather than the problem of—public lands misuse.

Although he did not mention Take Pride in his Earth Day campaign speech, President Bush made clear that he agreed with the program's operational belief that responsibility for environmental conservation should rest above all with the private sector. With a scenic coastal marsh backdropping his prepared remarks, he announced a wetlands initiative at the Wells National Estuarine Research Reserve in southern Maine, near the Bush family compound. Noting that 2004's Earth Day coincided with National Volunteer Week, the president acknowledged the 64 million Americans who served as volunteers, adding that it was his duty "to call people to a higher calling. If you're not volunteering, do so. It will make somebody else's life better, including your own." By way of example, he praised the 400 volunteers who helped maintain the beauty of the wetlands reserve in Wells, asserting, "good conservation and good stewardship will happen when people say, I'm just not going to rely upon the government to be the solution to the problem."[59]

In summer 2004, Norton and Allbright led a "Take Pride in America Western States Tour" aimed at promoting volunteer events on public lands in Colorado, Utah, Oregon, and California. The Council on Environmental Quality reported that the tour's cosponsor, Unilever, donated "100 percent recycled plastic lumber picnic tables to Estes Park [Colorado], as well as continuing their sustainable lumber donation to the National Park Service" and then listed all the Unilever activities as if a commercial for the company.[60]

Take Pride in America held its 2004 national awards ceremony in September at Interior headquarters, with secretary Norton, USA Freedom Corps director Desiree Sayle, and Take Pride executive director Allbright presiding. After Clint Eastwood greeted the attendees via a taped video message, Norton told the audience, "Cooperative conservation is essential to the long-term vitality of our nation's most prized treasure—our public lands."[61] American Recreation Coalition president Derrick Crandall accepted the special "Spirit of Take Pride in America" award. The Walt Disney Company received the Take Pride in America Charter Partner award for including a Take Pride promotional flyer in its *Brother Bear* DVDs and video packaging and for hosting a brainstorming session involving Interior Department personnel and Walt Disney Imagineers.[62]

The Take Pride program played a subliminal role in the 2004 presidential election, to the extent that the attention it gave to the administration's encouragement of volunteer efforts on public lands helped soften criticism of President Bush's environmental record. Nevertheless, Take Pride's political and monetary costs remained small. Voluntary public lands stewardship presented an ideal area where the private sector could assist, whether it be through individuals, corporations, or nongovernmental organizations. California and Florida, with their large populations and higher-than-average citizen concern for environmental matters, became key battleground states in the election. In 2004, both were headed by Republican governors—Arnold Schwarzenegger in California and the president's brother, Jeb Bush, in Florida—and in that year they both pushed their states into high visibility involvement in Take Pride in America activities, moves that were designed to signal their commitment to environmental stewardship, the Republican Party, and President Bush.

Natural disasters in the two states allowed Take Pride officials to emphasize high-visibility volunteer initiatives: wildfire restoration efforts in California and hurricane recovery efforts in Florida. In announcing the new Take Pride in Florida project in October 2004, the Council on Environmental Quality reported the unveiling of "the first of five mobile volunteer centers—trailers equipped with donated generators and filled with supplies that will be used to rehabilitate hurricane-ravaged areas in Florida and other public lands." Among the Take Pride partners underwriting the Mobile Volunteer Depot Project were the Walt Disney Company, Cummins, Featherlite, NASCAR, ReserveAmerica, Unilever, and Zodiac.[63]

Bush defeated his Democratic opponent, John Kerry, by a slim margin in the November 2004 election, and that ensured Take Pride's continuation. A year later, the program launched another ad campaign featuring Clint Eastwood. Since first lending them a hand in the late 1980s, Eastwood had become one of Hollywood's most renowned directors. In terms of his political and public service activities, he followed his 1986 election as the nonpartisan mayor of Carmel-by-the-Sea, California (serving a single, two-year term), by successfully running again for the mayoralty of the picturesque coastal town in 2001. In that year, Governor Gray Davis (D) appointed Eastwood to the California State Parks and Recreation Commission, and Governor Arnold Schwarzenegger (R) reappointed him in 2004. This voluntary position allowed Eastwood to engage with matters associated with state-owned public lands while making clear his deep-seated sympathies with Take Pride's objectives. The online newsletter *SeniorJournal.com* ran a story proclaiming, "Senior citizens interested in finding a way to contribute something back to America may want to heed the advice from fellow senior Clint Eastwood and volunteer for Take Pride in America." In a new set of public service announcements, Eastwood endorsed the campaign's tagline "It's Your Land, Lend a Hand," declaring, "I am very happy to help further the mission of Take Pride in America. It was a cause I supported when it was first launched 20 years ago, and the message of caring for our public lands is one that I continue to support." The newsletter reported that the public service announcement production took place in Carmel, where Eastwood, secretary Norton, and Take Pride director Allbright "joined students from Carmel

River School in a wetlands restoration project. That school was named the first Take Pride in America School following its agreement to participate in public land projects several times annually. The wetlands restoration project also involved the California State Parks staff and the California Conservation Corps."[64]

At its national awards ceremony in September 2005, Take Pride in America showcased its gardens initiative, which counted some 2,240 community and school gardens planted across all 50 states, thanks to the contributions of "more than 1,000,000 volunteers." Allbright emphasized the concept of "cooperative conservation" while telling the audience, "The winners that we celebrate today truly demonstrate the mission of Take Pride. They all embraced the spirit of cooperative conservation by working with other organizations and individuals to accomplish a shared goal."[65]

Conservation organizations had long appreciated the meaningful work performed by volunteers, yet there were growing concerns about how the Bush administration was using Take Pride in America and other agency-associated volunteer programs to make more palatable the labor shortages created by the underfunding of public lands departments. With regard to the National Park Service (NPS), Bill Wade of the Coalition of National Park Retirees noted in 2005 that "voluntarism has traditionally been viewed as a valuable, 'free' way for NPS to augment its staffing." From its establishment in 1970, the Volunteers in Parks (VIP) program, for example, explicitly stated that volunteers were "to augment, not supplant, the services provided by NPS employees." But rather than supplementing the work of uniformed, full-time employees, volunteers were, Wade reported, "replacing them through programs such as Take Pride in America and Volunteers in Parks." Wade and his colleagues did not question the motives of the park volunteers; it was the steady attrition of well-trained and accountable NPS staff that was troubling, as the resources management work they performed sustained "the very heart of the NPS mission."[66]

PASSING THE BATON

Both Norton and Allbright resigned in early 2006 and returned to the private sector. Even though Take Pride continued as a modest, low-profile activity projecting a sense of federal care and concern, the program no longer had an enthusiastic, senior-level advocate within the administration.[67] As the *New York Times* observed, Norton had shared the view of President Bush's cabinet members that natural resources policy should not skew too heavily toward preservation. "As the cheerful, upbeat face of a retrograde public policy, she may have been the most successful of them all," the newspaper wrote. "In public Ms. Norton spoke winningly of what she called her four C's: 'cooperation, communication and consultation, all in the service of conservation.' But this was little more than comfy language diverting attention from her main agenda, which was to open up Western lands, some of them fragile, to the extractive industries."[68] In fact, *High Country News* reporter Paul Larmer noted that many conservationists had viewed Norton's relaunching of Take Pride in America "as mostly talk."[69]

Dick Kempthorne, Norton's successor as Interior secretary, did little to alter the situation. The former Republican governor of Idaho, who had earlier cochaired the bipartisan Take Pride in America Governor's Council with Arizona's Democratic governor Janet Napolitano, continued the program, but with enhanced recognition of corporate participants. At the 2006 national awards ceremony, Clint Eastwood delivered words of encouragement via video broadcast prior to Kempthorne bestowing awards in 10 different categories and giving the Ford Motor Company special recognition for being the program's "Outstanding Supporter."[70]

Two years later, Take Pride received funding from Toyota to launch a three-week promotional tour of seven southern states. A series of road trips and festivities labeled "Voluntour Across America" began with a shoreline cleanup around Lake Grapevine in Texas as a way to introduce Take Pride's new "voluntourism" program, in which individuals, families, and groups were encouraged to organize holiday outings around voluntary service on public lands.[71] In coordination with the roving Voluntour Across America effort, an online travel service, Travelocity, sponsored a companion initiative offering small grants to "voluntourists" seeking volunteer opportunities near various vacation destinations. Travelocity also assisted in the development of a new portal on the Take Pride website describing options for "volunteer vacations" on public lands.[72] A second rolling event, the "Heartland Voluntour" trip, featured Take Pride staff traveling in a Toyota Highlander to six states over 15 days. According to the press release, by September 2008, Voluntour Across America had "already logged more than 5,200 miles."[73]

During President Bush's second term, a succession of directors—most of them White House staff alumna—cycled through the Take Pride in America office. Given the diminishing emphasis placed upon Take Pride, the program's executive directors were assigned expanded portfolios with more demanding, agency-wide responsibilities within the Department of the Interior.[74] In the week before the 2008 presidential election, Interior secretary Kempthorne signed an order extending Take Pride's authorization through 2010 and solidifying three programmatic priorities: "engaging youth in service, promoting voluntourism, and supporting beautification as an economic development strategy."[75]

In truth, Kempthorne had been a caretaker rather than a champion of Take Pride. His half-hearted promotion of the program was enough to keep it afloat, and ironically, the resulting low-priority status of Take Pride may have increased its chances of survival in the Democratic administration of Barack Obama. It simply failed to register as a political target, despite the new president's disagreement with Bush's environmental policies. Obama's Interior secretary nominee, Senator Ken Salazar (D-CO), faced questions about Take Pride at his January 2009 confirmation hearing. Senator Lisa Murkowski (R-AK) asked if he planned to "provide leadership and institutional support for seeking, managing, and recognizing volunteers on the lands and waters administered by Interior, whether through Take Pride in America or other programs." Salazar replied, "Volunteerism is essential in Interior's management and conservation of the lands and water we administer. I am a strong supporter of volunteerism, and will look for opportunities to take advantage of our fellow citizens' willingness to give their time and energy to our natural and cultural resources."[76]

Take Pride may have been promoted by Republican administrations for veiled reasons, but its public-facing advocacy of voluntarism resonated with Obama's personal experiences, such as his earlier work as a community organizer, his volunteer-infused presidential election campaign, and the numerous volunteer activities the Obamas collectively undertook as a family. Once in the White House, Obama launched "United We Serve," an umbrella program to advance voluntarism across the board.[77] Unfortunately for Take Pride in America, it failed to catch that wave of support. Throughout Salazar's four-year term as Interior secretary, Take Pride's budget stagnated, its full-time staff dwindled to two people, and its director, Lisa Young, reported to a "nonpolitical" assistant secretary rather than to a "political" assistant secretary, as had been the case during the Bush administration.[78] Yet while teetering on its narrow foothold within the Department of the Interior, the program still managed to host an annual awards ceremony and to expand the digital resources available on its website.

The economic downturn that gripped the country from 2008 through 2011 eroded resource allocations for public lands at the federal, state, and local levels, with ripple effects on volunteer organizations across the nation. Reductions in funds available for maintenance, information services, educational programming, and scientific projects increased the reliance of public lands administrators on volunteers. States in particular found their budgets bruised by high unemployment rates and the depressed economy, forcing difficult decisions for how they managed state parks. Some states closed selected parks, others imposed new user fees, a few allowed oil and gas drilling, and most increased their use of volunteers.[79] Take Pride in America did what it could to publicize the heightened need for donated labor, but because it functioned as a cheerleading operation rather than an organizer or supplier of volunteer help, it was unable to provide direct relief.

In assembling his second-term cabinet in early 2013, President Obama turned to Sally Jewell, the chief executive officer of the Seattle-based outdoor gear retailer Recreational Equipment, Inc. (REI), to head the Department of the Interior. Secretary Jewell retained Take Pride's small office in Interior's headquarters but suspended the program's annual awards ceremony. Two years later, she quietly ended support of Take Pride and had its website archived, although leaving its legal basis—the Take Pride in America Act—intact.

This decision preserved the opportunity for the next president to revive the program, and the election of the Republican candidate, Donald John Trump, sparked hope that that might happen. Although every president during his lifetime had fostered volunteer-based initiatives, Trump showed zero interest in following suit. Indeed, his budget proposals consistently called for defunding the Corporation for National and Community Service, an independent agency of the U.S. government that supports several prominent volunteer organizations, such as AmeriCorps and Senior Corps.[80] Unlike his three immediate Republican predecessors, who had perceived Take Pride in America as a useful public relations buffer against criticism of their environmental policies, Trump brashly flaunted his extreme anti-environmental policies. The Trump White House made no pretense of balance and no effort at subtlety and saw no reason to resuscitate Take Pride in America or promote any public lands stewardship projects. Thus, Take Pride in America, a Reagan era program that had encouraged citizen participation in caring for the nation's landed inheritance, was left by a Republican administration to wither on the vine.

CONCLUSION

Like the provision of national defense, the task of managing the country's 700 million acres of federal parks, forests, wildlife refuges, and other public lands is so large and complex that it stands as an inherent obligation of government. For well over a century, countless Americans have lightened some of the burden on federal authorities by donating time, labor, and expertise to assist with the care and study of those commonly held lands. When the recreational use of public lands surged in the decades following World War II, the volume and type of challenges facing land managers also increased. To counter that escalating workload, the federal government sought to heighten levels of voluntarism by turning to commercial advertising experts, via the nonprofit Advertising Council, and exploited popular culture for clever messaging, most notably through such icons as Smokey Bear and Iron Eyes Cody, aka the Crying Indian.

The tone and motivations of this government advertising effort shifted in the 1980s, modified to accommodate the Reagan administration's political goals. In 1985, the Ad Council worked with the Department of the Interior in launching Take Pride in America, a direct appeal for voluntary help in looking after public lands. Whereas previous Ad Council campaigns had relied upon cartoon mascots or fictional characters to spread their messages, Take Pride in America was distinguished by imaginative use of three Hollywood stars—Clint Eastwood, Charles Bronson, and Louis Gossett Jr.—whose tough-guy screen personae pressed Americans to assume greater responsibility for stewardship of the public domain.

Take Pride occupied a small programmatic niche within Interior. It neither created volunteer opportunities nor oversaw the work of volunteers. It essentially functioned as a public relations operation, one that advocated voluntarism and publicized the contributions of individuals and groups via press releases, newsletters, and annual awards ceremonies. For those reasons, it is impossible to measure the program's impact quantitatively. Thousands of conservation-oriented volunteer projects had existed before Take Pride's establishment, and only a handful ever associated themselves with the new government effort. Still, the national advertising campaign did drum home the need for, and significance of, voluntarism, and it created some notable pop culture moments.

The Hollywood glamour approach did succeed in motivating more people to pitch in. However, the impact of that volunteer labor pool was destined to be minimal without a commensurate increase in the strength and commitment of the federal agencies charged with overseeing the nation's land holdings. A parallel stream of substantive, coordinated government action would have made Take Pride in America more than a feel-good activity, but such a complementary effort was never a part of its intrinsic goal. Driven by an anti-regulatory ideology that called for reducing restrictions on how public land resources could be used, the White House was reining in conservation activities across the executive branch. Rather than buttressing larger efforts to improve public lands stewardship, Take Pride was exploited as a public relations vehicle to counter environmental critics and fend off calls for fuller funding of federal land management agencies.

Successive Republican administrations also found the Take Pride in America program a useful foil in the defense of their own political objectives of loosening environmental protections, expanding development on public lands, and trimming conservation agency budgets. The capture of Take Pride by the outdoor recreation industry merely moved the program's emphasis further away from environmental enhancement and toward private recreation.

The stated objectives of Take Pride—calls to curb littering, theft, and vandalism in public lands and encouragement of volunteers to assist with conservation, education, and maintenance programs—were easy for politicians on both sides of the aisle to embrace. Perhaps because the initiative appeared so innocuous, critics of Reagan's anti-environmentalism neither openly opposed nor openly embraced it. By and large, they ignored it. Take Pride was initially perceived from the outside as an exercise in minimalism—a modest gesture toward conservation, one serving as a tepid, inconsequential action intended to appease the public—even while the administration wielded this bit of green persuasion as a public relations cover for its efforts to advance economic development on public lands and to reduce federal environmental protections. The linking of public lands stewardship to personal responsibility and patriotism was also perfectly in tune with the administration's conservative agenda of diminishing the government's role in favor of the private sector.

The history of the Take Pride in America program, especially its use and marginalization by different administrations, ultimately reflected a widening partisan divide on environmental matters. Although the program's volunteer participants deserve recognition for their contributions, Take Pride's political trajectory raises deeper questions about what a nation's citizens should expect of their government with regard to the lands held in public trust. How should those commonly owned lands and their resources be managed, used, and protected? What responsibilities do citizens *and* their government have for preserving Earth? The answers to those questions are too important to be left to the clever slogans mouthed by cartoon characters.

ACKNOWLEDGMENTS

I have W. Elliot Brownlee and the late Hugh Davis Graham to thank for their initial invitation to explore the history of environmental policy during the Reagan administration and also Joel A. Tarr and Terrence Young for their persistent encouragement that I build upon the kernel of that earlier work. Daniel A. Cornford, John Fleckner, Marcel Chotkowski LaFollette, Bernard Mergen, Amanda Moniz, Martin Reuss, and Deborah Jean Warner gave me the gift of carefully reading early drafts, and I have benefitted enormously from their comments, as I have from the comments provided by the Smithsonian Institution Scholarly Press's three anonymous peer reviewers.

For their keen advice and generous facilitation of my research, I thank Lisa J. Young and Douglas J. Blankinship at the Department of the Interior; Katrina M. Brown, James Roan, and Alexia MacClain at the Smithsonian Libraries; Ellen Alers, Tad Bennicoff, Pamela Henson, Tammy Peters, and Heidi Stover at the Smithsonian Institution Archives; Mark Madison at the U.S. Fish and Wildlife Service; Lincoln Bramwell at the U.S. Forest Service; John Grabowska and Blyth McManus at the National Park Service; Jamie Lewis, Cheryl Oakes, and Steve Anderson at the Forest History Society; William J. Maher, Kaileigh Oldham, and Rory D. Grennan at the University Library, University of Illinois; Elizabeth Brake at Duke University's David M. Rubenstein Rare Book and Manuscript Library; Steve Branch and Kelly D. Barton at the Ronald Reagan Presidential Library; Joseph Schwarz at the National Archives and Records Administration; and Marcia Soling at the Advertising Educational Foundation.

I am especially grateful for the rich troves of primary documents gathered for me by Connie L. Holland in the Advertising Council Archives at the University of Illinois, the late Morton I. Goldman in the Office of the Secretary Correspondence Files at the Department of the Interior headquarters, and Sherri Sheu in the George B. Hartzog Jr. Papers at Clemson University.

My colleagues at the National Museum of American History possess a remarkable range of expertise and a collective readiness to share their knowledge. Although my indebtedness extends more broadly, I particularly thank Larry Bird, John Fleckner, Paul Forman, Kathleen Franz, Kristen Frederick-Frost, Alexandra Lord, Amanda Moniz, Ann Seeger, Barbara Clark Smith, Alana Staiti, the late Jeff Tinsley, Harold D. Wallace Jr., Deborah Jean Warner, Mallory Warner, Diane Wendt, Roger White, Timothy Winkle, and Helena Wright. It was my good fortune to have worked with Ginger Minkiewicz, the talented and indefatigable director of the Smithsonian Institution Scholarly Press.

No one volunteered more time and effort in helping me think through and improve this book than my wife, Marcel Chotkowski LaFollette. Your love, wit, and editorial skills have been priceless, my dear. I can't thank you enough.

NOTES

CHAPTER 1

1. See Glenn Porter and Harold C. Livesay, *Merchants and Manufacturers: Studies in the Changing Structure of Nineteenth Century Marketing* (Baltimore: Johns Hopkins University Press, 1971); and Gary Cross, "Origins of Modern Consumption: Advertising, New Goods, and a New Generation, 1890–1930," in *The Routledge Companion to Advertising and Promotional Culture*, ed. Matthew P. McAllister and Emily West (New York: Routledge, 2013), 11–22. The broader turn toward professionalism is examined in Robert H. Wiebe, *The Search for Order, 1877–1920* (New York: Hill and Wang, 1967); and Burton J. Bledstein, *The Culture of Professionalism: The Middle Class and the Development of Higher Education in America* (New York: W. W. Norton, 1976). For the evolution of advertising in the United States, see James Playsted Wood, *The Story of Advertising* (New York: Ronald Press, 1958); Otis Pease, *The Responsibilities of American Advertising: Private Control and Public Influence, 1920–1940* (New Haven, Conn.: Yale University Press, 1958); Daniel Pope, *The Making of Modern Advertising* (New York: Basic Books, 1983); Roland Marchand, *Advertising the American Dream: Making Way for Modernity, 1920–1940* (Berkeley: University of California Press, 1985); Susan Strasser, *Satisfaction Guaranteed: The Making of the American Mass Market* (New York: Pantheon Books, 1989); James D. Norris, *Advertising and the Transformation of American Society, 1865–1920* (Westport, Conn.: Greenwood, 1990); Jackson Lears, *Fables of Abundance: A Cultural History of Advertising in America* (New York: Basic Books, 1994); Pamela Walker Laird, *Advertising Progress: American Business and the Rise of Consumer Marketing* (Baltimore: Johns Hopkins University Press, 1998); Roland Marchand, *Creating the Corporate Soul:*

The Rise of Public Relations and Corporate Imagery in American Big Business (Berkeley: University of California Press, 1998); Robert Jackall and Janice M. Hirota, *Image Makers: Advertising, Public Relations, and the Ethos of Advocacy* (Chicago: University of Chicago Press, 2000); and Danielle Sarver Coombs and Bob Batchelor, eds., *We Are What We Sell: How Advertising Shapes American Life . . . and Always Has*, 3 vols. (Santa Barbara, Calif.: Praeger, 2014).

2. John Maxwell Hamilton, "How Our Information Wars Began—in WWI," *Washington Post*, 3 August 2014. See also George Creel, *How We Advertised America: The First Telling of the Amazing Story of the Committee on Public Information That Carried the Gospel of Americanism to Every Corner of the Globe* (New York: Harper & Brothers, 1920); James R. Mock and Cedric Larson, *Words That Won the War: The Story of the Committee on Public Information, 1917–1919* (Princeton, N.J.: Princeton University Press, 1939); Stephen Vaughn, *Holding Fast the Inner Lines: Democracy, Nationalism, and the Committee on Public Information* (Chapel Hill: University of North Carolina Press, 1980), 141–192; Daniel Pope, "The Advertising Industry and World War I," *The Public Historian*, 2 (Spring 1980): 4–25; Alan Axelrod, *Selling the Great War: The Making of American Propaganda* (New York: Palgrave Macmillan, 2009); and Jonathan Auerbach, *Weapons of Democracy: Propaganda, Progressivism, and American Public Opinion* (Baltimore: Johns Hopkins University Press, 2015).

3. Lears, *Fables of Abundance*, 219. See also Roland Marchand, "The Fitful Career of Advocacy Advertising: Political Protection, Client Cultivation, and Corporate Morale," *California Management Review*, 29 (Winter 1987): 128–156.

4. See Wood, *The Story of Advertising*, 417–431; Robert Griffith, "The Selling of America: The Advertising Council and American Politics, 1942–1960," *Business History Review*, 57 (Autumn 1983): 389; William L. Bird, *"Better Living": Advertising, Media, and the New Vocabulary of Business Leadership, 1935–1955* (Evanston, Ill.: Northwestern University Press, 1999); and Inger L. Stole, "Consumer Protection in Historical Perspective: The Five-Year Battle over Federal Regulation of Advertising, 1933 to 1938," *Mass Communication and Society*, 3, no. 4 (2000): 351–372.

5. Gerd Horten, *Radio Goes to War: The Cultural Politics of Propaganda during World War II* (Berkeley: University of California Press, 2002), 92. For a short biography of one of the key attendees at the November 1941 meeting, see Jeanne M. Knapp, *Don Belding: A Career of Advertising and Public Service* (Lubbock: Department of Mass Communications, Texas Tech University, 1983).

6. Franklin D. Roosevelt, Establishing the Office of Facts and Figures, Executive Order No. 8922, 24 October 1941, https://www.presidency.ucsb.edu/documents/executive-order-8922-establishing-the-office-facts-and-figures (accessed 5 May 2021). See also

David Greenberg, *Republic of Spin: An Inside History of the American Presidency* (New York: W. W. Norton, 2016), 238–249. The history of U.S. advertising during World War II is covered in Blake Clark, *The Advertising Smokescreen* (New York: Harper & Brothers, 1944), 201–213; Frank W. Fox, *Madison Avenue Goes to War: The Strange Military Career of American Advertising, 1941–1945* (Provo, Utah: Brigham Young University Press, 1975); and Inger L. Stole, *Advertising at War: Business, Consumers, and Government in the 1940s* (Urbana: University of Illinois Press, 2012).

7. The organization was initially incorporated as the Advertising Council. It rechristened itself the War Advertising Council in June 1943, then changed its name back to the Advertising Council in February 1946. See Inger L. Stole, "Persuasion, Patriotism and PR: US Advertising in the Second World War," *Journal of Historical Research in Marketing*, 5, no. 1 (2013): 27–46.

8. For the history of OWI, see Allan M. Winkler, *The Politics of Propaganda: The Office of War Information, 1942–1945* (New Haven, Conn.: Yale University Press, 1978). For OWI's efforts to shape the messages delivered by various media, see Clayton R. Koppes and Gregory D. Black, *Hollywood Goes to War: How Politics, Profits, and Propaganda Shaped World War II Movies* (New York: Free Press, 1987); Thomas Doherty, *Projections of War: Hollywood, American Culture, and World War II* (New York: Columbia University Press, 1993); Mei-ling Yang, "Selling Patriotism: The Representation of Women in Magazine Advertising in World War II," *American Journalism*, 12 (Summer 1995): 304–320; Horten, *Radio Goes to War*; Dannagal Goldthwaite Young, "Sacrifice, Consumption, and the American Way of Life: Advertising and Domestic Propaganda during World War II," *Communication Review*, 8 (March 2005): 27–52; and Mordecai Lee, *Promoting the War Effort: Robert Horton and Federal Propaganda, 1938–1946* (Baton Rouge: Louisiana State University Press, 2012).

9. The development of the Advertising Council is discussed in J. A. R. Pimlott, "Public Service Advertising: The Advertising Council," *Public Opinion Quarterly*, 12 (Summer 1948): 209–219; Harold B. Thomas, *The Background and Beginning of the Advertising Council* (New York: Advertising Council, 1952); Maurice I. Mandell, "A History of the Advertising Council" (Ph.D. diss., Indiana University, Bloomington, 1953); Fox, *Madison Avenue Goes to War*, 48–66; David L. Paletz, Roberta E. Pearson, and Donald L. Willis, *Politics in Public Service Advertising on Television* (New York: Praeger Publishers, 1977), 6–22; Erik Barnouw, *The Sponsor: Notes on a Modern Potentate* (New York: Oxford University Press, 1978), 39–40, 140–146; Griffith, "The Selling of America," 388–412; Robert P. Keim, *A Time in Advertising's Camelot: The Memoirs of a Do-Gooder* (Madison, Conn.: Longview Press, 2002); Daniel L. Lykins, *From Total War to Total Diplomacy: The Advertising Council and the Construction of the Cold War Consensus* (Westport, Conn.: Praeger, 2003), 9–24; Stole, *Advertising at War*; and Wendy Melillo,

How McGruff and the Crying Indian Changed America: A History of Iconic Ad Council Campaigns (Washington, D.C.: Smithsonian Books, 2013).

10. See "Twenty Years of Public Service by Business through Advertising: The Advertising Council Annual Report, 1961–62," Advertising Council Annual Reports, 1942–1975, record series 13/2/202, box 1, Advertising Council Archives, University Library, University of Illinois at Urbana-Champaign, Urbana (hereafter cited as Ad Council Archives); and F. Bradley Lynch, "A Short History of the Advertising Council," in *A Retrospective of Advertising Council Campaigns: A Half Century of Public Service* (New York: Museum of Television & Radio, 1991), 6–9.

11. "Memorandum on the work of the War Advertising Council, 1942–1943," p. 3, Advertising Council Annual Reports, 1942–1975, record series 13/2/202, box 1, Ad Council Archives.

12. "Memorandum on the work of the War Advertising Council, 1942–1943," p. 8. See also Anne Marie Todd, *Communicating Environmental Patriotism: A Rhetorical History of the American Environmental Movement* (New York: Routledge, 2013), 68–85.

13. Marchand, "The Fitful Career of Advocacy Advertising," 147. For the historical development of American advertising during the years bracketing World War II, see Fox, *Madison Avenue Goes to War*; Griffith, "The Selling of America," 388–412; Horten, *Radio Goes to War*; Kathy M. Newman, *Radio Active: Advertising and Consumer Activism, 1935–1947* (Berkeley: University of California Press, 2004); James J. Kimble, *Mobilizing the Home Front: War Bonds and Domestic Propaganda* (College Station: Texas A&M University Press, 2006); John Bush Jones, *All-Out for Victory! Magazine Advertising and the World War II Home Front* (Waltham, Mass.: Brandeis University Press, 2009); Inger L. Stole, "Politics as Patriotism: Advertising and Consumer Activism during World War II," in *A Moment of Danger: Critical Studies in the History of U.S. Communication since World War II*, ed. Janice Peck and Inger L. Stole (Milwaukee, Wis.: Marquette University Press, 2011), 13–34; Dawn Spring, *Advertising in the Age of Persuasion: Building Brand America, 1941–1961* (New York: Palgrave Macmillan, 2011); and Stole, *Advertising at War*.

14. "A Plan to Sell the Post-War Council," 9 August 1945, Advertising Council Minutes, 1942–98, record series 13/2/201, box 2, Ad Council Archives.

15. Griffith, "The Selling of America," 392.

16. See Griffith, "The Selling of America," 394.

17. "Twenty Years of Public Service by Business through Advertising," 2. See also "Ad Council Plans Campaign," *New York Times*, 24 January 1947.

18. "The Advertising Council's First 25 Years: A Report to the American People," 1966–67 annual report, p. 7, Advertising Council Annual Reports, 1942–1975, record series 13/2/202, box 1, Ad Council Archives.

19. See "Twenty Years of Public Service by Business through Advertising," 18. The Ad Council's board of directors comprised about 80 members drawn from corporations (often the heads of corporate advertising and marketing departments), advertising agencies, and the print and broadcast media.

20. Paul G. Hoffman, "Introduction," in *The Promise of Advertising*, ed. C. H. Sandage (Homewood, Ill.: Richard D. Irwin, 1961), xiii. See also Richard Earle, *The Art of Cause Marketing: How to Use Advertising to Change Personal Behavior and Public Policy* (Lincolnwood, Ill.: NTC Business Books, 2000).

21. The majority of the council's staff (which numbered about 50 in 1962) worked at the organization's New York City headquarters, with skeleton crews running smaller offices in Chicago, Los Angeles, and Washington, D.C. During the 1970s, expenses for producing the advertising material—plus overhead to the Ad Council—ran between $100,000 and $300,000 per campaign.

22. See "Twenty Years of Public Service by Business through Advertising," 13. The Ad Council's other constituent groups included the Magazine Publishers Association, Newspaper Advertising Bureau, National Association of Broadcasters, American Business Press, American Advertising Federation, and Outdoor Advertising Association. The council had changed the name of "volunteer coordinator" to "campaign director" by the mid-1970s. The economic value of the pro bono work provided by the ad agencies is not a charitable tax deduction. For the motivation of these firms to volunteer their time and talent, see Jock Elliott, "Advertising Agencies in the Public Service," in *A Retrospective of Advertising Council Campaigns*, 14.

23. "Twenty Years of Public Service by Business through Advertising," 14. Once the council approved a campaign, it appointed a campaign manager to monitor, facilitate, and oversee the campaign and to liaise with the client, volunteer advertising agency, volunteer coordinator, and the media. Council staff brokered free time or space with broadcasters, publishers, and transit officials to run the ads. They also prepared the final advertisements for mass duplication and distribution. See "Why the Ad Council Is Sending You These Campaigns," undated factsheet, Take Pride in America/Free Press—June 1987 folder, Magazine Campaign Issuances, 1987–, record series 13/2/215, box 1, Ad Council Archives.

24. See "The Advertising Council's First 25 Years," 19. For the council's continuing discussions of environmental matters, see "The Advertising Council, America's Catalyst for Change: Report to the American People," 89–90, p. 7, Advertising Council Annual Reports, 1976–1995, record series 13/2/202, box 2, Ad Council Archives; and Advertising Council, *Bringing the Issues Home: Report to the American People, '88–'89* (New York: Advertising Council, 1989), 20.

25. Gerald W. Williams, *The U.S. Forest Service in the Pacific Northwest: A History* (Corvallis: Oregon State University Press, 2009), 160–161; and Annie Hanshew, "Sky-Fighters of the Forest: Conscientious Objectors, African American Paratroopers, and the US Forest Service Smokejumping Program in World War II," in *The Land Speaks: New Voices at the Intersection of Oral and Environmental History*, ed. Debbie Lee and Kathryn Newfont (New York: Oxford University Press, 2017), 175–192. For the evolving attitudes toward wildfire in the United States, see Stephen J. Pyne, *Fire in America: A Cultural History of Wildland and Rural Fire* (Seattle: University of Washington Press, 1995); and Stephen J. Pyne, *Tending Fire: Coping with America's Wildland Fires* (Washington, D.C.: Island Press, 2005).

26. For an overview of the internment, see Brian Masaru Hayashi, *Democratizing the Enemy: The Japanese American Internment* (Princeton, N.J.: Princeton University Press, 2004); Greg Robinson, *A Tragedy of Democracy: Japanese Confinement in North America* (New York: Columbia University Press, 2009); Richard Reeves, *Infamy: The Shocking Story of the Japanese American Internment in World War II* (New York: Henry Holt, 2015); and Connie Y. Chiang, *Nature Behind Barbed Wire: An Environmental History of Japanese American Incarceration* (New York: Oxford University Press, 2018). Concerns about human-ignited wildfires are discussed in Jake Kosek, *Understories: The Political Life of Forests in Northern New Mexico* (Durham, N.C.: Duke University Press, 2006), 192; and Eric Rutkow, *American Canopy: Trees, Forests, and the Making of a Nation* (New York: Scribner, 2012), 266.

27. See Rutkow, *American Canopy*, 261–263.

28. Robert C. Mikesh, *Japan's World War II Balloon Bomb Attacks on North America* (Washington, D.C.: Smithsonian Institution Press, 1973), 1. See also John McPhee, "Balloons of War," *New Yorker*, 71 (29 January 1996): 52–60.

29. See Mikesh, *Japan's World War II Balloon Bomb Attacks*, 3.

30. See "1973 Report: Cooperative Forest Fire Prevention," April 1974, Forest Fire Prevention 1974 folder, Robert P. Keim Papers, 1967–87, record series 13/2/220, box 15, Ad Council Archives. For a brief period, the Cooperative Forest Fire Prevention Program operated under the name Wartime Forest Fire Prevention Program. The Ad Council's forest fire prevention campaign, which continues to this day, has retained its original orientation, sponsors, and volunteer ad agency. That agency, Foote, Cone & Belding (aka FCB), merged with Draft Worldwide in 2006, changing its name to Draftfcb. The firm rebranded itself FCB in 2014.

31. See Rutkow, *American Canopy*, 264–265. For an extensive compilation of fire prevention posters and outdoor signage, see Harry "Punky" McClellan, *Remember . . . Only You! A History of Forest Fire Prevention Outdoor Advertising* (Evansville, Ind.:

M. T. Publishing Company, 2010). The poster featuring Bambi appears on the National Agricultural Library's website at https://www.nal.usda.gov/exhibits/speccoll/exhibits/show/smokey-bear/item/457 (accessed 16 November 2020).

32. Quoted in U.S. Department of Agriculture, Forest Service, *"Remember—Only You . . .": 1944 to 1984, Forty Years of Preventing Forest Fires, Smokey's 40th Birthday* (Washington, D.C.: GPO, 1984), 2. See also Memorandum on the work of the War Advertising Council, 1942–1943, n.d. [probably produced by council staff in 1943 or 1944], Advertising Council Annual Reports, 1942–1975, record series 13/2/202, box 1, Ad Council Archives; J. Morgan Smith, "The Story of Smokey Bear," *Forestry Chronicle*, 32 (June 1956): 183–188; and William Clifford Lawter Jr., *Smokey Bear 20252: A Biography* (Alexandria, Va.: Lindsay Smith Publishers, 1994).

33. See Marjory Houston Staehle, "He Gave Us Smokey the Bear," *American Legion Magazine*, 102 (January 1977): 10, 48; Lawter, *Smokey Bear 20252*, 43–45; Melillo, *How McGruff and the Crying Indian Changed America*, 42–43; and James G. Lewis, "Smokey Bear: From Idea to Icon," *Forest History Today*, 24 (Spring/Fall 2018): 13–16. At the war's end, Staehle moved on to other work, whereas Smokey remained on the job. The first fire prevention poster featuring Staehle's painting of Smokey carried the caption "Smokey Says—Care *will* prevent 9 out of 10 forest fires!" and appears on the National Agricultural Library's website at https://www.nal.usda.gov/exhibits/speccoll/exhibits/show/smokey-bear/item/453 (accessed 16 November 2020).

34. See U.S. Department of Agriculture, Forest Service, *"Remember—Only You,"* 2.

35. See "Annual Report: Cooperative Forest Fire Prevention," 8; Harry A. Phillips, "Smokey Bear Dies: Creator from Norwich," *Bulletin* (Norwich, Conn.), 14 November 1976; U.S. Department of Agriculture, Forest Service, *Smokey Bear—The First 50 Years* (Washington, D.C.: GPO, 1993), 6; and Gerald W. Williams, *The Forest Service: Fighting for Public Lands* (Westport, Conn.: Greenwood Press, 2007), 155.

36. Act of May 23, 1952, Public Law No. 82-359, Ch. 327, 66 Stat. 92; 18 U.S.C. 711; 16 U.S.C. 580p-2 (1952). Colloquially known as the Smokey Bear Act, it was officially "an act prohibiting the manufacture or use of the character 'Smokey Bear' by unauthorized persons." By 1970, according to the sports columnist Stan Isaacs, "about 40 licensees promote Smokey with sweat shirts, cigarette snuffers, litter bags and, among others, wrist watches that have shovels for hands and the legend 'prevent forest fires.'" Stan Isaacs, "Smokey the Bear Is Just Like Tom Seaver," *Newsday*, 4 February 1970.

37. For a sympathetic account of the Cooperative Fire Prevention Campaign, which includes extensive discussion of the living Smokey, see Ellen Earnhardt Morrison, *Guardian of the Forest: A History of the Smokey Bear Program* (New York: Vantage Press, 1976). See also U.S. Department of Agriculture, Forest Service, "Cub Helps in Forest Fire

Prevention," press release, 8 July 1950, folder 1, box 83, record unit 326, Smithsonian Institution Archives, Washington, D.C. (hereafter cited as SIA); Albert E. Manchester, "An American Original," *American Forests*, 87 (October 1981): 48; Elliott S. Barker, *Smokey Bear and the Great Wilderness* (Santa Fe, N.M.: Sunstone Press, 1982), 37–41; Sue Houser, *Hot Foot Teddy: The True Story of Smokey Bear* (Evansville, Ind.: M. T. Publishing Company, 2006); Alice Wondrak Biel, *Do (Not) Feed the Bears: The Fitful History of Wildlife and Tourists in Yellowstone* (Lawrence: University Press of Kansas, 2006), 71; and Robert Julyan, *Hiking to History: A Guide to Off-Road New Mexico Historic Sites* (Albuquerque: University of New Mexico Press, 2016), 129–140.

38. See U.S. Department of Agriculture, Forest Service, *"Remember—Only You,"* 3; Lawter, *Smokey Bear 20252*; and Tad Bennicoff, "Bearly Survived to Become an Icon," *Bigger Picture*, https://siarchives.si.edu/blog/bearly-survived-become-icon (accessed 29 April 2019). The living Smokey's fame, especially among children, inspired the creation of the Smokey Bear Museum in Capitan, New Mexico. The museum, which opened in 1961, features displays of photographs, posters, and a smorgasbord of Smokey memorabilia, along with interpretative labels discussing the history of the forest fire prevention campaign. See Smokey Bear Museum and Gift Shop, Village of Capitan website, https://www.villageofcapitan.org/smokey-bear (accessed 5 May 2021).

39. See "Goldie Bear Heads for Red-Carpet U.S. Capital Reception, 'Wedding,'" *Albuquerque Journal*, 8 September 1962.

40. Billie Hamlet to Reed et al., 1 November 1971, folder 2, box 83, record unit 326, SIA. See also Tom Cobb, "So Long, Smokey," *American Forests*, 81 (August 1975): 30; and Bennicoff, "Bearly Survived to Become an Icon." After Smokey Bear II's death in August 1990, there were no successors to the living Smokey.

41. The clerical staff of the National Zoological Park's Office of Public Affairs carefully pasted nearly 400 obituaries for Smokey into four large scrapbooks. See boxes 66 and 67, record unit 365, SIA. For examples of the condolence letters sent to the zoo following Smokey's death, see Sharon Rucker to Dear Friends, 9 November 1976; Harrison Lofton Jr. to Theodore H. Reed, 10 November 1976; and Charles Henry Fletcher to Superintendent of the Washington National Zoo, 11 November 1976, folder 14, box 21, record unit 326, SIA. Assessments of the continuing high public recognition of Smokey Bear and the forest fire prevention campaign appear in AHF Marketing Research, *Forest Fire Prevention: An Awareness and Attitudes Study*, a report prepared for the Advertising Council (New York: AHF Marketing Research, 1976); and Kenneth Turan, "Smokey's Enduring Appeal," *Washington Post*, 10 November 1976. Smokey's remains were buried outside the Smokey Bear Museum in Capitan, New Mexico. See Steve Johnson, "Make That Smokey Bear," *Chicago Tribune*, 30 August 1990; and Gary Cozzens, *Capitan, New Mexico: From the Coalora Coal Mines to Smokey Bear* (Charleston, S.C.: History Press, 2012), 138–140.

42. Unfortunately, the Smokey Bear campaign—with its implied message that forest fires are inherently bad—proved too effective. The long-term effect of aggressive wildfire suppression not only caused serious harm to forest ecologies; it ironically fueled the proliferation of the devastating megafires that came to plague the American West in the twenty-first century. See Bil Gilbert, "Where There's Smokey, There's Fire," *Sports Illustrated*, 36 (12 June 1972): 88–92, 94, 97, 100–102, 104; Pete Cowgill, "Some Fires Help, Not Hurt, Forests," *Arizona Daily Star*, 11 November 1976; Geoffrey H. Donovan and Thomas C. Brown, "Be Careful What You Wish For: The Legacy of Smokey Bear," *Frontiers in Ecology and the Environment*, 5 (March 2007): 73–79; Michael Kodas, *Megafire: The Race to Extinguish a Deadly Epidemic of Flame* (Boston: Houghton Mifflin Harcourt, 2017); Stephen J. Pyne, *Here and There: A Fire Survey* (Tucson: University of Arizona Press, 2018), 61–63; and Chris D'Angelo, "Smokey Bear Is 75: Is It Time for Him to Retire?" *HuffPost*, 12 November 2019, https://www.huffpost.com/entry/smokey-bear-75th-birthday-legacy_n_5dc5cf48e4b0fcfb7f662fda (accessed 27 November 2019).

CHAPTER 2

1. The general shifts in post–World War II attitudes toward conservation are addressed in Samuel P. Hays, *Beauty, Health, and Permanence: Environmental Politics in the United States, 1955–1985* (New York: Cambridge University Press, 1987); Hal K. Rothman, *The Greening of a Nation? Environmentalism in the United States since 1945* (Fort Worth, Tex.: Harcourt Brace, 1998); and Thomas R. Wellock, *Preserving the Nation: The Conservation and Environmental Movements, 1870–2000* (Wheeling, Ill.: Harland Davidson, 2007). For discussions of littering and solid wastes, see Office of Technology Assessment, *Facing America's Trash: What Next for Municipal Solid Waste?* (Washington, D.C.: GPO, 1989); David Saphire, *Case Reopened: Reassessing Refillable Bottles* (New York: Inform, 1994); Heather Rogers, *Gone Tomorrow: The Hidden Life of Garbage* (New York: New Press, 2005); Greg Kennedy, *An Ontology of Trash: The Disposable and Its Problematic Nature* (Albany: State University of New York Press, 2007); and Finn Arne Jørgensen, *Making a Green Machine: The Infrastructure of Beverage Container Recycling* (New Brunswick, N.J.: Rutgers University Press, 2011).

2. Report of the Public Policy Committee Annual Meeting, 17 November 1964, Public Policy Committee File, 1954–1987, 1992, record series 13/2/209, box 1, Advertising Council Archives, University Library, University of Illinois at Urbana-Champaign, Urbana (hereafter cited as Ad Council Archives). See also Bartow J. Elmore, *Citizen Coke: The Making of Coca-Cola Capitalism* (New York: W. W. Norton, 2015), 233–238.

3. For the larger historical context of how the anti-littering campaign fitted into evolving concerns about cleanliness, see John A. Kouwenhoven, *The Beer Can by the Highway: Essays on What's American about America* (Garden City, N.Y.: Doubleday, 1961); Suellen Hoy, *Chasing Dirt: The American Pursuit of Cleanliness* (New York: Oxford University Press, 1995); and Martin V. Melosi, *Garbage in the Cities: Refuse, Reform, and the Environment*, rev. ed. (Pittsburgh: University of Pittsburgh Press, 2005).

4. "Twenty Years of Public Service by Business through Advertising: The Advertising Council Annual Report, 1961–62," p. 7, Advertising Council Annual Reports, 1942–1975, record series 13/2/202, box 1, Ad Council Archives.

5. "Working Together We Can Help Keep America Beautiful," Advertising Council order form for Keep America Beautiful campaign material, June 1962, Ad Council Historical File, 1941–1997, record series 13/2/207, box 23, Ad Council Archives.

6. *A Retrospective of Advertising Council Campaigns: A Half Century of Public Service* (New York: Museum of Television & Radio, 1991), 40. Keep America Beautiful's 1961 television spot "It Happens in the Best of Places," featuring Susan Spotless, is available at https://www.youtube.com/watch?v=-BCnGP-ktrQ (accessed 6 August 2019).

7. *Heritage of Splendor* is available under a Creative Commons license at the Prelinger Archives, https://archive.org/details/Heritage1963 (accessed 1 June 2019).

8. Highway Beautification Act of 1965, Public Law No. 89-285, 79 Stat. 1028–1033 (22 October 1965). For the general influence of Lady Bird Johnson's beautification campaign, see Lewis L. Gould, *Lady Bird Johnson: Our Environmental First Lady* (Lawrence: University Press of Kansas, 1999).

9. See U.S. Congress, House Subcommittee on Department of the Interior and Related Agencies, Committee on Appropriations, Hearing, *Department of the Interior and Related Agencies Appropriations for 1972*, 92nd Cong., 1st sess., March 31, 1971 (Washington, D.C.: GPO, 1971), 474–478; John Mattoon, "How the Johnny Horizon Program Came to Be," in *Pioneering Outdoor Recreation for the Bureau of Land Management*, by Gene Peterson (McLean, Va.: Public Lands Foundation, 1996), 60–62; James Lewis, "Forgotten Characters from Forest History: Johnny Horizon," *Peeling Back the Bark*, 17 March 2011, https://foresthistory.org/forgotten-characters-from-forest-history-johnny-horizon/ (accessed 29 April 2019); and Robert King, "Celebrating Earth Day with the Legacy of Johnny Horizon, 1968–1977," *My Public Lands*, 28 September 2013, https://mypubliclands.tumblr.com/johnnyhorizon (accessed 27 March 2020).

10. Gerald R. Ford, Johnny Horizon '76 Clean Up America Month, 1974, Proclamation No. 4315, 19 September 1974, https://www.presidency.ucsb.edu/node/269726 (accessed 5 May 2021).

11. See U.S. Department of Agriculture, "Woodsy Owl Launches Anti-Pollution Campaign," press release, 15 September 1971, https://foresthistory.org/wp-content/uploads/2018/07/Woodsy_Owl_press.pdf (accessed 28 August 2020); Lewis W. Shollenberger to Gordon C. Kinney, 11 April 1973, Forest Fire Prevention 1973 folder, Robert P. Keim Papers, 1967–87, record series 13/2/220, box 15, Ad Council Archives; U.S. Department of Agriculture, Forest Service, *Smokey Bear—The First 50 Years* (Washington, D.C.: GPO, 1993), 6; and Harald Fuller-Bennett and Iris Velez, "Woodsy Owl at 40," *Forest History Today*, 18 (Spring 2012): 22–27.

12. Robert P. Keim, *A Time in Advertising's Camelot: The Memoirs of a Do-Gooder* (Madison, Conn.: Longview Press, 2002), 29.

13. See Keim, *A Time in Advertising's Camelot*, 30.

14. Minutes of the Public Policy Committee Meeting, 7 October 1969, Public Policy Committee File, 1954–1987, 1992, record series 13/2/209, box 1, Ad Council Archives. The Ad Council's recalculations of its decision-making priorities during the late 1960s and early 1970s are summarized in Robert P. Keim, "'Nothing Succeeds Like Successors': An Open Letter to Ruth Wooden," in Annual Report to the Board of Directors, the Advertising Council, 23 September 1987, copy in Advertising Council Minutes, 1942–98, record series 13/2/201, box 16, Ad Council Archives.

15. Minutes of the Public Policy Committee Meeting, 9 September 1970, Public Policy Committee File, 1954–1987, 1992, record series 13/2/209, box 1, Ad Council Archives.

16. See Minutes of the Public Policy Committee Meeting, 14 September 1971, Public Policy Committee File, 1954–1987, 1992, record series 13/2/209, box 1, Ad Council Archives.

17. "Public Service Advertising for Magazines," *Magazine Service Bulletin*, no. 43 (January, February, March 1971): 1; a copy of this ephemeral Ad Council publication resides in Ad Council Historical File, 1941–1997, record series 13/2/207, box 46, folder 1677, Ad Council Archives.

18. Help Fight Pollution Campaign, Magazine Ad No. HFP-1615-71, Ad Council Historical File, 1941–1997, record series 13/2/207, box 46, folder 1677, Ad Council Archives.

19. The Advertising Council, Inc., Annual Report, 1972–1973, p. 9, Advertising Council Annual Reports, 1942–1975, record series 13/2/202, box 1, Ad Council Archives. Keep America Beautiful's 1971 Crying Indian public service announcement can been seen at https://www.youtube.com/watch?v=8Suu84khNGY (accessed 6 August 2019). For the development of this Ad Council campaign, see Richard Earle, *The Art of Cause Marketing: How to Use Advertising to Change Personal Behavior and Public Policy* (Lincolnwood, Ill.: NTC Business Books, 2000), 66–71; Keim, *A Time in Advertising's Camelot*, 29–32; and

Wendy Melillo, *How McGruff and the Crying Indian Changed America: A History of Iconic Ad Council Campaigns* (Washington, D.C.: Smithsonian Books, 2013), 103–127. Although not widely known at the time, Cody was born in Louisiana in 1904 as Espera Oscar de Corti, the son of parents who had both immigrated to the United States from Italy. He changed his name to Cody in 1924, before launching a prolific film career portraying Native Americans. For criticism of the Crying Indian advertising campaign and of Keep America Beautiful more generally, see "Corporate Advertising and the Environment," *Economic Priorities Report*, 2 (September–October 1971): 1–40; Jerry Mander, "EcoPornography: One Year and Nearly a Billion Dollars Later, Advertising Owns Ecology," *Communication Arts Magazine*, 14, no. 2 (1972): 45–47, 54–55; Bruce Howard, "The Advertising Council: Selling Lies," *Ramparts*, 13 (December 1974–January 1975): 25–26, 28–32; Tom LaFaille, "The Ad Council: Gatekeepers for PSA's," *Access*, no. 34 (17 May 1976): 17–19; Angela Aleiss, "Iron Eyes Cody: Wannabe Indian," *Cineaste*, 25, no. 1 (1999): 30–31; Ginger Strand, "The Crying Indian: How an Environmental Icon Helped Sell Cans—and Sell Out Environmentalism," *Orion*, 27 (November/December 2008): 20–27; Finis Dunaway, "Gas Masks, Pogo, and the Ecological Indian: Earth Day and the Visual Politics of American Environmentalism," *American Quarterly*, 60 (March 2008): 67–69, 84–89; and Finis Dunaway, *Seeing Green: The Use and Abuse of American Environmental Images* (Chicago: University of Chicago Press, 2015), 79–95. Cody's fictionalized autobiography—Iron Eyes Cody, *Iron Eyes: My Life as a Hollywood Indian*, as told to Collin Perry (New York: Everest House, 1982)—fed numerous published commentaries about the actor, such as Ted Williams, "The Metamorphosis of Keep America Beautiful," *Audubon*, 92 (March 1990): 124–134. See also Robert F. Berkhofer Jr., *The White Man's Indian: Images of the American Indian from Columbus to the Present* (New York: Knopf, 1978); Shepard Krech III, *The Ecological Indian: Myth and History* (New York: W. W. Norton, 1999); Peter C. Rollins and John E. O'Connor, eds., *Hollywood's Indian: The Portrayal of the Native American in Film*, expanded ed. (Lexington: University Press of Kentucky, 2003); Kevin C. Armitage, "Commercial Indians: Authenticity, Nature, and Industrial Capitalism in Advertising at the Turn of the Twentieth Century," *Michigan Historical Review*, 29 (Fall 2003): 70–95; and Daniel Belgrad, *The Culture of Feedback: Ecological Thinking in Seventies America* (Chicago: University of Chicago Press, 2019), 59–79.

20. Advertising Council, "Daddy, What Did You Do in the War Against Pollution?," Help Fight Pollution Campaign magazine ad No. HFP-1491-71 (distributed in May 1971), Ad Council Historical File, 1941–1997, record series 13/2/207, box 49, Ad Council Archives.

21. Copies of the 16 May 1972 magazine ads for the Keep America Beautiful campaign in Ad Council Historical File, 1941–1997, record series 13/2/207, box 48, folder 1709, Ad Council Archives.

22. Copies of the 11 July 1972 magazine ads for the Keep America Beautiful campaign in Ad Council Historical File, 1941–1997, record series 13/2/207, box 48, folder 1714, Ad Council Archives. These ads incorporated still photographs from the original 1971 KAB Iron Eyes Cody television spot.

23. Keep America Beautiful, Inc., 1975 television spot, Television Public Service Announcements, 1963, 1971–1992, record series 13/2/214, box 1, TV Ads March 1975 folder, Ad Council Archives. Keep America Beautiful's 1975 public service announcement featuring the Crying Indian on horseback can be seen at https://www.youtube.com/watch?v=8_QGBWaD-A4 (accessed 6 August 2019). The growing influence of environmentalism on savvy entrepreneurs is addressed in Michael Silverstein, *The Environmental Economic Revolution: How Business Will Thrive and the Earth Survive in Years to Come* (New York: St. Martin's Press, 1993), 64–80; Jacquelyn A. Ottman, *Green Marketing: Opportunity for Innovation*, 2nd ed. (Lincolnwood, Ill.: NTC Business Books, 1998); and Robin Anderson, "The 'Crying Indian,' Corporations, and Environmentalism: A Half-Century of Struggle over Environmental Messaging," in *The Routledge Companion to Advertising and Promotional Culture*, ed. Matthew P. McAllister and Emily West (New York: Routledge, 2013), 404–416.

24. "The Advertising Council: 40 Years of Communicating in the Public Interest," 1980–1981 annual report, p. 5, Advertising Council Annual Reports, 1976–1995, record series 13/2/202, box 2, Ad Council Archives.

25. Keim, "Nothing Succeeds Like Successors," 7.

CHAPTER 3

1. See Carol Wojtowciz, "Philadelphia, 1736: Ben Franklin Organizes His Volunteers," *Firehouse*, 3 (April 1978): 53, 56, 72. The larger context of American voluntary associations is examined in Peter Clark, *British Clubs and Societies, 1580–1800: The Origins of an Associational World* (New York: Oxford University Press, 2000); Jessica Choppin Roney, *Governed by a Spirit of Opposition: The Origins of American Political Practice in Colonial Philadelphia* (Baltimore: Johns Hopkins University Press, 2014); and Amanda B. Moniz, *From Empire to Humanity: The American Revolution and the Origins of Humanitarianism* (New York: Oxford University Press, 2016).

2. Alexis de Tocqueville, *Democracy in America* (1835; repr., New York: Alfred A. Knopf, 1945), 1:198. In their exhaustive survey of the topic, Constance Smith and Anne Freedman described the voluntary association as "a nonprofit, nongovernment, private

group which an individual joins by choice." Smith and Freedman, *Voluntary Associations: Perspectives on the Literature* (Cambridge, Mass.: Harvard University Press, 1972), viii. See also Arthur M. Schlesinger, "Biography of a Nation of Joiners," *American Historical Review*, 50 (October 1944): 1–25; Selskar M. Gunn and Philip S. Platt, *Voluntary Health Agencies: An Interpretive Study* (New York: Ronald Press Company, 1945); Anne Firor Scott, "Women's Voluntary Associations: From Charity to Reform," in *Lady Bountiful Revisited: Women, Philanthropy, and Power*, ed. Kathleen D. McCarthy (New Brunswick, N.J.: Rutgers University Press, 1990), 35–54; Gerald Gamm and Robert D. Putnam, "The Growth of Voluntary Associations in America, 1840–1940," *Journal of Interdisciplinary History*, 29 (April 1999): 511–557; Theda Skocpol, Marshall Ganz, and Ziad Munson, "A Nation of Organizers: The Institutional Origins of Civic Volunteerism in the United States," *American Political Science Review*, 94 (September 2000): 527–546; and Kathleen D. McCarthy, *American Creed: Philanthropy and the Rise of Civil Society, 1700–1865* (Chicago: University of Chicago Press, 2003).

3. As the federal government's highly acclaimed director of relief during the disastrous Mississippi River flood of 1927, secretary of Commerce Herbert Hoover tapped into this spirit of voluntarism by relying heavily on the assistance of tens of thousands of volunteers. See Kendrick A. Clements, *Hoover, Conservation, and Consumerism: Engineering the Good Life* (Lawrence: University Press of Kansas, 2000), 111–127. For Hoover's broadscale utilization of voluntarism during World War I, see Robert D. Cuff, "Herbert Hoover, the Ideology of Voluntarism and War Organization during the Great War," *Journal of American History*, 64 (September 1977): 358–372. The role of philanthropy and voluntarism in urban-oriented environmental reform is addressed in Barry Ross Harrison Muchnick, "Nature's Republic: Fresh Air Reform and the Moral Ecology of Citizenship in Turn of the Century America" (Ph.D. diss., Yale University, New Haven, Conn., 2010).

4. See David Macleod, "Original Intent: Establishing the Creed and Control of Boy Scouting in the United States," in *Scouting Frontiers: Youth and the Scout Movement's First Century*, ed. Nelson R. Block and Tammy M. Proctor (Newcastle upon Tyne, U.K.: Cambridge Scholars, 2009), 13–27; Tammy M. Proctor, *Scouting for Girls: A Century of Girl Guides and Girl Scouts* (Santa Barbara, Calif.: Praeger, 2009); and Benjamin René Jordan, *Modern Manhood and the Boy Scouts of America: Citizenship, Race, and the Environment, 1910–1930* (Chapel Hill: University of North Carolina Press, 2016).

5. Jordan, *Modern Manhood and the Boy Scouts of America*, 28.

6. See Emily Yellin, *Our Mothers' War: American Women at Home and at the Front during World War II* (New York: Free Press, 2004), 167–174. Yellin states that the Red Cross alone recruited more than 3.5 million women volunteers. The volunteer opportunities presented to women during World War II is the subject of Keith Ayling, *Calling All Women* (New York: Harper & Brothers, 1942), whereas Cecilia Gowdy-Wygant explores

how the intersections of patriotism and voluntarism influenced women's roles during the two world wars in her book, *Cultivating Victory: The Women's Land Army and the Victory Garden Movement* (Pittsburgh: University of Pittsburgh Press, 2013). See also Judith Weisenfeld, *African American Women and Christian Activism: New York's Black YWCA, 1905–1945* (Cambridge, Mass.: Harvard University Press, 1997); Char Miller, "In the Sweat of Our Brow: Citizenship in American Domestic Practice during WWII—Victory Gardens," *Journal of American Culture*, 26 (September 2003): 395–409; and David P. Forsythe, *The Humanitarians: The International Committee of the Red Cross* (New York: Cambridge University Press, 2005).

7. See, for example, Merle Curti, "American Philanthropy and the National Character," *American Quarterly*, 10 (Winter 1958): 432. Broader perspectives are offered in Anne Firor Scott, *Natural Allies: Women's Associations in American History* (Urbana: University of Illinois Press, 1991); Richard E. Flathman, *Willful Liberalism: Voluntarism and Individuality in Political Theory and Practice* (Ithaca, N.Y.: Cornell University Press, 1992); Peter Dobkin Hall, "A Historical Overview of Philanthropy, Voluntary Associations, and Nonprofit Organizations in the United States, 1600–2000," in *The Nonprofit Sector: A Research Handbook*, 2nd ed., ed. Walter W. Powell and Richard Steinberg (New Haven, Conn.: Yale University Press, 2006), 32–65; Andrew J. F. Morris, *The Limits of Voluntarism: Charity and Welfare from the New Deal through the Great Society* (New York: Cambridge University Press, 2009); Benjamin Soskis, "The Problem of Charity in Industrial America, 1873–1915" (Ph.D. diss., Columbia University, New York, 2010); and Elizabeth A. Harmon, "The Transformation of American Philanthropy: From Public Trust to Private Foundation, 1785–1917" (Ph.D. diss., University of Michigan, Ann Arbor, 2017).

8. *Americans Volunteer, 1974: A Statistical Study of Volunteers in the United States* (Washington, D.C.: ACTION, 1975), 3, 4. See also Brian O'Connell, *Effective Leadership in Voluntary Organizations: How to Make the Greatest Use of Citizen Service and Influence* (New York: Association Press, 1976).

9. For the continuing high rates of participation in voluntary associations during the last quarter of the twentieth century, see Stuart Langton, "The New Voluntarism," *Nonprofit and Voluntary Sector Quarterly*, 10 (January 1981): 7–20; Eva Schindler-Rainman, "Trends and Changes in the Volunteer World," *Nonprofit and Voluntary Sector Quarterly*, 11 (April 1982): 157–163; Thomas Rotolo, "Trends in Voluntary Association Participation," *Nonprofit and Voluntary Sector Quarterly*, 28 (June 1999): 199–212; John Wilson, "Volunteering," *Annual Review of Sociology*, 26 (2000): 215–240; and Robert D. Putnam, *Bowling Alone: The Collapse and Revival of American Community* (New York: Simon & Schuster, 2000). The deepening codependency of voluntary organizations and the state is analyzed in Jennifer R. Wolch, *The Shadow State: Government and Voluntary Sector in Transition* (New York: Foundation Center, 1990).

10. For the Smithsonian's origins, see Paul H. Oehser, *The Smithsonian Institution* (New York: Praeger, 1970); Nina Burleigh, *The Stranger and the Statesman: James Smithson, John Quincy Adams, and the Making of America's Greatest Museum: The Smithsonian* (New York: Morrow, 2003); and Heather P. Ewing, *The Lost World of James Smithson: Science, Revolution, and the Birth of the Smithsonian* (New York: Bloomsbury, 2007).

11. See Donald Robert Whitnah, *A History of the United States Weather Bureau* (Urbana: University of Illinois Press, 1961); Bruce Sinclair, "Gustavus A. Hyde, Professor Espy's Volunteers, and the Development of Systematic Weather Observation," *Bulletin of the American Meteorological Society*, 46 (December 1965): 779–784; and James Rodger Fleming, *Meteorology in America, 1800–1870* (Baltimore: Johns Hopkins University Press, 1990).

12. See Philip Kopper, *Volunteer! O Volunteer! A Salute to the Smithsonian's Unpaid Legions* (Washington, D.C.: Smithsonian Institution Press, 1983); W. Patrick McCray, *Keep Watching the Skies! The Story of Operation Moonwatch and the Dawn of the Space Age* (Princeton, N.J.: Princeton University Press, 2008); and David H. DeVorkin, *Fred Whipple's Empire: The Smithsonian Astrophysical Observatory, 1955–1973* (Washington, D.C.: Smithsonian Institution Scholarly Press, 2018), 50–51, 73, 88, 93, 95.

13. Theodore H. Reed to David P. Herman, 10 May 1965, folder 12, box 50, record unit 326, Smithsonian Institution Archives, Washington, D.C. (hereafter cited as SIA). For a brief history of FONZ, see the National Zoo's website, https://nationalzoo.si.edu/about/history (accessed 13 April 2019).

14. See Susan Trencher to Dr. Reed, 4 March 1974, folder 12, box 50, record unit 326, SIA. For the volunteer program's subsequent growth, see Jaren G. Horsley to All NZP Employees, 10 April 1974; and Sabin Robbins to Reed, Kohn, and Iliff, February 14, 1975, folder 12, box 50, record unit 326, SIA. Museums across the country also expanded their use of volunteers after the mid-twentieth century, which prompted the establishment of the American Association of Museum Volunteers in 1979. See the association's website, https://aamv.wildapricot.org/Who-We-Are (accessed 16 December 2019).

15. For the contributions of volunteers to science, see Abraham Miller-Rushing, Richard Primack, and Rick Bonney, "The History of Public Participation in Ecological Research," *Frontiers in Ecology and the Environment*, 10 (August 2012): 285–290; Janis L. Dickinson and Rick Bonney, eds., *Citizen Science: Public Participation in Environmental Research* (Ithaca, N.Y.: Comstock Publishing Associates, 2012); Akiko Busch, *The Incidental Steward: Reflections on Citizen Science* (New Haven, Conn.: Yale University Press, 2013); Sharman Apt Russell, *Diary of a Citizen Scientist: Chasing Tiger Beetles and Other New Ways of Engaging the World* (Corvallis: Oregon State University

Press, 2014); Mary Ellen Hannibal, *Citizen Scientist: Searching for Heroes and Hope in an Age of Extinction* (New York: The Experiment, 2016); Caren Cooper, *Citizen Science: How Ordinary People Are Changing the Face of Discovery* (New York: Overlook Press, 2016); and Thom Davies and Alice Mah, eds., *Toxic Truths: Environmental Justice and Citizen Science in a Post-Truth Age* (Manchester, U.K.: Manchester University Press, 2020). The journal *Citizen Science: Theory and Practice*, which the Citizen Science Association launched in 2016, is another useful source.

16. See Robin W. Winks, *Laurance S. Rockefeller: Catalyst for Conservation* (Washington, D.C.: Island Press, 1997); Tom Butler, *Wildlands Philanthropy: The Great American Tradition* (San Rafael, Calif.: Earth Aware, 2008); and Jacqueline Vaughn and Hanna J. Cortner, *Philanthropy and the National Park Service* (New York: Palgrave Macmillan, 2013). Complicating these assessments is Justin Farrell, *Billionaire Wilderness: The Ultra-Wealthy and the Remaking of the American West* (Princeton, N.J.: Princeton University Press, 2020).

17. See Dwight F. Rettie, *Our National Park System: Caring for America's Greatest Natural and Historic Treasures* (Urbana: University of Illinois Press, 1995), 187.

18. See Merle Schlesinger Lefkoff, "The Voluntary Citizens' Group as a Public Policy Alternative to the Political Party: A Case Study of the Georgia Conservancy" (Ph.D. diss., Emory University, Atlanta, 1975); Eve Endicott, ed., *Land Conservation through Public/Private Partnerships* (Washington, D.C.: Island Press, 1993); Richard Brewer, *Conservancy: The Land Trust Movement in America* (Hanover, N.H.: University Press of New England, 2003); Michael M. Gunter Jr., *Building the Next Ark: How NGOs Work to Protect Biodiversity* (Hanover, N.H.: Dartmouth College Press, 2004); Christopher J. Bosso, *Environment, Inc.: From Grassroots to Beltway* (Lawrence: University Press of Kansas, 2005); and Bill Birchard, *Nature's Keepers: The Remarkable Story of How the Nature Conservancy Became the Largest Environmental Organization in the World* (San Francisco: Jossey-Bass, 2005). The federal government modestly subsidized the philanthropy supporting most of the conservancies through the charitable tax deduction.

19. See David Callahan, "The Billionaires' Park," *New York Times*, 1 December 2014. Such philanthropic initiatives often generated controversy, especially when their benefits were skewed toward already privileged segments of society. For a much different story involving voluntary citizen activism aimed at preserving the widely vilified New Jersey swampland directly across from Manhattan, see Robert Sullivan, *The Meadowlands: Wilderness Adventures at the Edge of a City* (New York: Scribner, 1998); and Cheryl Ann Hendry, "Finding Nature in an Industrial Swamp: A Case Study of New Jersey's Hackensack Meadowlands" (Ph.D. diss., Montana State University, Bozeman, 2017).

20. Etienne S. Benson, "A Centrifuge of Calculation: Managing Data and Enthusiasm in Early Twentieth-Century Bird Banding," *Osiris*, 32 (2017): 286. See also Mark V. Barrow Jr., *A Passion for Birds: American Ornithology after Audubon* (Princeton, N.J.: Princeton University Press, 1998), 154–181.

21. A general overview of voluntarism in the United States is provided in Susan J. Ellis and Katherine H. Campbell, *By the People: A History of Americans as Volunteers*, 3rd ed. (Philadelphia: Energize, 2005). According to Ellis and Campbell, "To volunteer is to act in recognition of a need, with an attitude of social responsibility and without concern for monetary profit, going beyond one's basic obligation" (p. 4). See also Murray Hausknecht, *The Joiners: A Sociological Description of Voluntary Association Membership in the United States* (New York: Bedminster Press, 1962); J. Roland Pennock and John W. Chapman, eds., *Voluntary Associations* (New York: Atherton Press, 1969); Burton A. Weisbrod, *The Voluntary Nonprofit Sector: An Economic Analysis* (Lexington, Mass.: Lexington Books, 1977); David E. Mason, *Voluntary Nonprofit Enterprise Management* (New York: Plenum Press, 1984); Marc A. Musick and John Wilson, *Volunteers: A Social Profile* (Bloomington: Indiana University Press, 2008); Shirley Sagawa, *The American Way to Change: How National Service and Volunteers Are Transforming America* (San Francisco: Jossey-Bass, 2010); Melissa Bass, *The Politics and Civics of National Service: Lessons from the Civilian Conservation Corps, Vista, and AmeriCorps* (Washington, D.C.: Brookings Institution Press, 2013); and J. Steven Ott and Lisa A. Dicke, eds., *The Nature of the Nonprofit Sector*, 3rd ed. (Boulder, Colo.: Westview Press, 2016).

22. In 1992, the National Wildlife Federation's volunteer programs staff launched the newsletter *Volunteer Spirit*. See also National Wildlife Federation, Volunteer Handbook, 2007, https://www.nwf.org/~/media/PDFs/Volunteers/NWF-Volunteer-Handbook-2007.ashx (accessed 9 May 2019). For the essential role of volunteers within conservation and environmental organizations, see Ernest Swift, *A Conservation Saga* (Washington, D.C.: National Wildlife Federation, 1967); Clem L. Zinger, Richard Dalsemer, and Helen Magargle, *Environmental Volunteers in America* (Washington, D.C.: National Center for Voluntary Action, 1973); Stephen Fox, *John Muir and His Legacy: The American Conservation Movement* (Boston: Little, Brown and Company, 1981), 333–357; Stuart Langton, ed., *Environmental Leadership: A Sourcebook for Staff and Volunteer Leaders of Environmental Organizations* (Lexington, Mass.: Lexington Books, 1984); Donald Snow, *Inside the Environmental Movement: Meeting the Leadership Challenge* (Washington, D.C.: Island Press, 1992); Jack Lorenz, "Developing the Complete Volunteer," in *Voices from the Environmental Movement: Perspectives for a New Era*, ed. Donald Snow (Washington, D.C.: Island Press, 1992), 205–216; and Bill McMillon, Doug Cutchins, and Anne Geissinger, *Volunteer Vacations: Short-Term Adventures That Will Benefit You and Others*, 11th ed. (Chicago: Chicago Review Press, 2012).

23. Stewart L. Udall, *The Quiet Crisis* (New York: Holt, Rinehart and Winston, 1963), 157. Insights into the roles of hunters and anglers are provided in John F. Reiger, *American Sportsmen and the Origins of Conservation*, 3rd ed. (Corvallis: Oregon State University Press, 2001), whereas examples of how volunteers have contributed to state parks are discussed in William C. Forrey, *History of Pennsylvania's State Parks, 1984–2015* (Harrisburg: Bureau of State Parks, Office of Parks and Forestry, Department of Conservation and Natural Resources, Commonwealth of Pennsylvania, 2017). The contributions of women volunteers to conservation are explored in Carolyn Merchant, *Earthcare: Women and the Environment* (New York: Routledge, 1995), 109–166; Priscilla G. Massmann, "A Neglected Partnership: The General Federation of Women's Clubs and the Conservation Movement, 1890–1920" (Ph.D. diss., University of Connecticut, Storrs, 1997); Glenda Riley, *Women and Nature: Saving the "Wild" West* (Lincoln: University of Nebraska Press, 1999), 43–61, 97–113; Shana Miriam Cohen, "American Garden Clubs and the Fight for Nature Preservation, 1890–1980" (Ph.D. diss., University of California, Berkeley, 2005); and Nancy C. Unger, *Beyond Nature's Housekeepers: American Women in Environmental History* (New York: Oxford University Press, 2012). For a broad-ranging examination of voluntarism among women's groups in general, see McCarthy, *Lady Bountiful Revisited.*

24. For general discussions of Lady Bird Johnson's beautification initiative, see Lewis L. Gould, *Lady Bird Johnson: Our Environmental First Lady* (Lawrence: University Press of Kansas, 1999); Thomas G. Smith, *Stewart L. Udall: Steward of the Land* (Albuquerque: University of New Mexico Press, 2017), 196–215; and Scott Raymond Einberger, *With Distance in His Eyes: The Environmental Life and Legacy of Stewart Udall* (Reno: University of Nevada Press, 2018), 196–202.

25. See Christopher Johnson, *This Grand and Magnificent Place: The Wilderness Heritage of the White Mountains* (Durham: University of New Hampshire Press, 2006), 196, 201–205; Silas Chamberlin, "'To Ensure Permanency': Expanding and Protecting Hiking Opportunities in Twentieth-Century Pennsylvania," *Pennsylvania History*, 77 (Spring 2010): 193–216; and Silas Chamberlin, *On the Trail: A History of American Hiking* (New Haven, Conn.: Yale University Press, 2016).

26. See Sarah Mittlefehldt, *Tangled Roots: The Appalachian Trail and American Environmental Politics* (Seattle: University of Washington Press, 2013); and Vaughn and Cortner, *Philanthropy and the National Park Service*, 90–91. The Appalachian Trail Conservancy's quarterly magazine, *Journeys*, regularly comments on the work of trail volunteers.

27. See Thomas R. Dunlap, *Saving America's Wildlife* (Princeton, N.J.: Princeton University Press, 1988), 108–109; John C. Hendee, "Membership in Conservation Groups and Outdoor Clubs," in *The Forest Recreation Symposium*, ed. E. vH. Larson (Upper

Darby, Pa.: Northeastern Forest Experiment Station, Forest Service, U.S. Department of Agriculture, 1971), 123–127; and Rue E. Gordon, ed., *1995 Conservation Directory*, 40th ed. (Washington, D.C.: National Wildlife Federation, 1995).

28. See Adam Rome, *The Genius of Earth Day: How a 1970 Teach-in Unexpectedly Made the First Green Generation* (New York: Hill and Wang, 2013). For the entrenched use of volunteers within conservation and environmental organizations, see Snow, *Inside the Environmental Movement.*

29. See Riley E. Dunlap and Angela G. Mertig, eds., *American Environmentalism: The U.S. Environmental Movement, 1970–1990* (Philadelphia: Taylor & Francis, 1992); and Samuel P. Hays, *A History of Environmental Politics since 1945* (Pittsburgh: University of Pittsburgh Press, 2000).

30. Randall K. Wilson, *America's Public Lands: From Yellowstone to Smokey Bear and Beyond* (Lanham, Md.: Rowman & Littlefield, 2014), 4. The cruel irony is that many of these 650 million acres of "public" lands had involved the dispossession of Native Americans; millions of acres of ancestral Native American land had been wrested from Native Americans in treaties broken by the federal government. See also Marion Clawson and Burnell Held, *The Federal Lands: Their Use and Management* (Baltimore: Johns Hopkins University Press, 1957); Paul Wallace Gates, *History of Public Land Law Development* (Washington, D.C.: GPO, 1968); President's Commission on Americans Outdoors, *Americans Outdoors: The Legacy, the Challenge; The Report of the President's Commission* (Washington, D.C.: Island Press, 1987), 103–109; Dyan Zaslowsky and T. H. Watkins, *These American Lands: Parks, Wilderness, and the Public Lands*, rev. ed. (Washington, D.C.: Island Press, 1994); Char Miller, *Public Lands, Public Debates: A Century of Controversy* (Corvallis: Oregon State University Press, 2012); and Steven Davis, *In Defense of Public Lands: The Case against Privatization and Transfer* (Philadelphia: Temple University Press, 2018).

31. See Ronald F. Lee, *Public Use of the National Park System, 1972–2000* (Washington, D.C.: GPO, 1968); and Ethan Carr, *Mission 66: Modernism and the National Park Dilemma* (Amherst: University of Massachusetts Press, 2007).

32. See Emilie Martin, "Student Volunteers in the National Parks and Forests," *National Parks and Conservation Magazine*, 47 (February 1973): 24–27; John C. Miles, *Guardians of the Parks: A History of the National Parks and Conservation Association* (Washington, D.C.: Taylor & Francis, 1995), 199–204; Megan Anne Jones, "Stewards of Tomorrow: The Student Conservation Association, Youth Service, and Postwar American Environmentalism, 1953–1975" (Ph.D. diss., University of Delaware, Newark, 2011); and Vaughn and Cortner, *Philanthropy and the National Park Service*, 42–44. In 1984, the Student Conservation Association reached the milestone of having 10,000

alumni. A summary of the association's organizational history is provided in "The Student Conservation Association Turns 60: Part 1, a Look Back," 8 June 2017, https://www.thesca.org/connect/blog/student-conservation-association-turns-60-part-1-look-back (accessed 24 May 2019), and examples of the work performed by its first group of volunteers is given in "6 Excerpts from the Original 1957 SCA Crew Journals," 8 June 2017, https://www.thesca.org/connect/blog/6-excerpts-original-1957-sca-crew-journals (accessed 24 May 2019).

33. Lee, *Public Use of the National Park System*, 2.

34. Walter J. Hickel to Spiro T. Agnew (president of the Senate), 9 July 1969, Aspinall July 9–September 23, 1969 folder, box 65, George B. Hartzog Jr. Papers, Special Collections and Archives, Clemson University Libraries, Clemson, S.C. (hereafter cited as Hartzog papers). Hickel elaborated, stating, "Voluntary service is associated with citizenship, and it has helped to improve conditions in neighborhoods, cities, and across the Nation. Volunteers representing all segments of our population are today working in the fields of health, education, welfare, cultural affairs, and community activities." See also George Hartzog to Carl McMurray (assistant to secretary Hickel), 19 March 1969, folder 655, box 51, Hartzog papers; and "Secretary Hickel Asks Volunteer Program for Parks," Department of the Interior news release, 15 July 1969, folder 851, box 68, Hartzog papers.

35. See Volunteers in the Parks Act of 1969, Public Law No. 91-357, 84 Stat. 472 (29 July 1970); "Vols Help Smokey the Bear," *Voluntary Action News*, 3 (November 1972): 5; and https://www.nps.gov/getinvolved/volunteer.htm (accessed 5 May 2021).

36. The 30,000 volunteers assisting the National Park Service in 1989 grew to more than 75,000 by 1993, and by 2015 the VIP program had expanded to 200,000 volunteers. See James M. Ridenour, *The National Parks Compromised: Pork Barrel Politics and America's Treasures* (Merrillville, Ind.: ICS Books, 1994), 49; Rettie, *Our National Park System*, 196; Dylan Lewis, "Unpaid Protectors: Volunteerism and the Diminishing Role of Federal Responsibility in the National Park Service" (honors thesis, Northwestern University, Evanston, Ill., 2011); Dylan Lewis, "Unpaid Protectors: Volunteerism and the Diminishing Role of Federal Responsibility in the National Park Service," in *Protected Areas in a Changing World: Proceedings of the 2013 George Wright Society Conference on Parks, Protected Areas, and Cultural Sites*, ed. Samantha Weber (Hancock, Mich.: George Wright Society, 2014), 95–100; and Department of the Interior, National Park Service, Director's Order #7: Volunteers-in-Parks, rev. ed., 15 March 2016, https://www.nps.gov/policy/DOrders/DO_7_2016.htm (accessed 22 August 2018). For the volunteer opportunities created within the Bureau of Land Management and Fish and Wildlife Service, see U.S. Department of the Interior, *Bureau of Land Management: Volunteer Opportunities in Utah* (Washington, D.C.: GPO, 1990); U.S. Department of the Interior, *Volunteer Opportunities: Eastern States, Bureau of Land Management* (Washington,

D.C.: GPO, 1990); U.S. Department of the Interior, Bureau of Land Management, https://www.blm.gov/get-involved/volunteers/volunteer-opportunities (accessed 5 May 2021); U.S. Department of the Interior, Fish and Wildlife Service, Volunteers, https://www.fws.gov/volunteers/ (accessed 22 August 2018); and Bill Hartwig, "Volunteers Vital to Refuges," *Wildlife Refuge Magazine*, 1 (Autumn 2005): 19.

37. Quoted in "National Mall and Memorial Park's Volunteers-In-Parks," *Washington Post*, 4 January 2018. See also Scott Einberger, *A History of Rock Creek Park: Wilderness and Washington, D.C.* (Charleston, S.C.: History Press, 2014), 211–215; and "Park Rangers Outside the Woods: A Q&A with Park Ranger Jason Cangelosi," Student Conservation Association, 4 May 2018, https://www.thesca.org/connect/blog/park-rangers-outside-woods-qa-park-ranger-jason-cangelosi (accessed 13 May 2019).

38. Terry Tempest Williams, *The Hour of Land: A Personal Topography of America's National Parks* (New York: Sarah Crichton Books, 2016), 391. For a discussion of what motivated many of the volunteers concerned with ecological restoration projects, see Robert E. Grese, Rachel Kaplan, Robert L. Ryan, and Jane Buxton, "Psychological Benefits of Volunteering in Stewardship Programs," in *Restoring Nature: Perspectives from the Social Sciences and Humanities*, ed. Paul H. Gobster and R. Bruce Hull (Washington, D.C.: Island Press, 2000), 265–280.

39. George Hartzog to Directorate and All Field Directors, 17 November 1970, folder 656, box 52, Hartzog papers. For Hartzog's pride in the early success of the VIP program, see transcript, George Hartzog remarks to NPRA 50th Anniversary Conference, 19 September 1971, folder 1162, box 94A, Hartzog papers.

40. See *Volunteers in the National Forests: A Decade of Excellence*, FS 669 (Washington, D.C.: U.S. Department of Agriculture, Forest Service, 2000); and Gerald W. Williams, *The U.S. Forest Service in the Pacific Northwest: A History* (Corvallis: Oregon State University Press, 2009), 225. The Forest Service named its program Volunteers in Forests. Since 1968, the Forest Service has collaborated with the Student Conservation Association, which supplied summertime student volunteers.

41. President's Commission on Americans Outdoors, *Americans Outdoors*, 103.

42. See Wilson, *America's Public Lands*, 168–169. The U.S. Army Corps of Engineers, which manages nearly 2 million acres of developed recreational areas at more than 450 reservoirs and other water projects, is another federal agency that engaged volunteers in public lands stewardship. In 1996, for example, it claimed that its roughly 70,000 volunteers contributed more than 9 million dollars' worth of services. See Carter J. Betz, Donald B. K. English, and H. Ken Cordell, "Outdoor Recreation Resources," in *Outdoor Recreation in American Life: A National Assessment of Demand and Supply Trends*, by H. Ken Cordell, Carter Betz, J. Michael Bowker, Donald B. K. English, Shela H. Mou,

John C. Bergstrom, R. Jeff Teasley, Michael A. Tarrant, and John Loomis (Champaign, Ill.: Sagamore Publishing, 1999), 69.

43. See "The 1971 Annual Report of the Advertising Council, Inc.," Advertising Council Annual Reports, 1942–1975, record series 13/2/202, box 1, Advertising Council Archives, University Library, University of Illinois at Urbana-Champaign, Urbana (hereafter cited as Ad Council Archives).

44. See Marie Smith, "Volunteer Plan," *Washington Post*, 7 January 1970.

45. Charles B. Wilkinson to Robert P. Keim, 16 December 1969, Voluntarism—1969 folder, Robert P. Keim Papers, 1967–87, record series 13/2/220, box 17, Ad Council Archives. See also "The National Program for Voluntary Action," a two-page summary paper dated 23 January 1970 and attached to Charles B. Wilkinson to Robert P. Keim, 28 January 1970, Voluntarism—1969 folder, Robert P. Keim Papers, 1967–87, record series 13/2/220, box 17, Ad Council Archives.

46. For the Ad Council's agreement to take on the Nixon administration's voluntary action campaign, see "The Advertising Council Annual Report 1970," p. 32, Advertising Council Annual Reports, 1942–1975, record series 13/2/202, box 1, Ad Council Archives; and "Volunteers Pour In: 'We Need You' Ads Work," *Evening Star* (Washington, D.C.), 22 January 1973.

47. Ellis and Campbell, *By the People*, 246.

48. See Thomas F. Michaels, conference report, 14 July 1971, Voluntarism—1971–1972 folder, Robert P. Keim Papers, 1967–87, record series 13/2/220, box 17, Ad Council Archives. On the contributions of volunteers to government service, see Smith and Freedman, *Voluntary Associations*, 220–226. Nixon's motivation for creating the umbrella agency ACTION stemmed in part from his vindictive desire to defang the Peace Corps, following its former volunteers actively protesting the administration's escalation of the Vietnam War. See Jack Rosenthal, "Nixon Submits Plan to Merge 9 Volunteer Programs," *New York Times*, 25 March 1971; and Terence Smith, "Peace Corps: Alive but Not So Well," *New York Times*, 25 December 1977. General Peace Corps histories are provided in Gerard T. Rice, *The Bold Experiment: JFK's Peace Corps* (Notre Dame, Ind.: University of Notre Dame Press, 1985); T. Zane Reeves, *The Politics of the Peace Corps and VISTA* (Tuscaloosa: University of Alabama Press, 1988); and Elizabeth Cobbs Hoffman, *All You Need Is Love: The Peace Corps and the Spirit of the 1960s* (Cambridge, Mass.: Harvard University Press, 1998).

49. See Robert P. Keim to Edwin D. Etherington, 31 January 1972, Voluntarism—1971–1972 folder, Robert P. Keim Papers, 1967–87, record series 13/2/220, box 17, Ad Council Archives; and "Rules for Nominations for the National Volunteer Awards for 1975," *Voluntary Action News*, 6 (September/October 1975): 14.

50. See "Super Bowl Ratings History (1967–present)," http://www.sportsmediawatch. com/super-bowl-ratings-historical-viewership-chart-cbs-nbc-fox-abc/ (accessed 30 August 2018).

51. "Volunteers Pour In: 'We Need You' Ads Work." See also "The Advertising Council, Inc. Annual Report, 1972–1973," p. 14, Advertising Council Annual Reports, 1942–1975, record series 13/2/202, box 1, Ad Council Archives. Several years later, the Take Pride in America campaign partnered with the National Football League to develop a similar public service television ad featuring NFL players.

52. Richard Nixon, Earth Week, 1974, Proclamation No. 4287, 20 April 1974, http:// www.presidency.ucsb.edu/ws/index.php?pid=106843 (accessed 5 May 2021).

53. Richard Nixon, National Volunteer Week, 1974, Proclamation No. 4288, 20 April 1974, https://www.presidency.ucsb.edu/documents/proclamation-4288-national-volunteer-week-1974 (accessed 5 May 2021).

54. See "Lists of White House 'Enemies' and Memorandums Relating to Those Named," *New York Times*, 28 June 1973.

55. See Collingwood J. Harris to Robert E. Hill, 12 March 1975, Voluntarism—1975 folder, Robert P. Keim Papers, 1967–87, record series 13/2/220, box 17, Ad Council Archives. NBC Sports claimed that Super Bowl IX reached 29 million homes per minute.

56. "National Congress on Volunteerism and Citizenship," *Voluntary Action News*, 6 (September/October 1975): 2.

57. "Directors Announce New Role for NCVA," *Voluntary Action News*, 6 (September/ October 1975): 7.

58. "The Advertising Council Annual Report to the American People (1984–1985)," p. 1, Advertising Council Annual Reports, 1976–1995, record series 13/2/202, box 2, Ad Council Archives. For the growth of volunteerism in the 1980s, see Ellis and Campbell, *By the People*, 260–269.

59. Minutes of the Public Policy Committee Meeting, 15 December 1981, Public Policy Committee File, 1954–1987, 1992, record series 13/2/209, box 1, Ad Council Archives.

CHAPTER 4

1. For the bipartisan nature of environmental policy before Reagan's presidency, see Dennis L. Soden, ed., *The Environmental Presidency* (Albany: State University of New

York Press, 1999); William Cronon, "When the G.O.P. Was Green," *New York Times*, 8 January 2001; Brian Allen Drake, *Loving Nature, Fearing the State: Environmentalism and Antigovernmental Politics before Reagan* (Seattle: University of Washington Press, 2013); and James Morton Turner and Andrew C. Isenberg, *The Republican Reversal: Conservatives and the Environment from Nixon to Trump* (Cambridge, Mass.: Harvard University Press, 2018).

2. See C. Brant Short, *Ronald Reagan and the Public Lands: America's Conservation Debate, 1979–1984* (College Station: Texas A&M University Press, 1989); W. Kip Viscusi, "The Misspecified Agenda: The 1980s Reforms of Health, Safety, and Environmental Regulation," in *American Economic Policy in the 1980s*, ed. Martin Feldstein (Chicago: University of Chicago Press, 1994), 453–458; and Patrick Allitt, *A Climate of Crisis: America in the Age of Environmentalism* (New York: Penguin Press, 2014), 156–165. For the growing opposition to environmentalism among conservatives in the 1970s and thereafter, see R. McGreggor Cawley, *Federal Land, Western Anger: The Sagebrush Rebellion and Environmental Politics* (Lawrence: University Press of Kansas, 1993); Joshua Ross Ashenmiller, "The National Environmental Policy Act in the Green Decade, 1969–1981" (Ph.D. diss., University of California, Santa Barbara, 2004); James Morton Turner, *The Promise of Wilderness: American Environmental Politics since 1964* (Seattle: University of Washington Press, 2012); Judith A. Layzer, *Open for Business: Conservatives' Opposition to Environmental Regulation* (Cambridge, Mass.: MIT Press, 2012); Geoffrey Kabaservice, *Rule and Ruin: The Downfall of Moderation and the Destruction of the Republican Party* (New York: Oxford University Press, 2012); Alex John Boynton, "Confronting the Environmental Crisis? Anti-Environmentalism and the Transformation of Conservative Thought in the 1970s" (Ph.D. diss., University of Kansas, Lawrence, 2015); Jefferson Decker, *The Other Rights Revolution: Conservative Lawyers and the Remaking of American Government* (New York: Oxford University Press, 2016); and Turner and Isenberg, *The Republican Reversal*, who summarized the GOP's shift on public lands stewardship by stating "the Progressive-era Republican Party of conservation became the modern Republican Party of extraction" (p. 94).

3. Paul R. Portney, "Introduction," in *Natural Resources and the Environment: The Reagan Approach*, ed. Paul R. Portney (Washington, D.C.: Urban Institute Press, 1984), 10. See also Robert F. Durant, *The Administrative Presidency Revisited: Public Lands, the BLM, and the Reagan Revolution* (Albany: State University of New York Press, 1992); Jeffrey K. Stine, "Natural Resources and Environmental Policy," in *The Reagan Presidency: Pragmatic Conservatism and Its Legacies*, ed. W. Elliot Brownlee and Hugh Davis Graham (Lawrence: University Press of Kansas, 2003), 233–256; Holley Elizabeth Tankersley, "National and State Dimensions of Major Policy Change: The Reagan 'Revolution' Reexamined" (Ph.D. diss., University of Georgia, Athens, 2006); Joel D.

Aberbach, "Transforming the Presidency: The Administration of Ronald Reagan," in *Ronald Reagan and the 1980s: Perceptions, Policies, Legacies*, ed. Cheryl Hudson and Gareth Davies (New York: Palgrave Macmillan, 2008), 191–207; and Bruce J. Schulman, "The Privatization of Everyday Life: Public Policy, Public Services, and Public Space in the 1980s," in *Living in the Eighties*, ed. Gil Troy and Vincent J. Cannato (New York: Oxford University Press, 2009), 167–180.

4. See Lou Cannon, *President Reagan: The Role of a Lifetime* (New York: Simon & Schuster, 1991), 526–530; Lou Cannon, *Governor Reagan: His Rise to Power* (New York: PublicAffairs, 2003), 177–178, 298–299, 304–305, 319–320, 437–438; and Robert A. Goldberg, "The Western Hero in Politics: Barry Goldwater, Ronald Reagan, and the Rise of the American Conservation Movement," in *The Political Culture of the New West*, ed. Jeff Roche (Lawrence: University Press of Kansas, 2008), 13–50. During his eight years in the White House, Reagan spent 347 days at his secluded sanctuary—the 688-acre Rancho del Cielo (Sky Ranch)—perched atop the Santa Ynez Mountains 27 miles northwest of Santa Barbara, where he guarded his privacy by limiting the press's photo opportunities to orchestrated outdoor shots of him chopping wood or riding horses. See Peter Hannaford, *Ronald Reagan and His Ranch: The Western White House, 1981–89* (Bennington, Vt.: Images from the Past, 2002); and Peter Hannaford, *Presidential Retreats: Where They Went and Why They Went There* (New York: Threshold Editions, 2012), 258–267.

5. President Nixon's environmental attitudes and accomplishments are addressed in James Rathlesberger, ed., *Nixon and the Environment: The Politics of Devastation* (New York: Village Voice, 1972); Russell E. Train, "The Environmental Record of the Nixon Administration," *Presidential Studies Quarterly*, 26 (Winter 1996): 185–196; and J. Brooks Flippen, *Nixon and the Environment* (Albuquerque: University of New Mexico Press, 2000).

6. Governor Reagan's environmental record is discussed in Daniel J. Balz, *Ronald Reagan: A Trusty Script* (Washington, D.C.: Capitol Hill News Service, 1976), 2, 7–8; Bill Boyarsky, *Ronald Reagan: His Life and Rise to the Presidency* (New York: Random House, 1981), 166–176; Lou Cannon, *Reagan* (New York: Putnam, 1982), 350–354; Ted Simon, *The River Stops Here: How One Man's Battle to Save His Valley Changed the Fate of California* (New York: Random House, 1994), 210–220, 293–299, 339–344; Cannon, *Governor Reagan*, 297–321; Michael I. Muraki, "The Impacts of the State and Federal Wild and Scenic River Acts in Conservation Efforts on California's Trinity River" (M.A. thesis, California State University, Chico, 2018); Glenda Riley and Richard W. Etulain, *Presidents Who Shaped the American West* (Norman: University of Oklahoma Press, 2018), 220–224; and Bob Spitz, *Reagan: An American Journey* (New York: Penguin Press, 2018), 374–375. For the growth of environmental concern among Americans during

this time, see James McEvoy III, *The American Public's Concern with the Environment: A Study of Public Opinion* (Davis: Institute of Governmental Affairs, University of California, 1971); Ronald G. Faich and Richard P. Gale, "The Environmental Movement: From Recreation to Politics," *Pacific Sociological Review*, 14 (July 1971): 270–287; and Frederick H. Buttel and William L. Flinn, "The Structure of Support for the Environmental Movement, 1968–1970," *Rural Sociology*, 39 (Spring 1974): 56–69. For environmental concerns within California, see Robert Easton, *Black Tide: The Santa Barbara Oil Spill and Its Consequences* (New York: Delacorte Press, 1972); Ed Salzman, ed., *California Environment and Energy: Text and Readings on Contemporary Issues* (Sacramento: California Journal Press, 1980); Tim Palmer, ed., *California's Threatened Environment: Restoring the Dream* (Washington, D.C.: Island Press, 1993); Carolyn Merchant, ed., *Green Versus Gold: Sources in California's Environmental History* (Washington, D.C.: Island Press, 1998); Char Miller, *Not So Golden State: Sustainability vs. the California Dream* (San Antonio, Tex.: Trinity University Press, 2016); Teresa Sabol Spezio, *Slick Policy: Environmental and Science Policy in the Aftermath of the Santa Barbara Oil Spill* (Pittsburgh: University of Pittsburgh Press, 2018); and David Vogel, *California Greenin': How the Golden State Became an Environmental Leader* (Princeton, N.J.: Princeton University Press, 2018). The bipartisan nature of these environmental concerns was well represented in the pages of *Cry California*, a journal established in 1965 by the planning advocacy group California Tomorrow.

7. Cannon, *President Reagan*, 530. Reagan's thinking on environmental matters during the 1970s is addressed in Kiron K. Skinner, Annelise Anderson, and Martin Anderson, eds., *Reagan, in His Own Hand* (New York: Free Press, 2001), 307–308, 313–316, 318–341.

8. See John D. Leshy, "Natural Resource Policy," in Portney, *Natural Resources and the Environment*, 13; and C. Brant Short, "Conservation Reconsidered: Environmental Politics, Rhetoric, and the Reagan Revolution," in *Green Talk in the White House: The Rhetorical Presidency Encounters Ecology*, ed. Tarla Rai Peterson (College Station: Texas A&M University Press, 2004), 134–150.

9. See Michael E. Kraft, "A New Environmental Policy Agenda: The 1980 Presidential Campaign and Its Aftermath," in *Environmental Policy in the 1980s: Reagan's New Agenda*, ed. Norman J. Vig and Michael E. Kraft (Washington, D.C.: Congressional Quarterly, 1984), 44; Constance Holden, "The Reagan Years: Environmentalists Tremble," *Science*, 210 (28 November 1980): 988–989; Raymond Tatalovich and Mark J. Wattier, "Opinion Leadership: Elections, Campaigns, Agenda Setting, and Environmentalism," in Soden, *The Environmental Presidency*, 156–157; and Robert Kirby Green, "The Managerial Moralist: The Domestic Policy of Jimmy Carter, 1977–1981" (Ph.D. diss., Queen Mary University of London, London, 2018),

272–312. Carter's environmental record is covered in Jeffrey K. Stine, "Environmental Policy during the Carter Presidency," in *The Carter Presidency: Policy Choices in the Post-New Deal Era*, ed. Gary M Fink and Hugh Davis Graham (Lawrence: University Press of Kansas, 1998), 179–201. For the broader context of the 1980 presidential election, with special attention to the growth of political conservatism, see Andrew E. Busch, *Reagan's Victory: The Presidential Election of 1980 and the Rise of the Right* (Lawrence: University Press of Kansas, 2005); and Rick Perlstein, *Reaganland: America's Right Turn, 1976–1980* (New York: Simon & Schuster, 2020).

10. For the question of mandates in presidential elections, including how Reagan treated his victories in 1980 and 1984, see Patricia Heidotting Conley, *Presidential Mandates: How Elections Shape the National Agenda* (Chicago: University of Chicago Press, 2001); and Kraft, "A New Environmental Policy Agenda," 29–50.

11. Norman J. Vig, "Presidential Leadership and the Environment: From Reagan to Clinton," in *Environmental Policy in the 1990s: Reform or Reaction?*, 3rd ed., ed. Norman J. Vig and Michael E. Kraft (Washington. D.C.: CQ Press, 1997), 98.

12. Lewis Regenstein, quoted in Holden, "The Reagan Years," 988.

13. For an early report on this trend, see Constance Holden, "Public's Fear of Watt Is Environmentalists' Gain," *Science*, 212 (24 April 1981): 422. A broader assessment of Reagan's environmental attitudes and the impact of his election is provided in Paul Sabin, *The Bet: Paul Ehrlich, Julian Simon, and Our Gamble over Earth's Future* (New Haven, Conn.: Yale University Press, 2013), 137–150.

14. See Ray Lyman Wilbur and William Atherton Du Puy, *Conservation in the Department of the Interior* (Washington, D.C.: GPO, 1931); Norman O. Forness, "The Origins and Early History of the United States Department of the Interior" (Ph.D. diss., Pennsylvania State University, University Park, 1964); Paul Wallace Gates, *History of Public Land Law Development* (Washington, D.C.: GPO, 1968); Richard West Sellars, *Preserving Nature in the National Parks: A History* (New Haven, Conn.: Yale University Press, 1997); James R. Skillen, *The Nation's Largest Landlord: The Bureau of Land Management in the American West* (Lawrence: University Press of Kansas, 2009); and Megan Black, *The Global Interior: Mineral Frontiers and American Power* (Cambridge, Mass.: Harvard University Press, 2018).

15. See Lettie M. Wenner, *The Environmental Decade in Court* (Bloomington: Indiana University Press, 1982), 55; and Steven M. Teles, *The Rise of the Conservative Legal Movement: The Battle for Control of the Law* (Princeton, N.J.: Princeton University Press, 2008), 64.

16. The two classic hagiographies of Watt—Ron Arnold, *At the Eye of the Storm: James Watt and the Environmentalists* (Chicago: Regnery Gateway, 1982); and William

Perry Pendley, *Sagebrush Rebel: Reagan's Battle with Environmental Extremists and Why It Matters Today* (Washington, D.C.: Regnery Publishing, 2013)—are countered by the hypercritical assessment presented in Jonathan Lash, Katherine Gillman, and David Sheridan, *A Season of Spoils: The Reagan Administration's Attack on the Environment* (New York: Pantheon Books, 1984), 215–297. See also Ronald Brownstein and Nina Easton, *Reagan's Ruling Class: Portraits of the President's Top 100 Officials* (Washington, D.C.: Presidential Accountability Group, 1982), 107–114, 118–125; Jeff Radford, *The Chaco Coal Scandal: The People's Victory over James Watt* (Corrales, N.M.: Rhombus Publishing Company, 1986); Paul J. Culhane, "Sagebrush Rebels in Office: Jim Watt's Land and Water Politics," in Vig and Kraft, *Environmental Policy in the 1980s*, 293–314; George Cameron Coggins and Doris K. Nagel, "'Nothing Beside Remains': The Legal Legacy of James G. Watt's Tenure as Secretary of the Interior on Federal Land Law and Policy," *Boston College Environmental Affairs Law Review*, 17 (Spring 1990): 473–550; and Turner, *The Promise of Wilderness*, 232–238. Watt offers self-revealing insights into his political and philosophical perspective, as well as his vindictive disregard for environmentalists, in James G. Watt, *The Courage of a Conservative* (New York: Simon & Schuster, 1985). Similar insights are provided in his wife's memoir of their three years in Washington. See Leilani Watt, *Caught in the Conflict: My Life with James Watt*, with Al Janssen (Eugene, Ore.: Harvest House Publishers, 1984).

17. Watt, quoted in Philip Shabecoff, "Nearing Complete Renovation of Interior Department Rules," *New York Times*, 23 January 1983. Watt's criticism of centralized planning is addressed in "Watt Says Foes Want Centralization of Power," *New York Times*, 21 January 1983, whereas his administrative approach is discussed in Arnold, *At the Eye of the Storm*, 137.

18. Reagan's use of cabinet councils is covered in James P. Pfiffner, *The Strategic Presidency: Hitting the Ground Running* (Chicago: Dorsey Press, 1988), 58–64; Michael Turner, "The Reagan White House, the Cabinet, and the Bureaucracy," in *Reagan's First Four Years: A New Beginning?*, ed. John D. Lees and Michael Turner (Manchester, U.K.: Manchester University Press, 1988), 39–67; and Shirley Anne Warshaw, "White House Control of Domestic Policy Making: The Reagan Years," *Public Administration Review*, 55 (May/June 1995): 247–252.

19. See D. V. Feliciano, "President Reagan's Cabinet Councils: It's No Secret, Environment Is Second Priority to Natural Resources Development," *Journal (Water Pollution Control Federation)*, 54 (March 1982): 210–212; and Marc K. Landy, Marc J. Roberts, and Stephen R. Thomas, *The Environmental Protection Agency: Asking the Wrong Questions* (New York: Oxford University Press, 1990), 248.

20. See Lance Gay, "U.S. Parks Director Calls System Too Big," *Washington Star*, 1 February 1981.

21. For Watt's treatment of the National Park Service, see Michael Frome, *Regreening the National Parks* (Tucson: University of Arizona Press, 1992), 39–43, 98–102. The post-1950s conflicts within the Park Service are analyzed in Ronald A. Foresta, *America's National Parks and Their Keepers* (Washington, D.C.: Resources for the Future, 1984). Beyond his moratorium on acquiring additional lands for national parks, Watt abolished the Bureau of Outdoor Recreation, an agency within the Department of the Interior that helped states purchase recreational lands by providing 50% matching funds.

22. Richard Ganzel, "Maximizing Public Land Resource Values," in *Western Public Lands: The Management of Natural Resources in a Time of Declining Federalism*, ed. John G. Francis and Richard Ganzel (Totowa, N.J.: Rowan & Allanheld, 1984), 138. See also Bernard Shanks, *This Land Is Your Land: The Struggle to Save America's Public Lands* (San Francisco: Sierra Club Books, 1984).

23. National Wildlife Federation president Jay Hair, quoted in Philip Shabecoff, "Wildlife Unit Asks Watt's Ouster," *New York Times*, 15 July 1981.

24. See Short, *Ronald Reagan and the Public Lands*, 10–25; Charles I. Zinser, *Outdoor Recreation: United States National Parks, Forests, and Public Lands* (New York: John Wiley & Sons, 1995), 36–39; and George H. Siehl, *The Policy Path to the Great Outdoors: A History of the Outdoor Recreation Review Commissions*, Background Study 08-44 (Washington, D.C.: Resources for the Future, 2008), 7–8. A broader assessment of the challenges facing public lands policymakers is provided in Wayne Hage, *Storm over Rangelands: Private Rights in Federal Lands* (Bellevue, Wash.: Free Enterprise Press, 1989); William L. Graf, *Wilderness Preservation and the Sagebrush Rebellions* (Savage, Md.: Rowman & Littlefield, 1990); Cawley, *Federal Land, Western Anger*; Christopher McGrory Klyza, *Who Controls Public Lands? Mining, Forestry, and Grazing Policies, 1870–1990* (Chapel Hill: University of North Carolina Press, 1996); Martin Nie, *The Governance of Western Public Lands: Mapping Its Present and Future* (Lawrence: University Press of Kansas, 2008); and James R. Skillen, *This Land Is My Land: Rebellion in the West* (New York: Oxford University Press, 2020). The vituperative polemics put forth by proponents of the Sagebrush Rebellion (and, later, by the wise use movement) are exemplified in William Perry Pendley, *War on the West: Government Tyranny on America's Great Frontier* (Washington, D.C.: Regnery Publishing, 1995). For an examination of how radical environmentalists came to share the hardline conservatives' skepticism and distrust of the federal government, especially with regard to public land management, see Keith Makoto Woodhouse, *The Ecocentrists: A History of Radical Environmentalism* (New York: Columbia University Press, 2018), 143–182.

25. See Don H. Clausen et al. to Ronald Reagan, 18 March 1981, NR006 (019001–030000) folder, box 22, White House Office of Records Management (WHORM) subject file NR, Ronald Reagan Presidential Library, Simi Valley, Calif. (hereafter cited as RRL).

26. See Douglas D. Anderson to Secretary [Donald Regan], 19 April 1982, folder 1, box 128, Donald T. Regan Papers, Manuscript Division, Library of Congress, Washington, D.C. (hereafter cited as LC); minutes, Cabinet Council on Natural Resources and Environment, 29 April 1982, folder 1, box 128, Donald T. Regan Papers, LC; Dianne Feinstein to Reagan, 6 May 1982, NR006-01 Naval Petroleum Reserves (018955–080000) folder, box 30, WHORM subject file NR, RRL; and Robert Lindsey, "U.S. Oil Lease Sale in Coast's Waters Blocked in Court," *New York Times*, 28 July 1981.

27. "Watt Is Slowed on Oil Leasing," *New York Times*, 11 October 1982.

28. Watt, quoted in "Watt Unleashes Oil Explorers, to Some Dismay," *New York Times*, 25 July 1982. For an extended critique of Watt's plan, see Deni Greene's editorial, "To the Beaches! Oil Rigs Are Coming!," *New York Times*, 19 July 1982.

29. Form letter, Michael McCloskey to Dear Friend, n.d. [probably early 1982], Reagan Anti-environmental Program: Miscellaneous Articles and Materials folder, box 99, William Hoppen Papers, LC. See also J. Michael McCloskey, *In the Thick of It: My Life in the Sierra Club* (Washington, D.C.: Island Press/Shearwater Books, 2005), 210–219.

30. George B. Hartzog Jr., *Battling for the National Parks* (Mt. Kisco, N.Y.: Moyer Bell, 1988), 207.

31. Philip Shabecoff, "Questions Arise Not Just over Watt's Words," *New York Times*, 2 October 1983. In addition to invigorating environmentalist opposition, Watt fueled the news media's steady stream of negative reporting on the administration. An extensive sampling of the ways in which 36 political cartoonists from across the country lampooned Reagan's Interior secretary is provided in Carew Papritz, ed., *100 Watts: The James Watt Memorial Cartoon Collection* (Auburn, Wash.: Khyber Press, 1983). See also "Watt . . . We Worry!" *Mad*, no. 234 (October 1982): back cover.

32. Quoted in Shabecoff, "Questions Arise."

33. See Christopher J. Matthews, "Your Host, Ronald Reagan: From G.E. Theater to the Desk in the Oval Office," *New Republic*, 190 (26 March 1984): 15.

34. "What James Watt Said—and Did," *New York Times*, 11 October 1983. See also Philip Shabecoff, "Many Are Divided on Watt's Legacy," *New York Times*, 12 October 1983.

35. See Brownstein and Easton, *Reagan's Ruling Class*, 654–657; and "Nomination of William P. Clark to Be Secretary of the Interior," 13 October 1983, in *Public Papers of the Presidents of the United States, Ronald Reagan, 1983: Book II—July 2 to December 31, 1983* (Washington, D.C.: GPO, 1985), 1453. For the close, long-standing bond between Clark and Reagan, see Paul Kengor and Patricia Clark Doerner, *The Judge: William P. Clark, Ronald Reagan's Top Hand* (San Francisco: Ignatius Press, 2007).

36. Dunlap, Turnage, and Michel, quoted in Philip Shabecoff, "Environmental Groups Angered by Reagan Choice for Interior Job," *New York Times*, 14 October 1983. Clark's environmental critics did not mention his earlier role—as Governor Reagan's chief of staff—in supporting Norman "Ike" Livermore as director of resources. A Sierra Club member and avid outdoorsman, Livermore proved to be an effective proenvironmental force in Sacramento. See Lou Cannon, *Ronald Reagan: The Presidential Portfolio* (New York: PublicAffairs, 2001), 63–64.

37. "To Interior, a One-Way Secretary," *New York Times*, 15 October 1983. See also John B. Oakes, "Clark's Low Wattage," *New York Times*, 18 October 1983. For Clark's tenure at Interior, see Kengor and Doerner, *The Judge*, 257–279.

38. For the controversies encircling EPA during the Reagan administration's first term, see Landy et al., *The Environmental Protection Agency*, 245–273; Joel A. Mintz, *Enforcement at the EPA: High Stakes and Hard Choices* (Austin: University of Texas Press, 1995), 40–59; Richard N. L. Andrews, *Managing the Environment, Managing Ourselves: A History of American Environmental Policy* (New Haven, Conn.: Yale University Press, 1999), 257–261; and Marissa Martino Golden, *What Motivates Bureaucrats? Politics and Administration during the Reagan Years* (New York: Columbia University Press, 2000), 115–137.

39. See James Nathan Miller, "What Really Happened at EPA," *Reader's Digest*, 123 (July 1983): 64; and John Ehrman, *The Eighties: America in the Age of Reagan* (New Haven, Conn.: Yale University Press, 2005), 91–92. For political conservatives who found themselves disappointed in the Reagan administration (and Republican leaders in general) for turning a cold shoulder to environmental protection, see John R. E. Bliese, *The Greening of Conservative America* (Boulder, Colo.: Westview, 2001).

40. Philip Shabecoff, "Politics and the E.P.A. Crisis: Environment Emerges as a Mainstream Issue," *New York Times*, 29 April 1983. See also Andy Pasztor, "Reagan Policies Spur Big Revival of the Environmental Movement," *Wall Street Journal*, 9 August 1982; Philip Shabecoff, "Environmentalism Back in Spotlight as Activists and Administration Battle," *New York Times*, 19 September 1982; John M. Gillroy and Robert Y. Shapiro, "The Polls: Environmental Protection," *Public Opinion Quarterly*, 50 (1986): 270–279; and Gail Friedman, "Dumping the Pump: Bucks County, Pennsylvania, Community Activism and Eco-Politics in the Age of Reagan," *Pennsylvania History*, 85 (Summer 2018): 299–332.

41. For the White House's concern about negative press coverage of the administration's environmental record, see minutes, Cabinet Council on Natural Resources and Environment meeting, 9 February 1983, CCNRE February 9, 1983 folder, OA 12582, Randall E. Davis Files, RRL.

42. Andy Pasztor, "White House Acts to Change Image on Environment," *Wall Street Journal*, 11 March 1983.

43. "Radio Address to the Nation on Environmental and Natural Resources Management," 11 June 1983, in *Public Papers of the Presidents of the United States, Ronald Reagan, 1983: Book I—January 1 to July 1, 1983* (Washington, D.C.: GPO, 1984), 852–853.

44. For the response of environmental leaders to Reagan's radio address, see Steven R. Weisman, "Reagan, Assailing Critics, Defends His Environmental Policy as 'Sound,'" *New York Times*, 12 June 1983.

45. See "Debate between the President and Former Vice President Walter F. Mondale in Louisville, Kentucky," 7 October 1984, in *Public Papers of the Presidents of the United States, Ronald Reagan, 1984: Book II—June 30 to December 31, 1984* (Washington, D.C.: GPO, 1987), 1450.

46. See Cannon, *President Reagan*, 526.

47. Reagan won 58.8% of the popular vote, whereas Mondale succeeded in carrying only the District of Columbia and his home state of Minnesota.

48. For the limitations on Reagan's ability to modify environmental regulations, see Paul R. Portney, "Natural Resources and the Environment: More Controversy Than Change," in *The Reagan Record: An Assessment of America's Changing Domestic Priorities*, ed. John L. Palmer and Isabel V. Sawhill (Cambridge, Mass.: Ballinger, 1984), 141–175; George Hoberg, *Pluralism by Design: Environmental Policy and the American Regulatory State* (New York: Praeger, 1992), 169–194; and Michael E. Kraft, "U.S. Environmental Policy and Politics: From the 1960s to the 1990s," *Journal of Policy History*, 12, no. 1 (2000): 28–29.

49. R. Shep Melnick, "Risky Business: Government and the Environment after Earth Day," in *Taking Stock: American Government in the Twentieth Century*, ed. Morton Keller and R. Shep Melnick (New York: Cambridge University Press, 1999), 158. See also Everett Carll Ladd and Karlyn H. Bowman, *Attitudes toward the Environment: Twenty-Five Years after Earth Day* (Washington, D.C.: AEI Press, 1995); Robert H. Nelson, "Privatization of Federal Lands: What Did Not Happen," in *Regulation and the Reagan Era: Politics, Bureaucracy, and the Public Interest*, ed. Roger E. Meiners and Bruce Yandle (New York: Holmes and Meier, 1989), 132–165; and Daniel Nelson, *Nature's Burdens: Conservation and American Politics, the Reagan Era to the Present* (Logan: Utah State University Press, 2017).

50. Kraft, "A New Environmental Policy Agenda," 29–30.

CHAPTER 5

1. See Ronald Brownstein and Nina Easton, *Reagan's Ruling Class: Portraits of the President's Top 100 Officials* (Washington, D.C.: Presidential Accountability Group, 1982), 115–118; Jonathan Lash, Katherine Gillman, and David Sheridan, *A Season of Spoils: The Reagan Administration's Attack on the Environment* (New York: Pantheon Books, 1984), 235–236; Gerald M. Boyd, "Reagan Is Reported Set to Name Energy Secretary to Interior Post," *New York Times*, 10 January 1985; "Appendix I: Biography and Informational Statement of Donald Paul Hodel," in U.S. Congress, Senate Committee on Energy and Natural Resources, Hearing, *Nomination of Donald Paul Hodel to be Secretary of the Interior*, 99th Cong., 1st sess., 1 February 1985 (Washington, D.C.: GPO, 1985), 303–313; and Donald Hodel, interview by Bruce Collins, *The Reagan Legacy*, C-SPAN, 22 November 1988, https://www.c-span.org/video/?5721-1/interview-donald-hodel (accessed 9 May 2019). The history of the Bonneville Power Administration—the nation's second-largest electricity-marketing agency, after the Tennessee Valley Authority—is covered in Paul W. Hirt, *The Wired Northwest: The History of Electric Power, 1870s–1970s* (Lawrence: University Press of Kansas, 2012). Prior to Hodel's BPA appointment, he worked for a Portland, Oregon, law firm from 1960 to 1963 and for the general counsel of Georgia-Pacific Corporation from 1963 to 1969. He chaired the Republican State Central Committee of Oregon from 1966 to 1967. See "Nomination of Donald P. Hodel to Be Under Secretary of the Interior," 27 January 1981, in *Public Papers of the Presidents of the United States, Ronald Reagan, 1981: January 20 to December 31, 1981* (Washington, D.C.: GPO, 1982), 40. For the close friendships that developed between Donald and Barbara Hodel and James and Leilani Watt, see Leilani Watt, *Caught in the Conflict: My Life with James Watt*, with Al Janssen (Eugene, Ore.: Harvest House Publishers, 1984), 6.

2. "Statement of Donald Paul Hodel," in *Nomination of Donald Paul Hodel to be Secretary of the Interior*, 13.

3. "Statement of Hon. Howard M. Metzenbaum," in *Nomination of Donald Paul Hodel to be Secretary of the Interior*, 29. At that same Senate hearing, Wilderness Society vice president Charles M. Clusen testified, "There are many distinguished Republicans who have served in the Republican administrations of the past, but most recently in the Nixon and Ford administrations, who were very fine administrators who had a commitment to the environment. Unfortunately, this nomination of Mr. Hodel does not seem to represent a change from the Watt policies which still are in place at Interior" (p. 248). See also (in the same hearing report), National Wildlife Federation, "Issues Requiring Action by the New Secretary of the Interior," 144–197.

4. J. Michael McCloskey, *In the Thick of It: My Life in the Sierra Club* (Washington, D.C.: Island Press/Shearwater Books, 2005), 210. See also Susan Zakin, *Coyotes and*

Town Dogs: Earth First! and the Environmental Movement (New York: Viking, 1993), 414–415. Hodel had a history of antagonizing environmentalists, as exemplified by the address he delivered as head of the Bonneville Power Administration in July 1975, when he told business leaders, "The greatest threat to the environmental movement is the environmental movement itself. Over the past several years, it has fallen into the hands of a small, arrogant faction which is dedicated to bringing our society to a halt. I call this faction the Prophets of Shortage. They are the anti-producers, the anti-achievers. The doctrine they preach is scarcity and self-denial." Quoted in Barry Mitzman, "Abusing Public Power," *Environmental Action*, 7 (24 April 1976): 7.

5. Hodel's appeal extended beyond his genteel public face. As Philip Shabecoff observed, Hodel served "much the same political function as Mr. Watt served before his abrupt departure: He is a highly valued and effective Administration and Republican Party envoy and fund-raiser among the energy, mining and ranching interests of the West and in the conservative wing of the party." Philip Shabecoff, "Working Profile: Donald P. Hodel; Watt's Goals at Interior, but in a Different Style," *New York Times*, 3 March 1986.

6. For Hodel's conviction that federal lands and offshore waters should be opened to oil, gas, and mineral development and that the influence of environmental organizations should be curbed, see Reinier Lock, "Interview: Donald P. Hodel," *Natural Resources and Environment*, 2 (Spring 1986): 40–43, 75–76; Donald Paul Hodel and Robert Deitz, *Crisis in the Oil Patch: How America's Energy Industry Is Being Destroyed and What Must Be Done to Save It* (Washington, D.C.: Regnery Publishing, 1993); and Hodel, interview by Collins, 22 November 1988. For Hodel's holding fast to Watt's policies, see Rochelle L. Stanfield, "Tilting on Development: Interior Secretary Donald P. Hodel," *National Journal*, 19 (7 February 1987): 313–318; and R. McGreggor Cawley and William Chaloupka, "Federal Land Policy: The Conservative Challenge and Environmentalist Response," in *Federal Lands Policy*, ed. Phillip O. Foss (New York: Greenwood Press, 1987), 21–31.

7. Donald Hodel, address to the National Conference of State Legislatures, C-SPAN, 22 February 1985, https://www.c-span.org/video/?125324-1/national-conference-state-legislatures (accessed 9 May 2019). At the Department of Energy, Hodel had held open meetings with environmental leaders, who initially applauded the gestures, until they realized that those exchanges were purely window dressing. See Ruth Caplan, "From the Director," *Environmental Action*, 20 (January/February 1989): 2.

8. Donald P. Hodel, interview by Bruce Collins, with questions phoned in by the public, C-SPAN, 9 April 1985, https://www.c-span.org/video/?72472-1/department-interior (accessed 9 May 2019). Hodel and like-minded members of the Reagan administration found support for these beliefs in the nearly 600-page contrarian report, Julian L. Simon and Herman Kahn, eds., *The Resourceful Earth: A Response to Global 2000* (New York: Basil Blackwell, 1984). See also "Don Hodel, President Reagan's Point

Man for Parks and Recreation: A Conversation with the Secretary of the Interior," *Parks and Recreation*, 21 (August 1986): 52–58, 64; and "'NRPA Members Are Engaged in a Very Important Enterprise': Part Two of an Interview with Interior Secretary Don Hodel," *Parks and Recreation*, 21 (September 1986): 66–72.

9. U.S. Congress, Senate Committee on Energy and Natural Resources, *Proposed Fiscal Year 1986 Budget Request: Hearings to Review the President's Proposed Budget for Fiscal Year 1986 in Connection with the Preparation of the March 15 Report to the Senate Budget Committee*, 99th Cong., 1st sess., February 27, March 1 and 4, 1985 (Washington, D.C.: GPO, 1985), 69. The federal government manages approximately 640 million acres, or roughly 28%, of the U.S. land surface. Within the Department of the Interior, the Bureau of Land Management administers 248.3 million acres, the Fish and Wildlife Service 89.1 million acres, and the National Park Service 79.8 million acres. See Carol Hardy Vincent, Laura A. Hanson, and Carla N. Argueta, *Federal Land Ownership: Overview and Data*, CRS Report 7-5700 (Washington, D.C.: Congressional Research Service, 2017), 1. The main elements of the federal public lands are summarized in *A Guide to Our Federal Lands* (Washington, D.C.: National Geographic Society, 1984), whereas the largest public lands agency is addressed in James Muhn and Hanson R. Stuart, *Opportunity and Challenge: The Story of BLM* (Washington, D.C.: GPO, 1988); and U.S. Department of the Interior, Bureau of Land Management, *Managing the Nation's Public Lands* (Washington, D.C.: GPO, 1988). According to the latter report (p. 29), for the first time in history volunteers outnumbered BLM's employees in 1988 (14,077 volunteers to 10,810 employees). See also John D. Leshy, *Debunking Creation Myths about America's Public Lands* (Salt Lake City: University of Utah Press, 2018).

10. See Donald Paul Hodel to Stuart Upson, 7 August 1985, copy in Campaigns Review Committee minutes (19 September 1985), Campaigns Review Committee Minutes, 1948–69, 1981–97, record series 13/2/225, box 1, Advertising Council Archives, University Library, University of Illinois at Urbana-Champaign, Urbana (hereafter cited as Ad Council Archives).

11. "Inaugural Address," 20 January 1981, in *Public Papers of the Presidents of the United States, Ronald Reagan, 1981: January 20 to December 31, 1981* (Washington, D.C.: GPO, 1982), 1. Reagan asked the right-wing American Enterprise Institute to examine how the private sector—through voluntarism and philanthropy—could address social problems like health care, child welfare, and youth unemployment while advancing the conservative goal of reducing reliance on the federal government. The institute's 469-page report—Jack A. Meyer, ed., *Meeting Human Needs: Toward a New Public Philosophy* (Washington, D.C.: American Enterprise Institute for Public Policy Research, 1982)—proved too academic and philosophical to engage Reagan or directly influence White House initiatives.

12. "Remarks at the Annual Meeting of the National Alliance of Business," 5 October 1981, in *Public Papers of the Presidents of the United States, Ronald Reagan, 1981*, 882, 885, 886. See also David Harris, "Asking Too Much of the 'Spirit of Volunteerism,'" *New York Times*, 10 October 1981; David S. Adams, "Ronald Reagan's 'Revival': Voluntarism as a Theme in Reagan's Civil Religion," *Sociological Analysis*, 48 (Spring 1987), 17–29; Robert H. Bremner, *American Philanthropy*, 2nd ed. (Chicago: University of Chicago Press, 1988), 206–209; and Milton Goldin, "Ronald Reagan and the Commercialization of Giving," *Journal of American Culture*, 13 (Fall 1990): 31–36.

13. "Announcement of the Creation of the President's Volunteer Action Awards Program," 12 December 1981, in *Public Papers of the Presidents of the United States, Ronald Reagan, 1981*, 1151–1152. The other award categories were jobs, health, material resources, education, public safety, and the arts and humanities. Elizabeth Cushman Titus, the founder of the Student Conservation Association, received the first award in the recreation and environment category. See Donnie Radcliffe, "Honoring Deeds Well Done," *Washington Post*, 16 April 1982.

14. See Susan J. Ellis and Katherine H. Campbell, *By the People: A History of Americans as Volunteers*, 3rd ed. (Philadelphia: Energize, 2005), 262; and Ronald Reagan to Robert P. Keim, 6 December 1984, a facsimile of the letter is included as an appendix to Robert P. Keim, *A Time in Advertising's Camelot: The Memoirs of a Do-Gooder* (Madison, Conn.: Longview Press, 2002), xx.

15. Ronald Reagan, "Remarks at a Ceremony Honoring Youth Volunteers," 25 April 1985, https://www.presidency.ucsb.edu/node/260283 (accessed 5 May 2021).

16. For the general appeal of voluntarism among conservatives, see Richard C. Cornuelle, *Reclaiming the American Dream: The Role of Private Individuals and Voluntary Associations* (New Brunswick, N.J.: Transaction Publishers, 1993).

17. Hodel to Upson, 7 August 1985.

18. Proposal information for the Campaign Review Committee of the Advertising Council, attached to Hodel to Upson, 7 August 1985. The surge in thefts of cultural resources on public lands is examined in Derek V. Goodwin, "Raiders of the Sacred Sites," *New York Times*, 7 December 1986.

19. "Memorandum on the work of the War Advertising Council, 1942–1943," p. 3, Advertising Council Annual Reports, 1942–1975, record series 13/2/202, box 1, Ad Council Archives.

20. See Deputy Assistant Secretary—Policy, Budget and Administration [Joseph E. Doddridge] to Chief, Budget Branch, 20 September 1985, Education folder, Office of the Secretary Correspondence Files, Department of the Interior, Washington, D.C. (hereafter cited as DOI Office of Secretary files).

21. Principal Deputy Assistant Secretary—Policy, Budget and Administration [G. R. Riso] to Director, National Park Service, 18 September 1985, Education folder, DOI Office of Secretary files. Hodel established a full-time, six-person task force headed by his special assistant, Emily DeRocco, to oversee the project. He also set up a Policy Steering Committee consisting of the agency's assistant secretaries, bureau directors, and other senior officials. See "Update on Secretarial Initiative—Public Lands Educational Campaign," 4 November 1985 (an informational summary prepared by the Department of the Interior), NPLAC folder, box 608498, National Wildlife Federation Collection, National Conservation Training Center Archives, U.S. Fish and Wildlife Service, Shepherdstown, W.Va. (hereafter cited as NCTC).

22. "Take Pride in America: This Land Is Your Land," October 1985 (a brochure released by the Department of the Interior), NPLAC folder, box 608498, National Wildlife Federation Collection, NCTC. Emphasis in original.

23. See Ronald Reagan, "Address to the Nation on the Explosion of the Space Shuttle *Challenger*," 28 January 1986, in *Public Papers of the Presidents of the United States, Ronald Reagan, 1986: Book I—January 1 to June 27, 1986* (Washington, D.C.: GPO, 1988), 94–95; and Bernard Weinraub, "The Shuttle Explosion: Reagan Postpones State of Union Speech," *New York Times*, 29 January 1986.

24. Ronald Reagan, "Message to the Congress on America's Agenda for the Future," 6 February 1986, in *Public Papers of the Presidents of the United States, Ronald Reagan, 1986*, 153 and 158. When unveiled, Take Pride in America was described as a public-private partnership consisting of nine federal agencies, 44 states, and 12 national organizations. The federal agencies included the Departments of Interior, Agriculture, Commerce, Education, and Transportation, along with the Army Corps of Engineers, Environmental Protection Agency, Tennessee Valley Authority, and ACTION. The original private-sector partners included American Recreation Coalition; Chamber of Commerce of the United States; Council of Chief State School Officers; Keep America Beautiful, Inc.; Society for American Archaeology; National Association of Manufacturers; National Crime Prevention Council; National Recreation and Park Association; National Association of CCC Alumni; Touch American Project of the American Forestry Association; Travel for Tomorrow Council; and VOLUNTEER: The National Center. None of them were mainstream environmental organizations. See Council on Environmental Quality, *Environmental Quality*, 17th Annual Report (Washington, D.C.: GPO, 1988), 193.

25. Six members of the House of Representatives—Charles Pashayan Jr. (R-CA), George Miller (D-CA), Ron Marlenee (R-MT), Larry Craig (R-ID), Don Young (R-AK), and Nick Joe Rahall II (D-WV)—attended the breakfast meeting.

26. "Examples of Corporate Efforts in Behalf of Public Lands," March 1986 (a Department of the Interior handout accompanying Donald Paul Hodel's 24 March 1986 letter to Don Young), Committees folder, DOI Office of Secretary files.

27. "Prepared Remarks of Interior Secretary Don Hodel for the Annual Meeting of the Outdoor Writers Association of America," 9 June 1986, Harrisburg, Pennsylvania, https://www.fws.gov/news/Historic/NewsReleases/1986/19860609.pdf (accessed 15 September 2017). Emphasis in original. See also Donald Hodel, "Foreword," in *Audubon Wildlife Report 1986* (New York: National Audubon Society, 1986), xv–xvi.

28. Council on Environmental Quality, *Environmental Quality*, 216. For a prescient discussion of how conservation has been justified in terms of patriotism, see Roderick Nash, "The Potential of Conservation History," in *The American Environment: Readings in the History of Conservation*, ed. Roderick Nash (Reading, Mass.: Addison-Wesley, 1968), x–xi. See also Anne Marie Todd, *Communicating Environmental Patriotism: A Rhetorical History of the American Environmental Movement* (New York: Routledge, 2013).

29. Council on Environmental Quality, *Environmental Quality*, 185.

30. Council on Environmental Quality, *Environmental Quality*, 188.

31. The Ad Council had advocated volunteerism from its earliest years, but perhaps never more explicitly than with its early 1980s public service advertising theme, "Volunteer—Lend a Hand," which the U.S. Postal Service featured on a commemorative stamp in 1983. See Ellis and Campbell, *By the People*, 265.

32. See John O'Toole, "The Advertising Council's Oldest Customer," in *A Retrospective of Advertising Council Campaigns: A Half Century of Public Service* (New York: Museum of Television & Radio, 1991), 26.

33. See "The Advertising Council Inc. 1985–1986 Annual Report: Making a Difference in the Fabric of America," p. 16, Advertising Council Annual Reports, 1976–1995, record series 13/2/202, box 2, Ad Council Archives.

34. See Philip H. Dougherty, "Advertising: Doner Gets 'Good Guys' for Pride in America," *New York Times*, 10 April 1987. Doner's creative team included Paul Hagan, Steve Perrin, Dave Sackey, and Mark Westerman. Their intuitive reasoning for featuring tough-guy actors to overcome an environmental-feminine stereotype was later validated by social science research. See Aaron R. Brough, James E. B. Wilkie, Jingjing Ma, Matthew S. Isaac, and David Gal, "Is Eco-Friendly Unmanly? The Green-Feminine Stereotype and Its Effect on Sustainable Consumption," *Journal of Consumer Research*, 43 (December 2016): 567–582; and Aaron R. Brough and James E. B. Wilkie, "Men Resist Green Behavior as Un-Manly: A Surprising Reason for Resistance to Environmental Goods and Habits," *Scientific American Mind* (Behavior & Society;

26 December 2017), https://www.scientificamerican.com/article/men-resist-green-behavior-as-unmanly/ (accessed 5 May 2019).

35. Deborah Bright, "Of Mother Nature and Marlboro Men: An Inquiry into the Cultural Meanings of Landscape Photography," *Exposure*, 23 (Winter 1985): 8. See also Michael Schaller, *Reckoning with Reagan: America and Its President in the 1980s* (New York: Oxford University Press, 1992), viii; and Susan Jeffords, *Hard Bodies: Hollywood Masculinity in the Reagan Era* (New Brunswick, N.J.: Rutgers University Press, 1994).

36. Donald Paul Hodel to Al Kingon, 3 June 1986, Program Planning folder, DOI Office of Secretary files.

37. Draft letter, Ronald Reagan to Dear _____, attached to memo, Donald Paul Hodel to Al Kingon, 3 June 1986, Program Planning folder, DOI Office of Secretary files.

38. For the Ad Council's relations with Reagan, see Keim, *A Time in Advertising's Camelot*, 131–150. Another important factor, which historian Mike Wallace addresses in his essay "Ronald Reagan and the Politics of History," is the extent that the mythmaking of Hollywood's history films, which Reagan internalized, helped shape the president's sensibilities and his own image of reality. See Mike Wallace, *Mickey Mouse History and Other Essays on American Memory* (Philadelphia: Temple University Press, 1996), 249–268.

39. Keim, *A Time in Advertising's Camelot*, 132. In all likelihood, Nancy Reagan's active membership in the Los Angeles chapter of the Junior League (a prominent women's volunteer organization) during the 1950s predisposed her to endorse the volunteer premise of the Take Pride initiative. The league's activities are outlined in Janet Gordon and Diana Reische, *The Volunteer Powerhouse* (New York: Rutledge Press, 1982); and Nancy Beth Jackson, *The Junior League: 100 Years of Volunteer Service* (New York: Association of Junior Leagues International, 2001).

40. The Reagan administration's blending of celebrity and political leadership is examined in Douglas Kellner, "Presidential Politics: The Movie," *American Behavioral Scientist*, 46 (December 2002): 473–475. For insight into Reagan's exposure to the power of celebrity advertising from 1954 to 1962, when he hosted, and occasionally acted in, CBS's Sunday night television anthology series *General Electric Theater*, see Thomas W. Evans, *The Education of Ronald Reagan: The General Electric Years and the Untold Story of His Conversion to Conservatism* (New York: Columbia University Press, 2006); Timothy Raphael, *The President Electric: Ronald Reagan and the Politics of Performance* (Ann Arbor: University of Michigan Press, 2009), 153–194; and David Haven Blake, *Liking Ike: Eisenhower, Advertising, and the Rise of Celebrity Politics* (New York: Oxford University Press, 2016), 151–172. Reagan subsequently narrated the 1963 film *Heritage of Splendor*, which the Richfield Oil Company produced for Keep America Beautiful.

41. For examples of how Bronson, Eastwood, and Gossett were presented in the initial sets of print and audio ads, see the material assembled in the Take Pride in America folder, box 37, Advertising Council Records, 1935–2007, David M. Rubenstein Rare Book and Manuscript Library, Duke University, Durham, N.C.

42. See "Town Crier for a Nation: 1986–1987 Annual Report of the Advertising Council," p. 14, Advertising Council Annual Reports, 1976–1995, record series 13/2/202, box 2, Ad Council Archives.

43. See Frank Rich, "How Dirty Harry Turned Commie," *New York Times*, 13 February 2005; and Drucilla Cornell, *Clint Eastwood and Issues of American Masculinity* (New York: Fordham University Press, 2009). The *Dirty Harry* sequels included *Magnum Force* (1973), *The Enforcer* (1976), *Sudden Impact* (1983), and *The Dead Pool* (1988). Any questions about Eastwood's political aptitude and seriousness were laid to rest in the late 1980s, when he successfully ran for mayor of his adopted hometown of Carmel, California.

44. The *Death Wish* sequels included *Death Wish II* (1982), *Death Wish 3* (1985), *Death Wish 4: The Crackdown* (1987), and *Death Wish V: The Face of Death* (1994). As the host of *General Electric Theater*, Reagan had performed television sketches with Bronson during the 1950s. See Blake, *Liking Ike*, 164.

45. Other films that brandished Gossett's macho image included *The Laughing Policeman* (1974), *The Deep* (1979), *Enemy Mine* (1985), *Firewalker* (1986), and *Aces: Iron Eagle III* (1992).

46. This film tradition is discussed in Peter N. Stearns, *Be a Man! Males in Modern Society*, 2nd ed. (New York: Holmes & Meier, 1990), 226–227; Richard Slotkin, *Gunfighter Nation: The Myth of the Frontier in Twentieth-Century America* (New York: Antheneum, 1992); Ann Hornaday, "America Loves a Vigilante, Until We Meet One," *Washington Post*, 8 April 2012; and J. Hoberman, *Make My Day: Movie Culture in the Age of Reagan* (New York: New Press, 2019).

47. "Protect Your Public Lands Campaign" television public service announcement scripts accompanying the Advertising Council Guide & Fact Sheet for Take Pride in America, n.d. [probably March 1987], Take Pride in America/March 1987 folder, file 6242, Advertising Council Historical File, 1941–97, record series 13/2/207, box 80, Ad Council Archives. Examples of the original video clips of the 30-second television spots featuring Eastwood, Bronson, and Gossett are housed in Ad Council Campaign Video Recordings, 1961, 1965, 1972, 1982–, record series 13/2/280, box 1, cassette 14, Ad Council Archives. See also Clint Eastwood Take Pride in America PSA, 1987, https://www.youtube.com/watch?v=TTEteDDJu10 (accessed 14 January 2020); Charles Bronson "Take Pride in America" Commercial, 1987, https://www.youtube.com/watch?v=wfxp6HR6KwI (accessed 5 May 2021); Lou Gossett Jr. Take Pride in America

PSA, 1987, https://m.youtube.com/watch?v=tUdf7y2cN7c (accessed 12 December 2020); and Wayne King, "New Ad Drive: Call It a Fistful of Leaves," *New York Times*, 10 April 1987.

48. Take Pride in America Campaign Magazine Ad No. TPA-2228-87, attached to Donald G. Goldstrom to Dear Publisher, n.d. [probably June 1987], Take Pride in America/Free Press—June 1987 folder, Magazine Campaign Issuances, 1987–, record series 13/2/215, box 1, Ad Council Archives.

49. Take Pride in America Campaign Newspaper Ad No. TPA-87-1191, Forest Fire Prevention/Take Pride in America, June 1987 folder, Newspaper Advertisements, 1961–1968, 1987–, record series 13/2/212, box 1, Ad Council Archives.

50. Take Pride in America Campaign Guide & Fact Sheet, n.d., Forest Fire Prevention/Take Pride in America, June 1987 folder, Newspaper Advertisements, 1961–1968, 1987–, record series 13/2/212, box 1, Ad Council Archives.

51. Take Pride in America Campaign Business Press Ad No. TPA-2315-88, Take Pride in America (Business Press Kit), March 1988 folder, Business Press Campaign Material, 1987–, record series 13/2/211, box 1, Ad Council Archives.

CHAPTER 6

1. For background on the splintering of society (with implications for the splintering among outdoor recreation groups), see Robert H. Wiebe, *The Segmented Society: An Introduction to the Meaning of America* (New York: Oxford University Press, 1975); Robert A. Stebbins, *Amateurs, Professionals, and Serious Leisure* (Montreal: McGill-Queens University Press, 1992); Lizabeth Cohen, *A Consumers' Republic: The Politics of Mass Consumption in Postwar America* (New York: Alfred A. Knopf, 2003); Sam Binkley, *Getting Loose: Lifestyle Consumption in the 1970s* (Durham, N.C.: Duke University Press, 2007); and Kevin M. Kruse and Julian E. Zelizer, *Fault Lines: A History of the United States since 1974* (New York: W. W. Norton, 2019).

2. Richard Nixon, Use of Off-Road Vehicles on the Public Lands, Executive Order No. 11644, 37 *Federal Register* 2877–2878 (9 February 1972); and Jimmy Carter, Off-Road Vehicles on Public Lands, Executive Order No. 11989, 42 *Federal Register* 26959–26960 (25 May 1977). The environmental concerns raised by off-road vehicle use on public lands are discussed in Shaun Bennett, *A Trail Rider's Guide to the Environment* (Westerville, Ohio: American Motorcycle Association, 1973); Malcolm F. Baldwin and Dan H. Stoddard Jr., *The Off-Road Vehicle and Environmental Quality* (Washington,

D.C.: Conservation Foundation, 1973); David Sheridan, *Off-Road Vehicles on Public Lands* (Washington, D.C.: GPO, 1979); Robert H. Webb and Howard G. Wilshire, eds., *Environmental Effects of Off-Road Vehicles: Impacts and Management in Arid Regions* (New York: Springer-Verlag, 1983); and David G. Havlick, *No Place Distant: Roads and Motorized Recreation on America's Public Lands* (Washington, D.C.: Island Press, 2002).

3. For the general context of these concerns, see R. McGreggor Cawley, *Federal Land, Western Anger: The Sagebrush Rebellion and Environmental Politics* (Lawrence: University Press of Kansas, 1993); Jacqueline Vaughn Switzer, *Green Backlash: The History and Politics of Environmental Opposition in the U.S.* (Boulder, Colo.: Lynne Rienner Publishers, 1997), 93–96; and James R. Skillen, *This Land Is My Land: Rebellion in the West* (New York: Oxford University Press, 2020). For the Bureau of Land Management's early off-road vehicle policies, see James Muhn and Hanson R. Stuart, *Opportunity and Challenge: The Story of BLM* (Washington, D.C.: GPO, 1988), 129–131, 193–195.

4. See, for example, the letters from United Mobile Sportfishermen (p. 99), American Motorcyclist Association (p. 504), Travel Industry Association of America (p. 508), Marine Retailers Association of America (p. 516), Boating Trades Association of Texas (p. 518), and Recreational Vehicle Dealers Association (p. 520) in U.S. Congress, Senate Committee on Energy and Natural Resources, Hearing, *Nomination of Donald Paul Hodel to be Secretary of the Interior*, 99th Cong., 1st sess., 1 February 1985 (Washington, D.C.: GPO, 1985). Insights into why a nonthreatening program like Take Pride in America promised to appeal to firms interested in burnishing their environmental images are offered in Stan Sauerhaft and Chris Atkins, *Image Wars: Protecting Your Company When There's No Place to Hide* (New York: John Wiley & Sons, 1989), 98–108, 174–187. Exemplifying how the Ad Council worked to ensure such confidence within the business community, council chair James Rosenfield declared, "In these times, people are deeply and appropriately concerned about many problems, and they look to American business to share those concerns and do something about them. Through the Advertising Council, we are all doing something: Being part of the solution is the best way not to be part of the problem." James H. Rosenfield, "Inaugural Address," in Board of Directors minutes, 20 June 1985, Advertising Council Minutes, 1942–98, record series 13/2/201, box 15, Advertising Council Archives, University Library, University of Illinois at Urbana-Champaign, Urbana (hereafter cited as Ad Council Archives).

5. Statement of Derrick A. Crandall, in *Nomination of Donald Paul Hodel to be Secretary of the Interior*, 269.

6. See Martin Nie, *The Governance of Western Public Lands: Mapping Its Present and Future* (Lawrence: University Press of Kansas, 2008), 52–55; Michael J. Yochim, *Yellowstone and the Snowmobile: Locking Horns over National Park Use* (Lawrence: University Press of Kansas, 2009); Judith A. Layzer, *The Environmental Case: Translating*

Values into Policy, 3rd ed. (Washington, D.C.: CQ Press, 2012), 209–235; Randall K. Wilson, *America's Public Lands: From Yellowstone to Smokey Bear and Beyond* (Lanham, Md.: Rowman & Littlefield, 2014), 99–102; and Robert E. Manning, Laura E. Anderson, and Peter R. Pettengill, *Managing Outdoor Recreation: Case Studies in the National Parks*, 2nd ed. (Boston: CABI International, 2017), 142–145.

7. See James Morton Turner, *The Promise of Wilderness: American Environmental Politics since 1964* (Seattle: University of Washington Press, 2012), 91–94; Terence Young, *Heading Out: A History of American Camping* (Ithaca, N.Y.: Cornell University Press, 2017); Rachel Gross, "From Buckskin to Gore-Tex: Consumption as a Path to Mastery in Twentieth-Century American Wilderness Recreation," *Enterprise and Society*, 19 (December 2018): 826–835; and Jim Robbins, "Bears and Bikers Meet in Uncharted Territory," *New York Times*, 8 October 2019.

8. The challenges facing federal outdoor recreation managers during the 1960s are addressed in Edwin M. Fitch and John F. Shanklin, *The Bureau of Outdoor Recreation* (New York: Praeger, 1970), 155–162; Robert L. Prausa, "Multiple-Use Management for Recreation in the East," in *The Forest Recreation Symposium*, ed. E. vH. Larson (Upper Darby, Pa.: Northeastern Forest Experiment Station, Forest Service, U.S. Department of Agriculture, 1971), 96–102; and Paul J. Culhane, *Public Lands Politics: Interest Group Influence on the Forest Service and the Bureau of Land Management* (Baltimore: Johns Hopkins University Press, 1981). Interior secretary Watt had unsuccessfully tried to drive a wedge between sportsmen (particularly anglers and hunters) and conservationists. See Eleanor Randolph, "'Hook and Bullet Boys' vs. Environmentalists: Watt Courts Sportsmen to Back Policies," *Los Angeles Times*, 10 June 1981; and C. Brant Short, *Ronald Reagan and the Public Lands: America's Conservation Debate, 1979–1984* (College Station: Texas A&M University Press, 1989), 73.

9. Robert E. Manning, *Studies in Outdoor Recreation: Search and Research for Satisfaction*, 3rd ed. (Corvallis: Oregon State University Press, 2011), 206. See also Lary M. Dilsaver, "Resource Conflict in the High Sierra," in *The Mountainous West: Explorations in Historical Geography*, William Wyckoff and Lary M. Dilsaver (Lincoln: University of Nebraska Press, 1995), 296–298; Thomas R. Vale, *The American Wilderness: Reflections on Nature Protection in the United States* (Charlottesville: University of Virginia Press, 2005), 163–177; Kirk Johnson, "Bill Opening Wilderness to Biking Also Opens Debate on Conservation," *New York Times*, 20 August 2016; and Philip Dray, *The Fair Chase: The Epic Story of Hunting in America* (New York: Basic Books, 2018), 341–356.

10. Manning, *Studies in Outdoor Recreation*, 206–219. For general discussions of outdoor recreational planning on public lands, including the challenges of managing those lands for different (and sometimes incompatible) recreational uses, see Allan Jubenville, *Outdoor Recreation Planning* (Philadelphia: W. B. Saunders Co., 1976); John B. Loomis,

Integrated Public Lands Management: Principles and Applications to National Forests, Parks, Wildlife Refuges, and BLM Lands (New York: Columbia University Press, 1993); and Manning et al., *Managing Outdoor Recreation*. Trends in recreational demands are presented in Marion Clawson and Carlton S. Van Doren, eds., *Statistics on Outdoor Recreation* (Washington, D.C.: Resources for the Future, 1984), and the broader policy context is addressed in Peter Wolf, *Land in America: Its Value, Use, and Control* (New York: Pantheon Books, 1981), 469–487; Frank Gregg, "Public Land Policy: Controversial Beginnings for the Third Century," in *Government and Environmental Politics: Essays on Historical Developments since World War Two*, ed. Michael J. Lacey (Washington, D.C.: Wilson Center Press, 1989), 141–177; Walter A. Rosenbaum, *Environmental Politics and Policy*, 2nd ed. (Washington, D.C.: CQ Press, 1991), 270–299; and Robert B. Keiter, *Keeping Faith with Nature: Ecosystems, Democracy, and America's Public Lands* (New Haven, Conn.: Yale University Press, 2003).

11. For an example of the Recreational Vehicle Industry Association's involvement in Take Pride activities, see Donald Paul Hodel to Jackie Lang, 16 August 1988, Information And Public Relations—Courtesy Letters folder, Office of the Secretary Correspondence Files, Department of the Interior, Washington, D.C. (hereafter cited as DOI Office of Secretary files). Writing about the outpouring of voluntary citizen support of the Bureau of Land Management's archaeological work in Arizona, Gary Stumpf observed that some of the volunteers "belong to organizations we don't usually associate with cultural resource preservation. For example, members of the Arizona Desert Racing Association recently volunteered to help us construct a fence around an archaeological site to protect it from off-road vehicle damage. Every once in a while things like that happen to remind us that stereotypes are not valid." Gary Stumpf, "Cultural Resource Management in Arizona," in *Opportunity and Challenge: The Story of BLM*, James Muhn and Hanson R. Stuart (Washington, D.C.: GPO, 1988), 252.

12. William E. Miller to Donald Paul Hodel, 29 December 1985, Program Planning folder, DOI Office of Secretary files.

13. See Richard L. Stanton, *Potomac Journey: Fairfax Stone to Tidewater* (Washington, D.C.: Smithsonian Institution Press, 1993), 166–175; Karlyn Barker, "Canal, Towpath Flood Damage Set at $9.3 Million," *Washington Post*, 15 November 1985; and Claudia Levy, "Stretch of Canal Closed for Cleanup," *Washington Post*, 6 March 1986.

14. Jim Gilford, "Helping Clean Up the Canal," *Frederick* (Md.) *Post*, 12 February 1986.

15. See Ted Troxell, "About 20,000 Scouts to Spearhead C&O Canal Park Cleanup," *Sunday Times* (Cumberland, Md.), 2 March 1986; Lyle V. Harris, "Volunteers Help Clean C&O Canal," *Washington Post*, 31 July 1986; and "Stanton Will Address Society during Dinner," *Cumberland* (Md.) *News*, 15 October 1986.

16. "Prepared Remarks of Interior Secretary Don Hodel for the Annual Meeting of the Outdoor Writers Association of America," 9 June 1986, Harrisburg, Pennsylvania, U.S. Department of the Interior, Fish and Wildlife Service, https://www.fws.gov/news/Historic/NewsReleases/1986/19860609.pdf (accessed 15 September 2017).

17. Form letter, Dick Stanton to Dear Friend of the Canal, April 1986, Take Pride/History background material, Office of Service/Take Pride in America, Office of the Assistant Secretary for Policy, Management, and Budget, Department of the Interior, Washington, D.C. (hereafter cited as TPIA background files).

18. Donald Paul Hodel to Robert C. Byrd, 23 April 1987, Program Planning folder, DOI Office of Secretary files. For the Ad Council's portrayal of its role in the Take Pride campaign, see Robert P. Keim, remarks at the Protect Your Public Lands news conference, Department of the Interior, 15 April 1987, President's Speeches, 1966–, record series 13/2/221, box 4, Ad Council Archives.

19. Sidney R. Yates to Donald P. Hodel, 7 May 1987, Program Planning folder, DOI Office of Secretary files. For skepticism of Hodel among environmentalists, see Hal K. Rothman, *The Greening of a Nation? Environmentalism in the United States since 1945* (Fort Worth, Tex.: Harcourt Brace, 1998), 188–189. Criticism of Hodel's oversight of the National Park Service is discussed in George B. Hartzog Jr., *Battling for the National Parks* (Mt. Kisco, N.Y.: Moyer Bell, 1988), 269–272.

20. Donald Paul Hodel to Sidney R. Yates, 11 June 1987, Program Planning folder, DOI Office of Secretary files.

21. See Council on Environmental Quality, *Environmental Quality*, 17th Annual Report (Washington, D.C.: GPO, 1988), 191.

22. See form letter, Donald Paul Hodel to Dear Member [specific names to be inserted for each individual letter], 9 February 1987, Program Planning folder, DOI Office of Secretary files; and "Hodel Announces Finalists for Take Pride in America Awards," Department of the Interior news release, 9 February 1987, Program Planning folder, DOI Office of Secretary files. The judges ultimately selected 38 award winners. Participants were expected to cover their own travel expenses and room and board.

23. Department of the Interior news release, "Celebrities to Receive Awards for Serving as Spokesmen for the Take Pride in America Campaign," 16 July 1987, TPIA History folder, TPIA background files.

24. Ronald Reagan, "Remarks at the Presentation Ceremony for the Take Pride in America Awards," 21 July 1987, in Ronald Reagan, *Public Papers of the Presidents of the United States, Ronald Reagan, 1987: Book II—July 4 to December 31, 1987* (Washington, D.C.: GPO, 1989), 853. The Reagan Library released a video of those remarks, along with Reagan's pre-ceremonial meet-and-greet gathering with Gossett and Eastwood

in the Oval Office. See https://www.youtube.com/watch?v=3T9CvC3rYg8 (accessed 15 April 2019).

25. See Ronald Reagan, Take Pride in America Month, 1988, Proclamation No. 5827, 25 May 1988, in *Public Papers of the Presidents of the United States, Ronald Reagan, 1988: Book I—January 1 to July 1, 1988* (Washington, D.C.: GPO, 1990), 654; and Don Hodel to Malcolm Wallop, 25 May 1988, Information and Public Relations—Courtesy Letters folder, DOI Office of Secretary files.

26. Ronald Reagan, "Remarks at the Presentation Ceremony for the Take Pride in America Awards," 26 July 1988, in *Public Papers of the Presidents of the United States, Ronald Reagan, 1988–89: Book II—July 2, 1988 to January 19, 1989* (Washington, D.C.: GPO, 1991), 982. Among the award recipients, the Pennsylvania Bureau of State Parks was recognized for its environmental education program. See William C. Forrey, *History of Pennsylvania's State Parks, 1984–2015* (Harrisburg: Bureau of State Parks, Office of Parks and Forestry, Department of Conservation and Natural Resources, Commonwealth of Pennsylvania, 2017), 10.

27. Kim Freeman, conference/call report, 30 March 1988, Campaigns Review Committee Minutes, 1948–69, 1981–97, record series 13/2/225, box 2, Ad Council Archives. The comedian Paul Reubens created and portrayed the fictional character Pee-wee Herman.

28. The U.S. Department of the Interior Museum maintains the commissioned portraits of all the women and men who have served as secretary of Interior. They are displayed along the walls of the grand public corridor of the department's headquarters, on the floor housing the offices of Interior's top brass. The portraits are accompanied by labels summarizing each secretary's major accomplishments. The importance Donald Hodel attributed to Take Pride is reflected in the final sentence of the biographical caption hung beneath his official portrait: "Another hallmark of Hodel's tenure was the creation in 1985 of the 'Take Pride in America' campaign to enhance public lands through voluntarism." U.S. Department of the Interior Museum, "Portrait of an Agency," 2017, https://artsandculture.google.com/exhibit/portrait-of-an-agency%C2%AO-us-department-of-the-interior/WQLCE7mvTPURKQ?hl=en (accessed 14 December 2020).

CHAPTER 7

1. Bush, quoted in Bruce DeSilva and Charles F. J. Morse, "Bush Promises Cleanup: Candidate Decries Pollution in Sound and Boston Harbor," *Hartford Courant*, 2

September 1988. See also Philip Shabecoff, "Environmentalists Say Either Bush or Dukakis Will Be an Improvement," *New York Times*, 1 September 1988; Casey Bukro, "Harbor Taints Dukakis' Record on Pollution," *Chicago Tribune*, 2 September 1988; Bill Peterson, "In Boston, Bush Sails into Dukakis," *Washington Post*, 2 September 1988; Robin Toner, "Bush, in Enemy Waters, Says Rival Hindered Cleanup of Boston Harbor," *New York Times*, 2 September 1988; and Eric Jay Dolin, *Political Waters: The Long, Dirty, Contentious, Incredibly Expensive but Eventually Triumphant History of Boston Harbor—A Unique Environmental Success Story* (Amherst: University of Massachusetts Press, 2004), 143–144. Bush's environmental record is addressed in Byron W. Daynes and Glen Sussman, *White House Politics and the Environment: Franklin D. Roosevelt to George W. Bush* (College Station: Texas A&M University Press, 2010), 155–170; Paul Sabin, *The Bet: Paul Ehrlich, Julian Simon, and Our Gamble over Earth's Future* (New Haven, Conn.: Yale University Press, 2013), 190–195; and John Robert Greene, *The Presidency of George H. W. Bush*, 2nd ed. (Lawrence: University Press of Kansas, 2015), 92–94.

2. See Michael Duffy and Dan Goodgame, *Marching in Place: The Status Quo Presidency of George Bush* (New York: Simon & Schuster, 1992), 27–32; and David J. Lanoue, "Retrospective and Schematic Assessments of Presidential Candidates: The Environment and the 1988 Election," *Polity*, 25 (Summer 1993), 547–563.

3. See William K. Reilly, "The New Environmental Policy: Preventing Pollution," *Domestic Affairs*, 1 (Summer 1991): 73–98; and Ronald G. Westfall, "The Presidency and Environmental Policymaking: A Critical Assessment of George Bush" (M.A. thesis, University of Nevada, Las Vegas, 1994). Economic analyst Michael Silverstein observed that the administration's initial environmental orientation reflected Bush's "patrician background and longtime identification with the Republican Party's monied, ecopaternalistic, East Coast Teddy Roosevelt wing." Michael Silverstein, *The Environmental Economic Revolution: How Business Will Thrive and the Earth Survive in Years to Come* (New York: St. Martin's Press, 1993), 15.

4. See Samuel P. Hays, *Beauty, Health, and Permanence: Environmental Politics in the United States, 1955–1985* (New York: Cambridge University Press, 1987); Jerry W. Calvert, "Party Politics and Environmental Policy," in *Environmental Politics and Policy*, ed. James P. Lester (Durham, N.C.: Duke University Press, 1989), 158–178; Samuel P. Hays, *A History of Environmental Politics since 1945* (Pittsburgh: University of Pittsburgh Press, 2000); Thomas G. Smith, *Green Republican: John Saylor and the Preservation of America's Wilderness* (Pittsburgh: University of Pittsburgh Press, 2006); J. Brooks Flippen, *Conservative Conservationist: Russell E. Train and the Emergence of American Environmentalism* (Baton Rouge: Louisiana State University Press, 2006); Paul Charles Milazzo, *Unlikely Environmentalists: Congress and Clean Water, 1945–1972* (Lawrence: University Press of Kansas, 2006); Brian J. Glenn and Steven M. Teles, eds.,

Conservatism and American Political Development (New York: Oxford University Press, 2009); Brian Allen Drake, "The Skeptical Environmentalist: Senator Barry Goldwater and the Environmental Management State," *Environmental History*, 15 (October 2010): 587–611; and James Morton Turner and Andrew C. Isenberg, *The Republican Reversal: Conservatives and the Environment from Nixon to Trump* (Cambridge, Mass.: Harvard University Press, 2018).

5. See Michael E. Kraft, "U.S. Environmental Policy and Politics: From the 1960s to the 1990s," *Journal of Policy History*, 12, no. 1 (2000): 31; and Judith A. Layzer, "Environmental Policy from 1980 to 2008: The Politics of Prevention," in Glenn and Teles, *Conservatism and American Political Development*, 234–236. For a broader perspective on Bush's ideology and track record in the area of directing federal regulations, see Barry D. Friedman, *Regulation in the Reagan-Bush Era: The Eruption of Presidential Influence* (Pittsburgh: University of Pittsburgh Press, 1995).

6. See Robert Gottlieb, *Forcing the Spring: The Transformation of the American Environmental Movement* (Washington, D.C.: Island Press, 1993), 160; and Russell E. Train, *Politics, Pollution, and Pandas: An Environmental Memoir* (Washington, D.C.: Island Press/Shearwater Books, 2003), 269–271. Bush also appointed a well-regarded environmental administrator, Michael Deland, as chair of the Council on Environmental Quality. Deland had served as EPA regional administrator for New England, with oversight of the Boston Harbor cleanup. Summary assessments of Bush's initial appointments are provided in Rose Marie Audette, "The Bush Men: First Steps on the Environment from the New President, Hopeful Signs and Danger Warnings," *Environmental Action*, 20 (March/April 1989): 12–17.

7. George Bush, "Remarks at the Swearing-in Ceremony for William K. Reilly as Administrator of the Environmental Protection Agency," 8 February 1989, in *Public Papers of the Presidents of the United States, George Bush, 1989: Book I—January 20 to June 30, 1989* (Washington, D.C.: GPO, 1990), 69.

8. See George Bush, "Message to the Congress Reporting on Environmental Quality," 18 April 1991, in *Public Papers of the Presidents of the United States, George Bush, 1991: Book I—January 1 to June 30, 1991* (Washington, D.C.: GPO, 1992), 406.

9. See Donald C. Swain, *Wilderness Defender: Horace M. Albright and Conservation* (Chicago: University of Chicago Press, 1970), 251–252, 277–278; John C. Whitaker, *Striking a Balance: Environment and Natural Resources Policy in the Nixon-Ford Years* (Washington, D.C.: American Enterprise Institute for Public Policy Research, 1976), 31–33, 58–66; Dennis C. Le Master, *Decade of Change: The Remaking of Forest Service Statutory Authority during the 1970s* (Westport, Conn.: Greenwood Press, 1984), 106–128; T. H. Watkins, *Righteous Pilgrim: The Life and Times of Harold L. Ickes, 1874–*

1952 (New York: Henry Holt, 1990), 447–591; Marc K. Landy, Marc J. Roberts, and Stephen R. Thomas, *The Environmental Protection Agency: Asking the Wrong Questions* (New York: Oxford University Press, 1990), 30–33; J. Brooks Flippen, *Nixon and the Environment* (Albuquerque: University of New Mexico Press, 2000), 85–86, 143–145; Kendrick A. Clements, *Hoover, Conservation, and Consumerism: Engineering the Good Life* (Lawrence: University Press of Kansas, 2000), 78–79, 131–133, 178–179; and Otis L. Graham Jr., *Presidents and the American Environment* (Lawrence: University Press of Kansas, 2015). For the deliberations that took place between 1970 and 1972 regarding the likely impacts of President Nixon's proposed departmental reorganization on the National Park Service, see folders 824–826, box 65, George B. Hartzog Jr. Papers, Special Collections and Archives, Clemson University Libraries, Clemson, S.C.

10. George Bush, "Address Before a Joint Session of the Congress on the State of the Union," 31 January 1990, in *Public Papers of the Presidents of the United States, George Bush, 1990: Book I—January 1 to June 30, 1990* (Washington, D.C.: GPO, 1991), 132.

11. George Bush, "Remarks at a White House Tree-Planting Ceremony," 22 March 1990, in *Public Papers of the Presidents of the United States, George Bush, 1990: Book I*, 402.

12. George Bush, "Inaugural Address," 20 January 1989, in *Public Papers of the Presidents of the United States, George Bush, 1989: Book I*, 2. See also Duffy and Goodgame, *Marching in Place*, 209–213; David Mervin, "An Evaluation of the Presidency of George Bush," in *A Noble Calling: Character and the George H. W. Bush Presidency*, ed. William Levantrosser and Rosanna Perotti (Westport, Conn.: Praeger, 2004), 107–109; Robert Goodwin, Thomas Kinkade, and Pam Proctor, *Points of Light: A Celebration of the American Spirit of Giving* (New York: Center Street, 2006); and Greene, *The Presidency of George H. W. Bush*, 190–192.

13. President Bush presided as honorary chairman of the Points of Light Foundation, and Richard F. Schubert served as its president and chief executive officer. The foundation's board of directors included several high-profile members, among them Louis Gossett Jr., who lent a connection to the Take Pride in America initiative. See Points of Light (Business Press Kit), n.d. [probably September 1992], Business Press Campaign Material, 1987–, record series 13/2/211, box 1, Advertising Council Archives, University Library, University of Illinois at Urbana-Champaign, Urbana (hereafter cited as Ad Council Archives); "White House Fact Sheet on the Points of Light Initiative," 22 June 1989, in *Public Papers of the Presidents of the United States, George Bush, 1989: Book I*, 788; and David R. Francis, "Encouraging Volunteers: A Thousand Points of Light to Shine," *Christian Science Monitor*, 7 November 1989. For the rationale behind the Points of Light idea, see C. Gregg Petersmeyer to Ruth Wooden, 15 August 1989, attached to Mary Eagen, conference/call report, 24 August 1989, Campaigns Review Committee Minutes, 1948–69, 1981–97, record series 13/2/225, box 4, Ad Council Archives.

14. Lujan, who was born in 1928, received his B.A. in 1950 from the College of Santa Fe (New Mexico) and worked as an insurance salesperson until entering politics in the late 1960s. Former National Park Service director James Ridenour commented on Interior secretary Lujan's leadership style in James M. Ridenour, *The National Parks Compromised: Pork Barrel Politics and America's Treasures* (Merrillville, Ind.: ICS Books, 1994), 31–38. As Michael Frome explained, "Secretaries of the interior are not appointed to be two-fisted leaders, and they are certainly not supposed to be champions of conservation. They're chosen because they are good politicians, party regulars worthy of reward who come from the right part of the country and have an ability to make deals and accept deals. Presidents scarcely, if ever, ask, Who really is best qualified to define and face the tough, inescapable resource challenges?" Michael Frome, *Regreening the National Parks* (Tucson: University of Arizona Press, 1992), 23. Lujan's generally poor standing among environmentalists is surveyed in Audette, "The Bush Men," 16–17; and Zach Montague, "Manuel Luján Jr., Former Congressman and Interior Secretary, Is Dead at 90," *New York Times*, 27 April 2019.

15. See, for example, Manuel Lujan Jr. to Richard B. Groves, 23 February 1989, Information and Public Relations—Courtesy Letters folder, Office of the Secretary Correspondence Files, Department of the Interior, Washington, D.C. (hereafter cited as DOI Office of Secretary files).

16. Frank D. Boren to Manuel Lujan, 29 December 1988, Information and Public Relations—Courtesy Letters folder, DOI Office of Secretary files.

17. Manuel Lujan to Frank D. Boren, 8 March 1989, Information and Public Relations—Courtesy Letters folder, DOI Office of Secretary files.

18. George Bush, "Remarks at the Swearing-in Ceremony for Manuel Lujan, Jr., as Secretary of the Interior," 8 February 1989, in *Public Papers of the Presidents of the United States, George Bush, 1989: Book I*, 67.

19. For the president's rhetorical support of the program, see George Bush, "Remarks at the Presentation Ceremony for the Take Pride in America Awards," 24 July 1989, in *Public Papers of the Presidents of the United States, George Bush, 1989: Book II—July 1 to December 31, 1989* (Washington, D.C.: GPO, 1990), 1004–1006.

20. Manuel Lujan Jr. to Mrs. George Bush, 29 March 1989 and 3 July 1989, Information and Public Relations—Courtesy Letters folder, DOI Office of Secretary files.

21. Manuel Lujan Jr. to Clint Eastwood, 26 May 1989, Information and Public Relations—Courtesy Letters folder, DOI Office of Secretary files. Lujan sent identical letters to Charles Bronson and Louis Gossett Jr.

22. George Bush, "Remarks to Members of the Family Motor Coach Association in Richmond, Virginia," 21 June 1989, in *Public Papers of the Presidents of the United States, George Bush, 1989: Book I*, 769.

23. Bush, "Remarks to Members of the Family Motor Coach Association," 770. In his opening statement, Bush made a point of expressing his pleasure at seeing American Recreation Coalition president Derrick Crandall in the audience, a person, he said, "who has been a good friend of mine and who has shown me the wonders of some of our most beautiful parks, borrowing, I am sure, the vehicles to house us from some of you sitting right here" (p. 769). Crandall went on to become a staunch supporter of the Take Pride in America program.

24. See Manuel Lujan Jr. to Bill Humphries (Commissioner of Public Lands, New Mexico), 7 February 1990, Information and Public Relations—Courtesy Letters folder, DOI Office of Secretary files. This folder contains a long list of people who were sent similar invitations. The private-sector groups included Browning-Ferris Industries; National Parks and Conservation Association; America's Clean Water Foundation; Conservation Foundation; National Cattlemen's Association; National Campground Owners Association; Keep New Mexico Beautiful; PMI Parking, Inc. (Washington, DC); National Association of Black and Minority Chambers of Commerce; National Association of State Outdoor Recreation Liaison Officers; Girls Clubs of America; Ducks Unlimited; South Carolina Optimist International; American Farm Bureau Federation; and Izaak Walton League.

25. Although the Blue Ribbon Panel of Judges lacked members associated with mainstream environmental groups, the following organizations were represented: Bass Anglers Sportsman Society, Bass Pro Shops, American Farm Bureau Federation, National Recreation and Parks Association, American Camping Association, AARP, America's Clean Water Foundation, Lions Clubs International, Boy Scouts of America, Girl Scouts of the U.S.A., Future Farmers of America, and Camp Fire Clubs of America. See Manuel Lujan Jr. to Vice President and Mrs. Quayle, 2 April 1992, Information and Public Relations—Courtesy Letters folder, DOI Office of Secretary files.

26. "President Bush Hosts Awards Ceremony at White House," *National Campaign News*, August 1989, 1. Copies of Take Pride in America's ephemeral newsletter reside in Department of Interior folder, box 23, accession 93–066, Smithsonian Institution Archives, Washington, D.C. (hereafter cited as SIA).

27. George Bush, "Remarks at the Presentation Ceremony for the Take Pride in America Awards," 24 July 1989, in *Public Papers of the Presidents of the United States, George Bush, 1989: Book II*, 1004.

28. Manuel Lujan Jr. to Elizabeth H. Dole, 1 September 1989; and Manuel Lujan Jr. to Jack F. Kemp, 1 September 1989, Information and Public Relations—Courtesy Letters folder, DOI Office of Secretary files.

29. Manuel Lujan Jr. to Marvin Runyon (Chairman of the Board, Tennessee Valley Authority), 12 September 1989, Information and Public Relations—Courtesy Letters

folder, DOI Office of Secretary files. For his entreatments to the governors of the 48 states then participating in the campaign, see Manuel Lujan Jr. to Don Schaefer (governor of Maryland), 25 September 1989, Organization and Management—Awards folder, DOI Office of Secretary files. And for his similar appeals to the campaign's private-sector partners, see Manuel Lujan Jr. to Frank Stryczek (Rotary International), 4 October 1989, Information and Public Relations—Courtesy Letters folder, DOI Office of Secretary files.

30. Harold J. Handley to Public Service Director, undated form letter [probably May 1989], Take Pride in America folder, file 6695, Advertising Council Historical File, 1941–97, record series 13/2/207, box 91, Ad Council Archives. The Ad Council had approved the concept for an ALF campaign in May 1988. See Elenore Hangley, conference/call report, 16 October 1988, Campaigns Review Committee Minutes, 1948–69, 1981–97, record series 13/2/225, box 2, Ad Council Archives. The offbeat comedy began airing on NBC in September 1986. Earlier youth-oriented efforts included the Department of the Interior's work with the Mark Trail/Ed Dodd Foundation. See Jack Elrod, *Take Pride in America with Mark Trail: A Coloring Book* (Washington, D.C.: U.S. Department of the Interior, 1987).

31. "Protect Your Public Lands/Youth Campaign" Advertising Council Public Service Announcement, CNPL-8160/8130, n.d. [probably May 1989], Take Pride in America folder, file 6695, Advertising Council Historical File, 1941–97, record series 13/2/207, box 91, Ad Council Archives. See also "ALF—1989 Department of Interior PSA," https://www.youtube.com/watch?v=vrWDlNAM_f8 (accessed 10 October 2020); Advertising Council, *Bringing the Issues Home: Report to the American People, '88–'89* (New York: Advertising Council, 1989), 21; Jeanne McDowell, "The Greening of Hollywood," *Time*, 133 (12 June 1989): 76; and Barbara Hunt Lazerson, "Spokes-Terms," *American Speech*, 70 (Spring 1995): 108.

32. See Manuel Lujan Jr. to David Sackey (Executive Vice President, W. B. Doner and Company), 11 August 1989; and Manuel Lujan Jr. to Marvin Runyon, 12 September 1989, Information and Public Relations—Courtesy Letters folder, DOI Office of Secretary files; and "Take Pride's 'ALF' Campaign Has Surprise Results," *National Campaign News*, August 1989, 7 (copy in Department of Interior folder, box 23, accession 93-066, SIA).

33. Mary Eagen, conference/call report, 15 December 1989, p. 3, Campaigns Review Committee Minutes, 1948–69, 1981–97, record series 13/2/225, box 5, Ad Council Archives.

34. See Diane R. Soto, conference/call report, 24 January 1990, p. 2, Campaigns Review Committee Minutes, 1948–69, 1981–97, record series 13/2/225, box 5, Ad Council Archives.

35. "The Advertising Council, America's Catalyst for Change: Report to the American People, 89–90," p. 9, Advertising Council Annual Reports, 1976–1995, record series 13/2/202, box 2, Ad Council Archives. See also Diane R. Soto, conference/call report,

30 March 1990, p. 1, Campaigns Review Committee Minutes, 1948–69, 1981–97, record series 13/2/225, box 5, Ad Council Archives.

36. "The Results Are In: Annual Report to the American People, 1990–1991," p. 4, Advertising Council Annual Reports, 1976–1995, record series 13/2/202, box 2, Ad Council Archives.

37. Manuel Lujan Jr. to Ruth Wooden, 18 October 1990, Information and Public Relations—Courtesy Letters folder, DOI Office of Secretary files.

38. "Media Helps," *National Campaign News*, March 1989, 1 (copy in Information and Public Relations—Courtesy Letters folder, DOI Office of Secretary files).

39. "Media Helps," 3.

40. Take Pride in America Act, Public Law No. 101-628, Title XI, §1102, 104 Stat. 4469 (1990).

41. Steve Symms, "'Take Pride' Deserves to be Made Permanent," *National Campaign News*, October 1990, 2 (copy in Information and Public Relations—Courtesy Letters folder, DOI Office of Secretary files).

42. See *United States Code*, Title 16, Chapter 66—Take Pride in America Program, §4601–4608.

43. Charter, The Take Pride in America Advisory Board, 27 August 1990 (included as an appendix in the *Take Pride in America Advisory Board Recommendations* [Washington, D.C.: U.S. Department of the Interior, Office of the Secretary, 1992], 40–43). Copies of this internal document are kept in the DOI Office of the Secretary files. See also U.S. Department of the Interior, "Interior Secretary Lujan Launches Take Pride in America Advisory Board," Take Pride in America press release, 21 May 1991, TPIA History folder, Take Pride in America background files, Office of Service/Take Pride in America, Office of the Assistant Secretary for Policy, Management, and Budget, Department of the Interior, Washington, D.C. (hereafter cited as TPIA background files). The advisory board was limited to 20 voting members (with a maximum of two members representing "conservation, environmental or recreation organizations"), plus representatives from each state serving as ex officio, nonvoting members.

44. See M. L. to Vickie Burrios, n.d. [probably late October 1991]; Victoria E. Barrios to Carolyn L. Tillotson-Smith, 29 October 1991 (with Tillotson-Smith's attached resume); and Manuel Lujan Jr. to Carolyn L. Tillotson-Smith, 8 November 1991, all in Information and Public Relations—Courtesy Letters folder, DOI Office of Secretary files.

45. Anne House Quinn to the secretary of Interior, December 1992 (part of the front matter in the *Take Pride in America Advisory Board Recommendations*, 4). Quinn, who was director of events for Robert Dole's presidential campaign from 1987 to 1988, was

executive director of the National Aquarium when Lujan tapped her in 1991 to head the Take Pride in America program.

46. For the use of advocacy advertising by businesses and corporations to improve their environmental image, see Peter M. Sandman, "Eco-Pornography: Environmental Advertising and Advertising Acceptance in the San Francisco Bay Area" (Ph.D. diss., Stanford University, Stanford, Calif., 1971); Michael Howlett and Rebecca Raglon, "Constructing the Environmental Spectacle: Green Advertisements and the Greening of the Corporate Image, 1910–1990," *Environmental History Review*, 16 (Winter 1992): 53–68; John C. Stauber and Sheldon Rampton, *Toxic Sludge Is Good for You: Lies, Damn Lies, and the Public Relations Industry* (Monroe, Maine: Common Courage Press, 1995); Joe Greene Conley II, "Environmentalism Contained: A History of Corporate Responses to the New Environmentalism" (Ph.D. diss., Princeton University, Princeton, N.J., 2006); Finis Dunaway, *Seeing Green: The Use and Abuse of American Environmental Images* (Chicago: University of Chicago Press, 2015); and Melissa Aronczyk, "Public Relations, Issue Management, and the Transformation of American Environmentalism, 1948–1992," *Enterprise and Society*, 19 (December 2018): 836–863.

47. "May Is Declared Take Pride in America Month," undated Take Pride in America news release, Office of the Secretary [U.S. Department of the Interior] (copies of the two-page release were attached to the 11 May 1989 letter Manuel Lujan mailed to the 46 governors participating in the Take Pride in America campaign; Information and Public Relations—Courtesy Letters folder, DOI Office of Secretary files). Congress had endorsed Reagan's May 1988 proclamation but not Lujan's subsequent (unofficial) declaration, which evaporated after he left office.

48. Manuel Lujan Jr. to Guy Hunt (Governor of Alabama), 11 May 1989, Information and Public Relations—Courtesy Letters folder, DOI Office of Secretary files. Lujan sent similar letters to 45 other governors.

49. Manuel Lujan Jr. to All Employees, 25 April 1989, Take Pride/History background material, TPIA background files.

50. Identical text to the two letters of invitation: Manuel Lujan Jr. to Constance Horner, 8 May 1989; and Manuel Lujan Jr. to Richard Austin, 8 May 1989, Information and Public Relations—Courtesy Letters folder, DOI Office of Secretary files.

51. Manuel Lujan Jr. to Bureau Directors, 8 May 1989, Information and Public Relations—Courtesy Letters folder, DOI Office of Secretary files.

52. Manuel Lujan Jr. to Ben Love, 8 February 1990, Information and Public Relations—Courtesy Letters folder, DOI Office of Secretary files.

53. Director, National Park Service to Department Liaison, Boy Scouts of America, n.d. [probably written in December 1989 or January 1990], attached to Manuel Lujan

Jr. to Ben Love, 8 February 1990, Information and Public Relations—Courtesy Letters folder, DOI Office the Secretary files. The report explained that "most of the Scout projects involved such traditional activities as trash and litter cleanup; trail building, maintenance, and/or rehabilitation; vegetative planting; erosion control; traffic control and auto parking; ushering and escort services; flag ceremonies; removal of exotics; posting of No Hunting and Safety zones; construction and cleaning/painting of campground equipment and/or structures; boundary clearing and patrol; wall/fence building and/or stabilization; grounds maintenance and landscaping; removal of graffiti; building and placement of birdhouses and nesting boxes; preparation of literature mailings; and tree/shrubbery enclosures to prevent deer/beaver damage."

54. "Boy Scout TPIA Patch Program," *National Campaign News*, April 1990, 6.

55. See form letter, Manuel Lujan Jr. to Blue Ribbon Panel Members, 31 May 1990, Information and Public Relations—Courtesy Letters folder, DOI Office of Secretary files.

56. Manuel Lujan Jr. to Green Watch Editor, Good Housekeeping Magazine, 7 May 1990, Information and Public Relations—Courtesy Letters folder, DOI Office of Secretary files.

57. "Take Pride in America Announces 1989 National Award Winners," Take Pride in America news release, 31 May 1990, Department of Interior folder, box 23, accession no. 93–066, SIA.

58. Manuel Lujan Jr. to Public Service Director, 11 July 1990, Information and Public Relations—Courtesy Letters folder, DOI Office of Secretary files.

59. Luce Press Clippings/Television News Transcripts, *Entertainment Tonight*, 7 June 1990, 6:30 pm, Take Pride folder, Advertising Council Press Clippings and Publicity file, 1942–2003, record series 13/2/228, box 8, Ad Council Archives. For a video clip of this interview, see "Linda Evans Discusses Her 'Take Pride in America' Ad," https://m.youtube.com/watch?v=pw_9MJTRrIQ (accessed 3 October 2019).

60. See Philip Shabecoff, *A Fierce Green Fire: The American Environmental Movement*, rev. ed. (Washington, D.C.: Island Press, 2003), 243–246; and J. Michael McCloskey, *In the Thick of It: My Life in the Sierra Club* (Washington, D.C.: Island Press, 2005), 269–272.

61. For a summary of the president's self-assessment of his 1990 accomplishments, see George Bush, "Message to the Congress Reporting on Environmental Quality," 18 April 1991, in *Public Papers of the Presidents of the United States, George Bush, 1991: Book I*, 404–406. For his self-assessment two years later, see George Bush, "Message to the Congress on Environmental Goals," 24 March 1992, in *Public Papers of the Presidents of the United States, George Bush, 1992–93: Book I—January 1 to July 31, 1992* (Washington, D.C.: GPO, 1993), 498–502.

CHAPTER 8

1. Transcripts of Bush's campaign speeches and press conferences are reprinted in *Public Papers of the Presidents of the United States*. For examples of references to his environmental record, see "Question-and-Answer Session in Secaucus, New Jersey," 22 October 1992, and "Remarks and a Question-and-Answer Session in Des Moines, Iowa," 27 October 1992, in *Public Papers of the Presidents of the United States, George Bush, 1992–93: Book II—August 1, 1992 to January 20, 1993* (Washington, D.C.: GPO, 1993), 1929–1930, 2009.

2. "Question-and-Answer Session in Paducah," 27 October 1992, in *Public Papers of the Presidents of the United States, George Bush, 1992–93: Book II*, 2021. The book Bush referred to was Al Gore, *Earth in the Balance: Ecology and the Human Spirit* (Boston: Houghton Mifflin, 1992). For Gore's sharp criticisms of Bush's environmental record, see pp. 174, 181, 192–196.

3. See Steven Greenhouse, "The 1992 Campaign: The Economy; Despite Recession's End, Bush May Face Unusually Harsh Public Judgment," *New York Times*, 11 May 1992; "The Meaning of the Victory of Bill Clinton and Al Gore: Agonized by Recession and Gridlock, America Asks for Change," *Los Angeles Times*, 4 November 1992; and Paul Sabin, "The Decline of Republican Environmentalism," *Boston Globe*, 31 August 2013. For the generally low salience of environmental concerns in national elections, see Deborah Lynn Guber, *The Grassroots of a Green Revolution: Polling America on the Environment* (Cambridge, Mass.: MIT Press, 2003), 105–123.

4. See Riley E. Dunlap and Rik Scarce, "Poll Trends: Environmental Problems and Protection," *Public Opinion Quarterly*, 55 (Winter 1991): 651–672; and John C. Hendee and Randall C. Pitstick, "The Growth of Environmental and Conservation-Related Organizations: 1989–1991," *Renewable Resources Journal*, 10 (Summer 1992): 6–19.

5. Manuel Lujan Jr. to Bruce Babbitt, 19 January 1993, Reprints and Statistics file, Office of the Secretary correspondence files, Department of the Interior, Washington, D.C. (hereafter cited as DOI Office of Secretary files). Babbitt outlined his viewpoints on the environmental challenges facing the nation in Bruce Babbitt, "The Future Environmental Agenda for the United States," *University of Colorado Law Review*, 64, no. 2 (1993): 513–522. For the broader policy efforts of the Bush administration during its final weeks, see David M. Shafie, *Eleventh Hour: The Politics of Policy Initiatives in Presidential Transitions* (College Station: Texas A&M University Press, 2013), 87–105.

6. Timothy S. Elliott to Chief of Staff, 16 March 1993, Information and Public Relations—Courtesy Letters file, DOI Office of Secretary files.

7. Order, Bruce Babbitt, Cessation of the Activity of the Take Pride in America Program, 6 April 1993, Take Pride in America background files, Office of Service/Take Pride in America, Office of the Assistant Secretary for Policy, Management and Budget, Department of the Interior, Washington, D.C. (hereafter cited as TPIA background files). The Clinton administration's environmental record is discussed in Byron Daynes, "Bill Clinton: Environmental President," in *The Environmental Presidency*, ed. Dennis L. Soden (Albany: State University of New York Press, 1999), 259–302; Michael P. Dombeck, Christopher A. Wood, and Jack E. Williams, *From Conquest to Conservation: Our Public Lands Legacy* (Washington, D.C.: Island Press, 2003); J. Robert Cox, "The (Re)Making of the 'Environmental President': Clinton/Gore and the Rhetoric of U.S. Environmental Politics, 1992–1996," in *Green Talk in the White House: The Rhetorical Presidency Encounters Ecology*, ed. Tarla Rai Peterson (College Station: Texas A&M University Press, 2004), 157–175; Judith A. Layzer, "Environmental Policy from 1980 to 2008: The Politics of Prevention," in *Conservatism and American Political Development*, ed. Brian J. Glenn and Steven M. Teles (New York: Oxford University Press, 2009), 236–244; Byron W. Daynes and Glen Sussman, *White House Politics and the Environment: Franklin D. Roosevelt to George W. Bush* (College Station: Texas A&M University Press, 2010), 101–119; and Daniel Nelson, *Nature's Burdens: Conservation and American Politics, the Reagan Era to the Present* (Logan: Utah State University Press, 2017), 147–173.

8. Bonnie R. Cohen to Sydney R. Yates, 25 June 1993, Accounting—Transfer file, DOI Office of Secretary files. Cohen sent a similar letter to Yates's Senate counterpart, Robert C. Byrd (D-WV).

9. Bruce Babbitt to Jose F. Nino (president, U.S. Hispanic Chamber of Commerce), 18 June 1993, Information and Public Relations—Courtesy Letters file, DOI Office of Secretary files. Babbitt also sent a separate batch of letters to the 1992 Take Pride in America national award nominees. See Bruce Babbitt to Cynthia P. Grove, 29 June 1993, Information and Public Relations—Courtesy Letters file, DOI Office of Secretary files. Babbitt's administrative style as Interior secretary is discussed in John D. Leshy, "The Babbitt Legacy at the Department of the Interior: A Preliminary View," *Environmental Law*, 31 (2001): 199–227. For Clinton's campaign positions on national service and related issues, see Bill Clinton and Al Gore, *Putting People First: How We Can All Change America* (New York: Times Books, 1992).

10. See Stephen Barr, "Advisory Panels Nosing Out: Tea Sniffers and Others Bow to Budget Agency's Thriftiness," *Washington Post*, 31 March 1994.

11. See Derrick A. Crandall to John Garamendi (deputy secretary of the Interior), 1 November 1995, Take Pride in America folder, box 28, Office of Deputy Secretary correspondence, Department of the Interior records, accession no. 048-06-0787, NN3-048-11-002, National Archives and Records Administration, College Park, Md. Crandall's

lobbying got him nowhere with Garamendi; see Garamendi to Crandall, 7 November 1995, in the same file.

12. See "Bush's 'Points of Light' Volunteerism Burns On, with Clinton's Aid," *New York Times*, 22 April 1993. An overall assessment of AmeriCorps is provided in Will Marshall and Marc Porter Magee, eds., *The AmeriCorps Experiment and the Future of National Service* (Washington, D.C.: Progressive Policy Institute, 2005); Peter Frumkin and JoAnn Jastrzab, *Serving Country and Community: Who Benefits from National Service?* (Cambridge, Mass.: Harvard University Press, 2010); and Melissa Bass, *The Politics and Civics of National Service: Lessons from the Civilian Conservation Corps, Vista, and AmeriCorps* (Washington, D.C.: Brookings Institution Press, 2013), 147–225.

13. For insight into how the environmental movement changed its political strategies in light of the Republican takeover of Congress in 1994, see Robert J. Duffy, *The Green Agenda in American Politics: New Strategies for the Twenty-First Century* (Lawrence: University Press of Kansas, 2003); and David M. Shafie, *Presidential Administration and the Environment: Executive Leadership in the Age of Gridlock* (New York: Routledge, 2014).

14. The outlines of the USA Freedom Corps are discussed in John M. Bridgeland, *Heart of the Nation: Volunteering and America's Civic Spirit* (Lanham, Md.: Rowman & Littlefield, 2013). See also E. J. Dionne Jr., Kayla Meltzer Drogosz, and Robert E. Litan, eds., *United We Serve: National Service and the Future of Citizenship* (Washington, D.C.: Brookings Institution Press, 2003); and James L. Perry and Ann Marie Thomson, *Civic Service: What Difference Does It Make?* (Armonk, N.Y.: M. E. Sharpe, 2004). A critical assessment of the Bush administration's environmental strategy in the wake of the terrorist attacks of 11 September 2001 is provided in David W. Orr, *The Last Refuge: Patriotism, Politics, and the Environment in an Age of Terror* (Washington, D.C.: Island Press, 2004), 11–46.

15. The contours of Bush's environmental policy agenda are outlined in Victoria Sutton, "The George W. Bush Administration and the Environment," *Western New England Law Review*, 25, no. 2 (2003): 221–242; Richard J. Lazarus, *The Making of Environmental Law* (Chicago: University of Chicago Press, 2004), 239–242; David H. Getches, "The Legacy of the Bush II Administration in Natural Resources: A Work in Progress," *Ecology Law Quarterly*, 32, no. 2 (2005): 235–248; Jacqueline Vaughn and Hanna J. Cortner, *George W. Bush's Healthy Forests: Reframing the Environmental Debate* (Boulder: University Press of Colorado, 2005); Layzer, "Environmental Policy from 1980 to 2008," 244–247; and Daynes and Sussman, *White House Politics and the Environment*, 189–209. For scathing political assessments of Bush's environmental record, see Robert F. Kennedy Jr., *Crimes Against Nature: How George W. Bush and His Corporate Pals Are Plundering the Country and Hijacking Our Democracy* (New York:

HarperCollins, 2004); Robert S. Devine, *Bush versus the Environment* (New York: Anchor Books, 2004); and Carl Pope and Paul Rauber, *Strategic Ignorance: Why the Bush Administration Is Recklessly Destroying a Century of Environmental Progress* (San Francisco: Sierra Club Books, 2004).

16. See Douglas Jehl, "Norton Record Often at Odds with Laws She Would Enforce," *New York Times*, 13 January 2001.

17. Lazarus, *The Making of Environmental Law*, 241. For the hardening partisan divide over federal lands, see James R. Skillen, *This Land Is My Land: Rebellion in the West* (New York: Oxford University Press, 2020).

18. See Getches, "The Legacy of the Bush II Administration in Natural Resources," 240. Bush's abandonment of the Clinton administration's public land policies is discussed in Michael C. Blumm, "The Bush Administration's Sweetheart Settlement Policy: A Trojan Horse Strategy for Advancing Commodity Production on Public Lands," *Environmental Law Reporter*, 34 (May 2004): 10397–10420. See also Barton H. Thompson Jr., "Conservative Environmental Thought: The Bush Administration and Environmental Policy," *Ecology Law Quarterly*, 32, no. 2 (2005): 307–347.

19. See Trudy Harlow, briefing for the Secretary, 14 March 2001, TPIA History folder, TPIA background files.

20. Draft Strategic Plan—Take Pride in America, 9 March 2006, State of Events Briefing Binder: Michelle Cangelosi, TPIA background files.

21. Derrick A. Crandall to Gale Norton, 25 September 2001, TPIA History folder, TPIA background files.

22. See Donna L. Margelos to Eric Ruff, 27 September 2001, TPIA History folder, TPIA background files.

23. Meeting between Interior secretary Gale Norton and key recreation industry leaders, 18 October 2001 briefing document, TPIA History folder, TPIA background files. This paper contains a detailed "company biography" of the American Recreation Coalition and an equally detailed bio of its president, both of them written by Derrick Crandall, who pressed hard for a prominent seat at the table.

24. Deputy Director, Office of External and Intergovernmental Affairs to Bureau and Office Heads, n.d. [probably mid-November 2002], Program Paper folder, TPIA background files.

25. Lynn Scarlett and Kit Kimball to Gale Norton, n.d. [probably November 2002], Program Paper folder, TPIA background files.

26. Lynn Scarlett and Kit Kimball to John Bridgeland and James Connaughton, 16 January 2003, Timetable folder, TPIA background files.

27. Lynn Scarlett and Kit Kimball to John Bridgeland and James Connaughton, 16 January 2003, Timetable folder, TPIA background files.

28. Ralph Knoll to Gale A. Norton, 14 March 2003, Partners 2003–2006 folder, TPIA background files.

29. Derrick Crandall to Steve Griles, 2 April 2003, Partnership Notes/Email folder, TPIA background files.

30. Department of the Interior, "Interior Secretary Norton Launches National Volunteer Program to Restore and Improve America's Public Lands," press release, 16 April 2003, National Press Club (16 April 2003) folder, TPIA background files. See also "Pitching in for Parks," *Washington Post*, 19 April 2003. For the abuse inflicted upon the Anacostia River, see John R. Wennersten, *Anacostia: The Death and Life of an American River* (Baltimore: Chesapeake Book Company, 2008).

31. Memorandum of understanding between the United States Department of the Interior and the American Recreation Coalition, 28 April 2003, Partners 2003–2006 folder, TPIA background files.

32. Bob Ashley, "'Take Pride in America' Program Back in Action," *RV Business*, 53 (June 2003): 45.

33. With the assistance of the American Recreation Coalition, Take Pride had recruited 100 nonprofit and corporate "charter partners" (including the National Geographic Society, Keep America Beautiful, and Walt Disney Company), an effort intended to highlight Take Pride's new public-private cooperative model. See U.S. Department of the Interior, "Secretary Norton Announces the Walt Disney Co. Is Recipient of 2004 National Take Pride in America Outstanding Charter Partner Award," press release, 21 September 2004, TPIA background files; and Derrick A. Crandall to Gale Norton, 28 February 2006, State of Events Briefing Binder: Michelle Cangelosi, TPIA background files.

34. See, for example, Derrick A. Crandall to Gale Norton, 7 July 2003; Derrick A. Crandall to Marti Allbright, 15 July 2003; and Michael A. Molino to Derrick Crandall, 10 October 2003, Partners 2003–2006 folder, TPIA background files.

35. Michael A. Molino to Gale Norton, 24 October 2003, Partners 2003–2006 folder, TPIA background files.

36. Allbright had also served as general counsel of the U.S. Senate Committee on Commerce, Science, and Transportation from 1999 to 2000. See "Interior Secretary Norton Names Marti Allbright Head of Take Pride in America."

37. P. Lynn Scarlett to All DOI Employees (Subject: Adding the Take Pride in America logo to all DOI Letterhead), 26 June 2003, TPIA Letterhead Memo folder, TPIA background files.

38. See U.S. Department of the Interior, Office of the Secretary, "Interior Secretary Gale Norton Announces Designation of First Take Pride in America School," press release, 24 May 2005, https://web.archive.org/web/20060929090043/http://www.doi.gov/news/050525a1.htm (accessed 30 August 2019).

39. See Karlyn Barker, "NFL Tries Play for Fans on Mall," *Washington Post*, 31 August 2003; David Montgomery, "The NFL's New Turf," *Washington Post*, 1 September 2003; and Eric Fisher, "Live Show Kicks Off NFL Year," *Washington Times*, 4 September 2003.

40. U.S. Department of the Interior, "Secretary Norton to Join KaBOOM!, NFL Greats, and Others to Build a 'Playground of Hope' as Part of NFL KickOff Celebration," press release, 2 September 2003, https://www.doi.gov/sites/doi.gov/files/archive/news/archive/03_News_Releases/030902.htm (accessed 6 May 2021).

41. See Site Design Drawings, 18 August 2003, in "NFL Kick-Off" folder, TPIA background files.

42. See U.S. Department of the Interior, "NFL Helps Carry the Ball for Take Pride in America," press release, 3 September 2003, https://www.doi.gov/sites/doi.gov/files/archive/news/archive/03_News_Releases/030903a.htm (accessed 6 May 2021).

43. See "Marketing the Mall," *Washington Post*, 3 September 2003.

44. Karlyn Barker, "Ad Rules Don't Apply for NFL Bash," *Washington Post*, 4 September 2003.

45. Samantha King, "Offensive Lines: Sport-State Synergy in an Era of Perpetual War," *Cultural Studies ↔ Critical Methodologies*, 8 (November 2008): 536. See also Fisher, "Live Show Kicks Off NFL Year."

46. King, "Offensive Lines," 537. For the controversy the NFL Kickoff event raised in Congress over the blatantly commercial use of the National Mall, see U.S. Government Accountability Office, *National Park Service: Revenues Could Increase by Charging Allowed Fees for Some Special Uses Permits* (Washington, D.C.: Government Accountability Office, 2005).

47. See U.S. Department of the Interior, "Take Pride in America and Presidential Awards Presented to Outstanding Volunteers," press release, 26 September 2003, https://www.doi.gov/sites/doi.gov/files/archive/news/archive/03_News_Releases/030926a.htm (accessed 6 May 2021).

48. "Take Pride in America," American Horse Council, http://www.horsecouncil.org/issues/2005%20summer%20fall%20issues/TAKE%20PRIDE (accessed 20 June 2007; no longer available).

49. Derrick A. Crandall to Marti Allbright, 1 August 2003, Partners 2003–2006 folder, TPIA background files.

50. U.S. Department of the Interior, "Secretary Norton Saddles Up for Rose Bowl Parade, Highlights New Year's Volunteer Pledge Drive," press release, 31 December 2003, California—12/30–1/1/04 folder, TPIA background files. The Wonderful Outdoor World, for example, had pledged 25,000 hours of volunteer service to assist with the rehabilitation of California's fire-damaged forests. See U.S. Department of the Interior, "Secretary Norton to Announce Volunteer Hours to Restore Southern California's Forests and Communities," press release, 24 December 2003, https://www.doi.gov/sites/doi.gov/files/archive/news/archive/03_News_Releases/031224.htm (accessed 6 May 2021).

51. John Stewart, "Take Pride in America: New Year's Resolution Pledge Drive," posted on the United Four Wheel Drive Associations' website on 7 January 2004 (print copy in Clips—Master Copy folder, TPIA background files). The recreation organizations pledging volunteer hours included United Four Wheel Drive Associations, Cleveland National Forest Off Highway Volunteers, San Bernardino National Forest Off Highway Volunteers, Society for the Conservation of Bighorn Sheep, Friends of the Rubicon, Warrior's Society, Tierra del Sol Four Wheel Drive Club of San Diego, California Association of Four Wheel Drive Clubs, American Sand Association, American Motorcycle Association—District 37, Arizona State Association of Four Wheel Drive Clubs, Colorado Association of Four Wheel Drive Clubs, North East Association of Four Wheel Drive Clubs, Rubicon Owners Club of America, and Back Country Horsemen of California.

52. See "Good Sam Leads the Way with Take Pride Program," *Highways*, 38 (March 2004): 10.

53. J. Steven Giles to Anthony L. Lombardo, 23 February 2004, Clint Eastwood folder, TPIA background files.

54. Marti Allbright to Judy Hoyt, 18 May 2004, Clint Eastwood folder, TPIA background files. See also U.S. Department of the Interior, "Clint Eastwood Reprises Role as Spokesman for Take Pride in America," press release, 25 May 2004, Clint Eastwood folder, TPIA background files.

55. Home page on Take Pride in America's website, http://www.takepride.gov/aboutus.html (accessed 22 April 2004; no longer available).

56. U.S. Department of the Interior, "Take Pride in America Recruits Mayors to Become Stewards of Our Public Lands," press release, 21 January 2003, Handbook folder, TPIA background files. One indicator of the growth in volunteerism was the establishment of the bimonthly magazine *Inspire Your World: Celebrating the People, Companies and Causes That Inspire Us to Give Back*, which described itself as "the first consumer magazine on volunteering and philanthropy." Gary Schneider, "From the Publisher," volume 1, issue 1 (April/May 2004): 4. See also the "Special Volunteer Edition" of *Continental Divide Trail News*, 11 (Fall 2005).

57. Information on the American Sand Association and its activities over the years is best acquired by browsing ASA's newsletter, *In the Dunes*. Downloadable copies of back issues are available at https://americansandassociation.org/all-downloads/newsletters-2/whats-new-archive (accessed 6 May 2021).

58. See Michael Sommer to Jennifer Garrison et al., 14 February 2006, Feature Media Pitch/Track folder, TPIA background files; and Taking Pride in the Dunes, *In the Dunes*, 6 (May 2006): 19.

59. "President Announces Wetlands Initiative on Earth Day," 22 April 2004, https://georgewbush-whitehouse.archives.gov/news/releases/2004/04/20040422-4.html (accessed 29 January 2019). See also Amy Goldstein and Lois Romano, "Earth Day's Point, Counterpoint," *Washington Post*, 23 April 2004.

60. "Secretary Norton Announces the Designation of Estes Park, Colo. as a Take Pride in America City," *CEQ E-Notes*, 2, no. 30 (28 July 2004).

61. Norton, quoted in "Secretary Norton Commends 2004 National Take Pride in America Award Winners at Department of Interior Ceremony," *CEQ E-Notes*, 2, no. 37 (22 September 2004).

62. "Secretary Norton Commends 2004 National Take Pride in America Award Winners."

63. "Interior Department and State Launch Take Pride in Florida Project to Help Hurricane Ravaged Public Lands," *CEQ E-Notes*, 2, no. 42 (27 October 2004).

64. "Eastwood Asks Fellow Seniors to Help Improve Public Recreational Areas," *SeniorJournal.com*, 18 August 2005, http://www.seniorjournal.com/NEWS/Volunteers/5-08-18EastwoodVolunteers.htm (accessed 20 June 2007; no longer available). See also Paul Rogers, "Clint Eastwood on Parks and Recreation Commission," *San Jose Mercury News*, 2 December 2001.

65. Marti Allbright, quoted in U.S. Department of the Interior, "Secretary Norton Awards 2005 National Take Pride in America Award Winners at Department of Interior Ceremony," press release, 30 September 2005, https://www.doi.gov/sites/doi.gov/files/archive/news/archive/05_News_Releases/050930.htm (accessed 16 April 2019).

66. Bill Wade, "A New Tragedy for the Commons: The Threat of Privatization to National Parks (and Other Public Lands)," *George Wright Forum*, 22, no. 2 (2005): 65.

67. When Allbright left her post in December 2005 to return to private law practice, her deputy director, Michelle L. Cangelosi, replaced her. Before joining the Take Pride in America staff in 2003, Cangelosi had served as secretary Norton's associate director for external and intergovernmental affairs. Prior to that, she had worked as an environmental scientist with the Florida Department of Environmental Protection. See U.S. Department

of the Interior, "Cangelosi Named Executive Director of Take Pride in America," press release, 16 February 2006, https://www.doi.gov/sites/doi.gov/files/archive/news/archive/06_News_Releases/060216b.htm (accessed 6 May 2021). Norton's March 2006 resignation prompted Matthew Wald to note her emphasis on "voluntary conservation measures and 'cooperative conservation,' in partnership with landowners, rather than regulation." Matthew L. Wald, "Key Player for President Is Resigning as Head of the Interior Dept.," *New York Times*, 11 March 2006.

68. "Gale Norton Resigns," *New York Times*, 12 March 2006. For changes in environmental policymaking in the years since Reagan left office, when expanding partisan divisions led to legislative gridlock but when enduring public support of environmentalism continued to find expression through nonlegislative venues, see Christopher McGrory Klyza and David J. Sousa, *American Environmental Policy: Beyond Gridlock*, updated and expanded ed. (Cambridge, Mass.: MIT Press, 2013); and David J. Sousa and Christopher McGrory Klyza, "'Whither We Are Trending': Interrogating the Retrenchment Narrative in U.S. Environmental Policy," *Political Science Quarterly*, 132 (September 2017): 467–494.

69. Paul Larmer, "Norton Departs: A Look at Interior's Counterrevolution—And Its Unintended Consequences," *High Country News*, 3 April 2006.

70. U.S. Department of the Interior, "Take Pride in America Announces 2006 National Awards Winners," press release, 20 July 2006, www.TakePride.gov (accessed 17 August 2006; no longer available). That summer the nation's largest—and most politically conservative—conservation membership organization, the National Wildlife Federation, officially endorsed Take Pride in America. See Melinda Hughes, "NWF Becomes a Partner of the Take Pride in America Initiative," *Volunteer Spirit*, 14 (July/August 2006): 1.

71. See Take Pride in America, "Take Pride in America Joins Travelocity Employees for Cleanup Event at Lake Grapevine," press release, 18 April 2008, http://www.takepride.gov/mediaroom/news051308e.html (accessed 12 June 2009; no longer available).

72. See "Driving Resources and Opportunities to Volunteers from Coast to Coast," Take Pride in America fact sheet, n.d. [probably issued June or July 2008], http://www.takepride/mediaroom/factsheet.pdf (accessed 12 June 2009; no longer available).

73. Take Pride in America, "Take Pride in America and Toyota Take Voluntour Across America to the Heartland," press release, 16 September 2008, http://www.takepride.gov/mediaroom/news09172008.html (accessed 12 June 2009; no longer available). Take Pride's assistant director, Lisa Young, was on this trip. She went on to become the program's executive director in 2010.

74. Michelle Cangelosi, who replaced Marti Allbright as Take Pride director in December 2005, left in 2007, passing the baton to Heather M. Roebke, who transferred

from the White House office staff where she held the post of executive assistant to the counsel to the president. A year later, Roebke handed the executive director reins to another White House alumna, Katie R. Loovis, Bush's associate director of public liaison. Take Pride, however, took a back seat in Loovis's new portfolio, as she simultaneously held the more demanding position of director of external affairs within the Office of the Secretary of the Interior, where she focused on the agency's interactions with the private and nonprofit sectors. See U.S. Department of the Interior, "2008 Take Pride in America National Award Winners Announced," press release, 9 June 2008, http://www.takepride. gov/mediaroom/news06092008.html (accessed 24 June 2008; no longer available); and "Katie Loovis," biography posted on the Take Pride in America website, http://www. takepride.gov/aboutus/katie_bio.html (accessed 24 June 2008; no longer available).

75. Take Pride in America, "Secretary of the Interior Signs Order to Continue Take Pride in America," press release, 28 October 2008, http://www.takepride.gov/mediaroom/ news10282008.html (accessed 12 June 2009; no longer available).

76. "Appendix I: Responses to Additional Questions," in U.S. Congress, Senate Committee on Energy and Natural Resources, Hearing, *Consider the Nomination of Ken Salazar to be Secretary of the Interior,* 111th Cong., 1st sess., 15 January 2009 (Washington, D.C.: GPO, 2009), 61. The 53-year-old Salazar was born in Colorado. He earned a B.A. from Colorado College and a J.D. from the University of Michigan Law School. His public service included terms as director of the Colorado Department of Natural Resources (1990–1994), attorney general of Colorado (1999–2005), and Colorado's U.S. senator (2005–2009).

77. On 15 July 2013, Obama invited the 89-year-old George H. W. Bush to the White House, where they jointly bestowed the 5,000th Daily Point of Light Award. As *New York Times* reporter Mark Landler observed, the two men were "separated by nearly four decades but united in their fervor for volunteer service." Mark Landler, "At White House Homecoming, Former President's 'Points of Light' Shine On," *New York Times*, 16 July 2013.

78. Young, who grew up in Utah, began her association with Take Pride in America as a college student volunteer in summer 2003 helping with the NFL Kickoff event on the National Mall in Washington. She joined the Take Pride staff as a program assistant in 2005, becoming assistant director of events and awards in 2006. She replaced Katie Loovis as executive director during the Obama administration.

79. See, for example, William Yardley, "In State Parks, the Sharpest Ax Is the Budget's," *New York Times*, 7 June 2011.

80. See Megan O'Neil, "Volunteer Numbers Surge after Trump Election," *Chronicle of Philanthropy*, 2 February 2017, https://www.philanthropy.com/article/volunteer-

numbers-surge-after-trump-election/ (accessed 16 December 2020); Elena Souris, "Volunteering as Civic Engagement at Home and Abroad," *New America*, 23 October 2017, https://www.newamerica.org/political-reform/participatory-democracy-project/civic-engagement/volunteering-civic-engagement-home-and-abroad/ (accessed 11 December 2020); Benjamin Soskis, "Republicans Used to Celebrate Voluntarism and Service. What Happened?," *Washington Post*, 3 August 2018; Susan N. Dreyfus, "Volunteerism and US Civil Society," *Stanford Social Innovation Review*, 29 August 2018, https://ssir.org/articles/entry/volunteerism_and_us_civil_society (accessed 15 January 2021); and Elham Khatami, "Trump Seeks to Get Rid of Service Programs Like AmeriCorps, Senior Corps in Budget Proposal," *Think Progress*, 13 March 2019, https://archive.thinkprogress.org/trump-white-house-2020-budget-scraps-americorps-senior-corps-799fd69177e0/ (accessed 11 December 2020). Ironically, Trump's coolness toward volunteer service sparked a surge in the number of Americans donating their time and talent to various causes. Megan O'Neil reported the agreement among the heads of nonprofit organizations that "the increase in volunteerism probably is due to opposition to the new president: People are feeling a need to do something to counter Trump's policies."

BIBLIOGRAPHY

MANUSCRIPT COLLECTIONS

Advertising Council Archives. University of Illinois Archives, University Library, University of Illinois at Urbana-Champaign, Urbana.

Advertising Council Records. David M. Rubenstein Rare Book and Manuscript Library, Duke University, Durham, N.C.

Davis, Randall E. Files. Ronald Reagan Presidential Library, Simi Valley, Calif.

Hartzog, George B., Jr. Papers. Special Collections and Archives, Clemson University Libraries, Clemson, S.C.

Hoppen, William. Papers. Manuscript Division, Library of Congress, Washington, D.C.

Keim, Robert P. Papers. Advertising Council Archives. University of Illinois Archives, University Library, University of Illinois at Urbana-Champaign, Urbana.

National Wildlife Federation Collection. National Conservation Training Center Archives, U.S. Fish and Wildlife Service, Shepherdstown, W.Va.

National Zoological Park. Office of Public Affairs Records, 1899–1988. Record unit 365. Smithsonian Institution Archives, Washington, D.C.

National Zoological Park. Office of the Director Records, circa 1920–1984. Record unit 326. Smithsonian Institution Archives, Washington, D.C.

Reagan, Ronald. Gubernatorial Papers, 1966–1975. Ronald Reagan Presidential Library, Simi Valley, Calif.

Regan, Donald T. Papers. Manuscript Division, Library of Congress, Washington, D.C.

Smithsonian Institution Office of the Secretary. Administrative Records, 1990. Accession No. 93–066. Smithsonian Institution Archives, Washington, D.C.

U.S. Department of the Interior. National Park Service Records. Record group 79. National Archives and Records Administration, College Park, Md.

U.S. Department of the Interior. Office of the Assistant Secretary for Policy, Management, and Budget, Office of Service/Take Pride in America Records. U.S. Department of the Interior, Washington, D.C.

U.S. Department of the Interior. Office of the Secretary Correspondence Files. U.S. Department of the Interior, Washington, D.C.

White House Office of Records Management (WHORM) subject files. Ronald Reagan Presidential Library, Simi Valley, Calif.

THESES AND DISSERTATIONS

Ashenmiller, Joshua Ross. "The National Environmental Policy Act in the Green Decade, 1969–1981." Ph.D. diss., University of California, Santa Barbara, 2004.

Boynton, Alex John. "Confronting the Environmental Crisis? Anti-Environmentalism and the Transformation of Conservative Thought in the 1970s." Ph.D. diss., University of Kansas, Lawrence, 2015.

Cohen, Shana Miriam. "American Garden Clubs and the Fight for Nature Preservation, 1890–1980." Ph.D. diss., University of California, Berkeley, 2005.

Conley, Joe Greene, II. "Environmentalism Contained: A History of Corporate Responses to the New Environmentalism." Ph.D. diss., Princeton University, Princeton, N.J., 2006.

Forness, Norman O. "The Origins and Early History of the United States Department of the Interior." Ph.D. diss., Pennsylvania State University, University Park, 1964.

Green, Robert Kirby. "The Managerial Moralist: The Domestic Policy of Jimmy Carter, 1977–1981." Ph.D. diss., Queen Mary University of London, London, 2018.

Harmon, Elizabeth A. "The Transformation of American Philanthropy: From Public Trust to Private Foundation, 1785–1917." Ph.D. diss., University of Michigan, Ann Arbor, 2017.

Hendry, Cheryl Ann. "Finding Nature in an Industrial Swamp: A Case Study of New Jersey's Hackensack Meadowlands." Ph.D. diss., Montana State University, Bozeman, 2017.

Jones, Megan Anne. "Stewards of Tomorrow: The Student Conservation Association, Youth Service, and Postwar American Environmentalism, 1953–1975." Ph.D. diss., University of Delaware, Newark, 2011.

Lefkoff, Merle Schlesinger. "The Voluntary Citizens' Group as a Public Policy Alternative to the Political Party: A Case Study of the Georgia Conservancy." Ph.D. diss., Emory University, Atlanta, 1975.

Lewis, Dylan. "Unpaid Protectors: Volunteerism and the Diminishing Role of Federal Responsibility in the National Park Service." Honors thesis, Northwestern University, Evanston, Ill., 2011.

Mandell, Maurice I. "A History of the Advertising Council." Ph.D. diss., Indiana University, Bloomington, 1953.

Massmann, Priscilla G. "A Neglected Partnership: The General Federation of Women's Clubs and the Conservation Movement, 1890–1920." Ph.D. diss., University of Connecticut, Storrs, 1997.

Muchnick, Barry Ross Harrison. "Nature's Republic: Fresh Air Reform and the Moral Ecology of Citizenship in Turn of the Century America." Ph.D. diss., Yale University, New Haven, Conn., 2010.

Muraki, Michael I. "The Impacts of the State and Federal Wild and Scenic River Acts in Conservation Efforts on California's Trinity River." M.A. thesis, California State University, Chico, 2018.

Sandman, Peter M. "Eco-Pornography: Environmental Advertising and Advertising Acceptance in the San Francisco Bay Area." Ph.D. diss., Stanford University, Stanford, Calif., 1971.

Soskis, Benjamin. "The Problem of Charity in Industrial America, 1873–1915." Ph.D. diss., Columbia University, New York, 2010.

Tankersley, Holley Elizabeth. "National and State Dimensions of Major Policy Change: The Reagan 'Revolution' Reexamined." Ph.D. diss., University of Georgia, Athens, 2006.

Westfall, Ronald G. "The Presidency and Environmental Policymaking: A Critical Assessment of George Bush." M.A. thesis, University of Nevada, Las Vegas, 1994.

GOVERNMENT DOCUMENTS

Bush, George. *Public Papers of the Presidents of the United States, George Bush, 1989: Book I—January 20 to June 30, 1989*. Washington, D.C.: U.S. Government Printing Office (GPO), 1990.

Bush, George. *Public Papers of the Presidents of the United States, George Bush, 1989: Book II—July 1 to December 31, 1989*. Washington, D.C.: GPO, 1990.

Bush, George. *Public Papers of the Presidents of the United States, George Bush, 1990: Book I—January 1 to June 30, 1990*. Washington, D.C.: GPO, 1991.

Bush, George. *Public Papers of the Presidents of the United States, George Bush, 1991: Book I—January 1 to June 30, 1991*. Washington, D.C.: GPO, 1992.

Bush, George. *Public Papers of the Presidents of the United States, George Bush, 1992–93: Book I—January 1 to July 31, 1992*. Washington, D.C.: GPO, 1993.

Bush, George. *Public Papers of the Presidents of the United States, George Bush, 1992–93: Book II—August 1, 1992 to January 20, 1993*. Washington, D.C.: GPO, 1993.

Carter, Jimmy. Off-Road Vehicles on Public Lands. Executive Order No. 11989. 42 *Federal Register* 26959–26960 (25 May 1977).

Council on Environmental Quality. *Environmental Quality*. 17th Annual Report. Washington, D.C.: GPO, 1988.

Elrod, Jack. *Take Pride in America with Mark Trail: A Coloring Book*. Washington, D.C.: U.S. Department of the Interior, 1987.

Ford, Gerald R. Johnny Horizon '76 Clean Up America Month, 1974. Proclamation No. 4315. 19 September 1974. https://www.presidency.ucsb.edu/node/269726 (accessed 5 May 2021).

Forrey, William C. *History of Pennsylvania's State Parks, 1984–2015*. Harrisburg: Bureau of State Parks, Office of Parks and Forestry, Department of Conservation and Natural Resources, Commonwealth of Pennsylvania, 2017.

Highway Beautification Act of 1965. Public Law No. 89-285, 79 Stat. 1028–1033 (22 October 1965).

Larson, E. vH., ed. *The Forest Recreation Symposium*. Upper Darby, Pa.: Northeastern Forest Experiment Station, Forest Service, U.S. Department of Agriculture, 1971.

Lee, Ronald F. *Public Use of the National Park System, 1972–2000*. Washington, D.C.: GPO, 1968.

Muhn, James, and Hanson R. Stuart. *Opportunity and Challenge: The Story of BLM*. Washington, D.C.: GPO, 1988.

Nixon, Richard. Use of Off-Road Vehicles on the Public Lands. Executive Order No. 11644. 37 *Federal Register* 2877–2878 (9 February 1972).

Nixon, Richard. Earth Week, 1974. Proclamation No. 4287. 20 April 1974. http://www.presidency.ucsb.edu/ws/index.php?pid=106843 (accessed 5 May 2021).

Nixon, Richard. National Volunteer Week, 1974. Proclamation No. 4288. 20 April 1974. https://www.presidency.ucsb.edu/documents/proclamation-4288-national-volunteer-week-1974 (accessed 5 May 2021).

Office of Technology Assessment. *Facing America's Trash: What Next for Municipal Solid Waste?* Washington, D.C.: GPO, 1989.

President's Commission on Americans Outdoors. *Americans Outdoors: The Legacy, the Challenge; The Report of the President's Commission*. Washington, D.C.: Island Press, 1987.

Reagan, Ronald. *Public Papers of the Presidents of the United States, Ronald Reagan, 1981: January 20 to December 31, 1981*. Washington, D.C.: GPO, 1982.

Reagan, Ronald. *Public Papers of the Presidents of the United States, Ronald Reagan, 1983: Book I—January 1 to July 1, 1983*. Washington, D.C.: GPO, 1984.

Reagan, Ronald. *Public Papers of the Presidents of the United States, Ronald Reagan, 1983: Book II—July 2 to December 31, 1983*. Washington, D.C.: GPO, 1985.

Reagan, Ronald. *Public Papers of the Presidents of the United States, Ronald Reagan, 1984: Book II—June 30 to December 31, 1984*. Washington, D.C.: GPO, 1987.

Reagan, Ronald. *Public Papers of the Presidents of the United States, Ronald Reagan, 1986: Book I—January 1 to June 27, 1986*. Washington, D.C.: GPO, 1988.

Reagan, Ronald. *Public Papers of the Presidents of the United States, Ronald Reagan, 1987: Book II—July 4 to December 31, 1987*. Washington, D.C.: GPO, 1989.

Reagan, Ronald. *Public Papers of the Presidents of the United States, Ronald Reagan, 1988: Book I—January 1 to July 1, 1988*. Washington, D.C.: GPO, 1990.

Reagan, Ronald. *Public Papers of the Presidents of the United States, Ronald Reagan, 1988–89: Book II—July 2, 1988 to January 19, 1989*. Washington, D.C.: GPO, 1991.

Reagan, Ronald. "Remarks at a Ceremony Honoring Youth Volunteers." 25 April 1985. https://www.presidency.ucsb.edu/node/260283 (accessed 5 May 2021).

Roosevelt, Franklin D. Establishing the Office of Facts and Figures. Executive Order No. 8922. 24 October 1941. https://www.presidency.ucsb.edu/documents/executive-order-8922-establishing-the-office-facts-and-figures (accessed 5 May 2021).

Sheridan, David. *Off-Road Vehicles on Public Lands*. Washington, D.C.: GPO, 1979.

Smokey Bear Act of 1952. Public Law No. 82-359, Ch. 327, 66 Stat. 92; 18 U.S.C. 711; 16 U.S.C. 580p-2 (1952).

Take Pride in America Act of 1990. Public Law No. 101-628, Title XI, §1102, 104 Stat. 4469 (1990).

United States Code. Title 16, Chapter 66—Take Pride in America Program, §4601–4608.

U.S. Congress, House Subcommittee on Department of the Interior and Related Agencies, Committee on Appropriations. Hearing. *Department of the Interior and Related Agencies Appropriations for 1972*. 92nd Cong., 1st sess. (March 31, 1971). Washington, D.C.: GPO, 1971.

U.S. Congress, Senate Committee on Energy and Natural Resources. Hearing. *Nomination of Ken Salazar to be Secretary of the Interior*. 111th Cong., 1st sess. (January 15, 2009). Washington, D.C.: GPO, 2009.

U.S. Congress, Senate Committee on Energy and Natural Resources. Hearing. *Nomination of Donald Paul Hodel to be Secretary of the Interior*. 99th Cong., 1st sess. (February 1, 1985). Washington, D.C.: GPO, 1985.

U.S. Congress, Senate Committee on Energy and Natural Resources. *Proposed Fiscal Year 1986 Budget Request: Hearings to Review the President's Proposed Budget for Fiscal Year 1986 in Connection with the Preparation of the March 15 Report to the Senate Budget Committee*. 99th Cong., 1st sess. (February 27; March 1 and 4, 1985). Washington, D.C.: GPO, 1985.

U.S. Department of Agriculture. Woodsy Owl Launches Anti-pollution Campaign. Press release, 15 September 1971. https://foresthistory.org/wp-content/uploads/2018/07/Woodsy_Owl_press.pdf (accessed 28 August 2020).

U.S. Department of Agriculture, Forest Service. *"Remember—Only You . . .": 1944 to 1984, Forty Years of Preventing Forest Fires, Smokey's 40th Birthday*. Washington, D.C.: GPO, 1984.

U.S. Department of Agriculture, Forest Service. *Smokey Bear—The First 50 Years*. Washington, D.C.: GPO, 1993.

U.S. Department of the Interior. *Bureau of Land Management: Volunteer Opportunities in Utah*. Washington, D.C.: GPO, 1990.

U.S. Department of the Interior. *Volunteer Opportunities: Eastern States, Bureau of Land Management*. Washington, D.C.: GPO, 1990.

U.S. Department of the Interior, Bureau of Land Management. *Managing the Nation's Public Lands*. Washington, D.C.: GPO, 1988.

U.S. Department of the Interior. Cangelosi Named Executive Director of Take Pride in America. Press release, 16 February 2006, https://www.doi.gov/sites/doi.gov/files/archive/news/archive/06_News_Releases/060216b.htm (accessed 6 May 2021).

U.S. Department of the Interior, Fish and Wildlife Service. Prepared Remarks of Interior Secretary Don Hodel for the Annual Meeting of the Outdoor Writers Association of America. 9 June 1986. https://www.fws.gov/news/Historic/NewsReleases/1986/19860609.pdf (accessed 15 September 2017).

U.S. Department of the Interior, National Park Service. Director's Order #7: Volunteers-in-Parks. Rev. ed. 15 March 2016. https://www.nps.gov/policy/DOrders/DO_7_2016.htm (accessed 22 August 2018).

U.S. Department of the Interior. NFL Helps Carry the Ball for Take Pride in America. Press release, 3 September 2003. https://www.doi.gov/sites/doi.gov/files/archive/news/archive/03_News_Releases/030903a.htm (accessed 6 May 2021).

U.S. Department of the Interior, Office of the Secretary. Interior Secretary Gale Norton Announces Designation of First Take Pride in America School. Press release, 24 May 2005.

https://web.archive.org/web/20060929090043/http://www.doi.gov/news/050525a1.htm (accessed 30 August 2019).

U.S. Department of the Interior, Office of the Secretary. Secretary Norton Awards 2005 National Take Pride in America Award Winners at Department of Interior Ceremony. Press release, 30 September 2005. https://www.doi.gov/sites/doi.gov/files/archive/news/archive/05_News_Releases/050930.htm (accessed 16 April 2019).

U.S. Department of the Interior, Office of the Secretary. Take Pride in America and Presidential Awards Presented to Outstanding Volunteers. Press release, 26 September 2003. https://www.doi.gov/sites/doi.gov/files/archive/news/archive/03_News_Releases/030926a.htm (accessed 6 May 2021).

U.S. Department of the Interior. Secretary Norton to Announce Volunteer Hours to Restore Southern California's Forests and Communities. Press release, 24 December 2003. https://www.doi.gov/sites/doi.gov/files/archive/news/archive/03_News_Releases/031224.htm (accessed 6 May 2021).

U.S. Department of the Interior. Secretary Norton to Join KaBOOM!, NFL Greats, and Others to Build a "Playground of Hope" as Part of NFL KickOff Celebration. Press release, 2 September 2003. https://www.doi.gov/sites/doi.gov/files/archive/news/archive/03_News_Releases/030902.htm (accessed 6 May 2021).

U.S. Government Accountability Office. *National Park Service: Revenues Could Increase by Charging Allowed Fees for Some Special Uses Permits*. Washington, D.C.: Government Accountability Office, 2005.

Vincent, Carol Hardy, Laura A. Hanson, and Carla N. Argueta. *Federal Land Ownership: Overview and Data*. CRS Report 7-5700. Washington, D.C.: Congressional Research Service, 2017.

Volunteers in the National Forests: A Decade of Excellence. FS 669. Washington, D.C.: U.S. Department of Agriculture, Forest Service, 2000.

Volunteers in the Parks Act of 1969. Public Law No. 91-357, 84 Stat. 472 (29 July 1970).

The White House. President Announces Wetlands Initiative on Earth Day, 22 April 2004. https://georgewbush-whitehouse.archives.gov/news/releases/2004/04/20040422-4.html (accessed 16 April 2019).

BOOKS, PAMPHLETS, AND NONGOVERNMENT REPORTS

Advertising Council. *Bringing the Issues Home: Report to the American People, '88–'89*. New York: Advertising Council, 1989.

Advertising Council. *10th Annual Report of the Advertising Council, 1951–1952*. New York: Advertising Council, 1952.

AHF Marketing Research. *Forest Fire Prevention: An Awareness and Attitudes Study*. A report prepared for the Advertising Council. New York: AHF Marketing Research, 1976.

Allitt, Patrick. *A Climate of Crisis: America in the Age of Environmentalism*. New York: Penguin Press, 2014.

Americans Volunteer, 1974: A Statistical Study of Volunteers in the United States. Washington, D.C.: ACTION, 1975.

Andrews, Richard N. L. *Managing the Environment, Managing Ourselves: A History of American Environmental Policy*. New Haven, Conn.: Yale University Press, 1999. https://doi.org/10.2307/j.ctt2250wm9

Arnold, Ron. *At the Eye of the Storm: James Watt and the Environmentalists*. Chicago: Regnery Gateway, 1982.

Auerbach, Jonathan. *Weapons of Democracy: Propaganda, Progressivism, and American Public Opinion*. Baltimore: Johns Hopkins University Press, 2015.

Axelrod, Alan. *Selling the Great War: The Making of American Propaganda*. New York: Palgrave Macmillan, 2009.

Ayling, Keith. *Calling All Women*. New York: Harper & Brothers, 1942.

Baldwin, Malcolm F., and Dan H. Stoddard Jr. *The Off-Road Vehicle and Environmental Quality*. Washington, D.C.: Conservation Foundation, 1973.

Balz, Daniel J. *Ronald Reagan: A Trusty Script*. Washington, D.C.: Capitol Hill News Service, 1976.

Barker, Elliott S. *Smokey Bear and the Great Wilderness*. Santa Fe, N.M.: Sunstone Press, 1982.

Barnouw, Erik. *The Sponsor: Notes on a Modern Potentate*. New York: Oxford University Press, 1978.

Barrow, Mark V., Jr. *A Passion for Birds: American Ornithology after Audubon*. Princeton, N.J.: Princeton University Press, 1998.

Bass, Melissa. *The Politics and Civics of National Service: Lessons from the Civilian Conservation Corps, Vista, and AmeriCorps*. Washington, D.C.: Brookings Institution Press, 2013.

Belgrad, Daniel. *The Culture of Feedback: Ecological Thinking in Seventies America*. Chicago: University of Chicago Press, 2019. https://doi.org/10.7208/chicago/9780226652672.001.0001

Bennett, Shaun. *A Trail Rider's Guide to the Environment*. Westerville, Ohio: American Motorcycle Association, 1973.

Berkhofer, Robert F., Jr. *The White Man's Indian: Images of the American Indian from Columbus to the Present*. New York: Knopf, 1978.

Biel, Alice Wondrak. *Do (Not) Feed the Bears: The Fitful History of Wildlife and Tourists in Yellowstone*. Lawrence: University Press of Kansas, 2006.

Binkley, Sam. *Getting Loose: Lifestyle Consumption in the 1970s*. Durham, N.C.: Duke University Press, 2007. https://doi.org/10.1215/9780822389514

Birchard, Bill. *Nature's Keepers: The Remarkable Story of How the Nature Conservancy Became the Largest Environmental Organization in the World*. San Francisco: Jossey-Bass, 2005.

Bird, William L. *"Better Living": Advertising, Media, and the New Vocabulary of Business Leadership, 1935–1955*. Evanston, Ill.: Northwestern University Press, 1999.

Black, Megan. *The Global Interior: Mineral Frontiers and American Power*. Cambridge, Mass.: Harvard University Press, 2018. https://doi.org/10.4159/9780674989580

Blake, David Haven. *Liking Ike: Eisenhower, Advertising, and the Rise of Celebrity Politics*. New York: Oxford University Press, 2016. https://doi.org/10.1093/acprof:oso/9780190278182.001.0001

Bledstein, Burton J. *The Culture of Professionalism: The Middle Class and the Development of Higher Education in America*. New York: W. W. Norton, 1976.

Bliese, John R. E. *The Greening of Conservative America.* Boulder, Colo.: Westview, 2001.

Block, Nelson R., and Tammy M. Proctor, eds. *Scouting Frontiers: Youth and the Scout Movement's First Century.* Newcastle upon Tyne, U.K.: Cambridge Scholars, 2009.

Bosso, Christopher J. *Environment, Inc.: From Grassroots to Beltway.* Lawrence: University Press of Kansas, 2005.

Boyarsky, Bill. *Ronald Reagan: His Life and Rise to the Presidency.* New York: Random House, 1981.

Bremner, Robert H. *American Philanthropy.* 2nd ed. Chicago: University of Chicago Press, 1988.

Brewer, Richard. *Conservancy: The Land Trust Movement in America.* Hanover, N.H.: University Press of New England, 2003.

Bridgeland, John M. *Heart of the Nation: Volunteering and America's Civic Spirit.* Lanham, Md.: Rowman & Littlefield, 2013.

Brownlee, W. Elliot, and Hugh Davis Graham, eds. *The Reagan Presidency: Pragmatic Conservatism and Its Legacies.* Lawrence: University Press of Kansas, 2003.

Brownstein, Ronald, and Nina Easton. *Reagan's Ruling Class: Portraits of the President's Top 100 Officials.* Washington, D.C.: Presidential Accountability Group, 1982.

Burleigh, Nina. *The Stranger and the Statesman: James Smithson, John Quincy Adams, and the Making of America's Greatest Museum: The Smithsonian.* New York: Morrow, 2003.

Busch, Akiko. *The Incidental Steward: Reflections on Citizen Science.* New Haven, Conn.: Yale University Press, 2013.

Busch, Andrew E. *Reagan's Victory: The Presidential Election of 1980 and the Rise of the Right.* Lawrence: University Press of Kansas, 2005.

Butler, Tom. *Wildlands Philanthropy: The Great American Tradition.* San Rafael, Calif.: Earth Aware, 2008.

Cannon, Lou. *Governor Reagan: His Rise to Power.* New York: PublicAffairs, 2003.

Cannon, Lou. *President Reagan: The Role of a Lifetime.* New York: Simon & Schuster, 1991.

Cannon, Lou. *Reagan.* New York: Putnam, 1982.

Cannon, Lou. *Ronald Reagan: The Presidential Portfolio.* New York: PublicAffairs, 2001.

Carr, Ethan. *Mission 66: Modernism and the National Park Dilemma.* Amherst: University of Massachusetts Press, 2007.

Cawley, R. McGreggor. *Federal Land, Western Anger: The Sagebrush Rebellion and Environmental Politics.* Lawrence: University Press of Kansas, 1993.

Chamberlin, Silas. *On the Trail: A History of American Hiking.* New Haven, Conn.: Yale University Press, 2016.

Chiang, Connie Y. *Nature Behind Barbed Wire: An Environmental History of Japanese American Incarceration.* New York: Oxford University Press, 2018. https://doi.org/10.1093/oso/9780190842062.001.0001

Clark, Blake. *The Advertising Smokescreen.* New York: Harper & Brothers, 1944.

Clark, Peter. *British Clubs and Societies, 1580–1800: The Origins of an Associational World.* New York: Oxford University Press, 2000.

Clawson, Marion, and Burnell Held. *The Federal Lands: Their Use and Management.* Baltimore: Johns Hopkins University Press, 1957.

Clawson, Marion, and Carlton S. Van Doren, eds. *Statistics on Outdoor Recreation.* Washington, D.C.: Resources for the Future, 1984.

Clements, Kendrick A. *Hoover, Conservation, and Consumerism: Engineering the Good Life*. Lawrence: University Press of Kansas, 2000.

Clinton, Bill, and Al Gore. *Putting People First: How We Can All Change America*. New York: Times Books, 1992.

Cobbs Hoffman, Elizabeth. *All You Need Is Love: The Peace Corps and the Spirit of the 1960s*. Cambridge, Mass.: Harvard University Press, 1998.

Cody, Iron Eyes. *Iron Eyes: My Life as a Hollywood Indian*. As told to Collin Perry. New York: Everest House, 1982.

Cohen, Lizabeth. *A Consumers' Republic: The Politics of Mass Consumption in Postwar America*. New York: Alfred A. Knopf, 2003.

Conley, Patricia Heidotting. *Presidential Mandates: How Elections Shape the National Agenda*. Chicago: University of Chicago Press, 2001.

Coombs, Danielle Sarver, and Bob Batchelor, eds. *We Are What We Sell: How Advertising Shapes American Life . . . and Always Has*. 3 vols. Santa Barbara, Calif.: Praeger, 2014.

Cooper, Caren. *Citizen Science: How Ordinary People Are Changing the Face of Discovery*. New York: Overlook Press, 2016.

Cordell, H. Ken, Carter Betz, J. Michael Bowker, Donald B. K. English, Shela H. Mou, John C. Bergstrom, R. Jeff Teasley, Michael A. Tarrant, and John Loomis. *Outdoor Recreation in American Life: A National Assessment of Demand and Supply Trends*. Champaign, Ill.: Sagamore Publishing, 1999.

Cornell, Drucilla. *Clint Eastwood and Issues of American Masculinity*. New York: Fordham University Press, 2009. https://doi.org/10.5422/fso/9780823230129.001.0001

Cornuelle, Richard C. *Reclaiming the American Dream: The Role of Private Individuals and Voluntary Associations*. New Brunswick, N.J.: Transaction Publishers, 1993.

Cozzens, Gary. *Capitan, New Mexico: From the Coalora Coal Mines to Smokey Bear*. Charleston, S.C.: History Press, 2012.

Creel, George. *How We Advertised America: The First Telling of the Amazing Story of the Committee on Public Information That Carried the Gospel of Americanism to Every Corner of the Globe*. New York: Harper & Brothers, 1920.

Culhane, Paul J. *Public Lands Politics: Interest Group Influence on the Forest Service and the Bureau of Land Management*. Baltimore: Johns Hopkins University Press, 1981.

Davies, Thom, and Alice Mah, eds. *Toxic Truths: Environmental Justice and Citizen Science in a Post-Truth Age*. Manchester, U.K.: Manchester University Press, 2020. https://doi.org/10.7765/9781526137005

Davis, Steven. *In Defense of Public Lands: The Case against Privatization and Transfer*. Philadelphia: Temple University Press, 2018.

Daynes, Byron W., and Glen Sussman. *White House Politics and the Environment: Franklin D. Roosevelt to George W. Bush*. College Station: Texas A&M University Press, 2010.

Decker, Jefferson. *The Other Rights Revolution: Conservative Lawyers and the Remaking of American Government*. New York: Oxford University Press, 2016. https://doi.org/10.1093/acprof:oso/9780190467302.001.0001

de Tocqueville, Alexis. *Democracy in America*. Volume 1. 1835. Reprint, New York: Alfred A. Knopf, 1945.

Devine, Robert S. *Bush versus the Environment*. New York: Anchor Books, 2004.

DeVorkin, David H. *Fred Whipple's Empire: The Smithsonian Astrophysical Observatory, 1955–1973*. Washington, D.C.: Smithsonian Institution Scholarly Press, 2018. https://doi.org/10.5479/si.9781944466176

Dickinson, Janis L., and Rick Bonney, eds. *Citizen Science: Public Participation in Environmental Research*. Ithaca, N.Y.: Comstock Publishing Associates, 2012.

Dionne, E. J., Jr., Kayla Meltzer Drogosz, and Robert E. Litan, eds. *United We Serve: National Service and the Future of Citizenship*. Washington, D.C.: Brookings Institution Press, 2003.

Doherty, Thomas. *Projections of War: Hollywood, American Culture, and World War II*. New York: Columbia University Press, 1993.

Dolin, Eric Jay. *Political Waters: The Long, Dirty, Contentious, Incredibly Expensive but Eventually Triumphant History of Boston Harbor—A Unique Environmental Success Story*. Amherst: University of Massachusetts Press, 2004.

Dombeck, Michael P., Christopher A. Wood, and Jack E. Williams. *From Conquest to Conservation: Our Public Lands Legacy*. Washington, D.C.: Island Press, 2003.

Drake, Brian Allen. *Loving Nature, Fearing the State: Environmentalism and Antigovernmental Politics before Reagan*. Seattle: University of Washington Press, 2013.

Dray, Philip. *The Fair Chase: The Epic Story of Hunting in America*. New York: Basic Books, 2018.

Duffy, Michael, and Dan Goodgame. *Marching in Place: The Status Quo Presidency of George Bush*. New York: Simon & Schuster, 1992.

Duffy, Robert J. *The Green Agenda in American Politics: New Strategies for the Twenty-First Century*. Lawrence: University Press of Kansas, 2003.

Dunaway, Finis. *Seeing Green: The Use and Abuse of American Environmental Images*. Chicago: University of Chicago Press, 2015. https://doi.org/10.7208/chicago/9780226169934.001.0001

Dunlap, Riley E., and Angela G. Mertig, eds. *American Environmentalism: The U.S. Environmental Movement, 1970–1990*. Philadelphia: Taylor & Francis, 1992.

Dunlap, Thomas R. *Saving America's Wildlife*. Princeton, N.J.: Princeton University Press, 1988.

Durant, Robert F. *The Administrative Presidency Revisited: Public Lands, the BLM, and the Reagan Revolution*. Albany: State University of New York Press, 1992.

Earle, Richard. *The Art of Cause Marketing: How to Use Advertising to Change Personal Behavior and Public Policy*. Lincolnwood, Ill.: NTC Business Books, 2000.

Easton, Robert. *Black Tide: The Santa Barbara Oil Spill and Its Consequences*. New York: Delacorte Press, 1972.

Ehrman, John. *The Eighties: America in the Age of Reagan*. New Haven, Conn.: Yale University Press, 2005.

Einberger, Scott. *A History of Rock Creek Park: Wilderness and Washington, D.C.* Charleston, S.C.: History Press, 2014.

Einberger, Scott Raymond. *With Distance in His Eyes: The Environmental Life and Legacy of Stewart Udall*. Reno: University of Nevada Press, 2018.

Ellis, Susan J., and Katherine H. Campbell. *By the People: A History of Americans as Volunteers*. 3rd ed. Philadelphia: Energize, 2005.

Elmore, Bartow J. *Citizen Coke: The Making of Coca-Cola Capitalism*. New York: W. W. Norton, 2015.

Endicott, Eve, ed. *Land Conservation through Public/Private Partnerships*. Washington, D.C.: Island Press, 1993.

Evans, Thomas W. *The Education of Ronald Reagan: The General Electric Years and the Untold Story of His Conversion to Conservatism*. New York: Columbia University Press, 2006. https://doi.org/10.7312/evan13860

Ewing, Heather P. *The Lost World of James Smithson: Science, Revolution, and the Birth of the Smithsonian*. New York: Bloomsbury, 2007.

Farrell, Justin. *Billionaire Wilderness: The Ultra-Wealthy and the Remaking of the American West*. Princeton, N.J.: Princeton University Press, 2020. https://doi.org/10.1515/9780691185811

Fink, Gary M, and Hugh Davis Graham, eds. *The Carter Presidency: Policy Choices in the Post-New Deal Era*. Lawrence: University Press of Kansas, 1998.

Fitch, Edwin M., and John F. Shanklin. *The Bureau of Outdoor Recreation*. New York: Praeger, 1970.

Flathman, Richard E. *Willful Liberalism: Voluntarism and Individuality in Political Theory and Practice*. Ithaca, N.Y.: Cornell University Press, 1992. https://doi.org/10.7591/9781501724091

Fleming, James Rodger. *Meteorology in America, 1800–1870*. Baltimore: Johns Hopkins University Press, 1990.

Flippen, J. Brooks. *Conservative Conservationist: Russell E. Train and the Emergence of American Environmentalism*. Baton Rouge: Louisiana State University Press, 2006.

Flippen, J. Brooks. *Nixon and the Environment*. Albuquerque: University of New Mexico Press, 2000.

Foresta, Ronald A. *America's National Parks and Their Keepers*. Washington, D.C.: Resources for the Future, 1984.

Forsythe, David P. *The Humanitarians: The International Committee of the Red Cross*. New York: Cambridge University Press, 2005. https://doi.org/10.1017/CBO9780511755958

Foss, Phillip O., ed. *Federal Lands Policy*. New York: Greenwood Press, 1987.

Fox, Frank W. *Madison Avenue Goes to War: The Strange Military Career of American Advertising, 1941–1945*. Provo, Utah: Brigham Young University Press, 1975.

Fox, Stephen. *John Muir and His Legacy: The American Conservation Movement*. Boston: Little, Brown and Company, 1981.

Francis, John G., and Richard Ganzel, eds. *Western Public Lands: The Management of Natural Resources in a Time of Declining Federalism*. Totowa, N.J.: Rowan & Allanheld, 1984.

Friedman, Barry D. *Regulation in the Reagan-Bush Era: The Eruption of Presidential Influence*. Pittsburgh: University of Pittsburgh Press, 1995.

Frome, Michael. *Regreening the National Parks*. Tucson: University of Arizona Press, 1992.

Frumkin, Peter, and JoAnn Jastrzab. *Serving Country and Community: Who Benefits from National Service?* Cambridge, Mass.: Harvard University Press, 2010.

Gates, Paul Wallace. *History of Public Land Law Development*. Washington, D.C.: GPO, 1968.

Glenn, Brian J., and Steven M. Teles, eds. *Conservatism and American Political Development*. New York: Oxford University Press, 2009.

Gobster, Paul H., and R. Bruce Hull, eds. *Restoring Nature: Perspectives from the Social Sciences and Humanities*. Washington, D.C.: Island Press, 2000.

Golden, Marissa Martino. *What Motivates Bureaucrats? Politics and Administration during the Reagan Years*. New York: Columbia University Press, 2000. https://doi.org/10.7312/gold10696

Goodwin, Robert, Thomas Kinkade, and Pam Proctor. *Points of Light: A Celebration of the American Spirit of Giving*. New York: Center Street, 2006.

Gordon, Janet, and Diana Reische. *The Volunteer Powerhouse*. New York: Rutledge Press, 1982.

Gordon, Rue E., ed. *1995 Conservation Directory*. 40th ed. Washington, D.C.: National Wildlife Federation, 1995.

Gore, Al. *Earth in the Balance: Ecology and the Human Spirit*. Boston: Houghton Mifflin, 1992.

Gottlieb, Robert. *Forcing the Spring: The Transformation of the American Environmental Movement*. Washington, D.C.: Island Press, 1993.

Gould, Lewis L. *Lady Bird Johnson: Our Environmental First Lady*. Lawrence: University Press of Kansas, 1999.

Gowdy-Wygant, Cecilia. *Cultivating Victory: The Women's Land Army and the Victory Garden Movement*. Pittsburgh: University of Pittsburgh Press, 2013. https://doi.org/10.2307/j.ctt9qh5qk

Graf, William L. *Wilderness Preservation and the Sagebrush Rebellions*. Savage, Md.: Rowman & Littlefield, 1990.

Graham, Otis L., Jr. *Presidents and the American Environment*. Lawrence: University Press of Kansas, 2015.

Greenberg, David. *Republic of Spin: An Inside History of the American Presidency*. New York: W. W. Norton, 2016.

Greene, John Robert. *The Presidency of George H. W. Bush*. 2nd ed. Lawrence: University Press of Kansas, 2015.

Guber, Deborah Lynn. *The Grassroots of a Green Revolution: Polling America on the Environment*. Cambridge, Mass.: MIT Press, 2003. https://doi.org/10.7551/mitpress/3351.001.0001

A Guide to Our Federal Lands. Washington: National Geographic Society, 1984.

Gunn, Selskar M., and Philip S. Platt. *Voluntary Health Agencies: An Interpretive Study*. New York: Ronald Press Company, 1945.

Gunter, Michael M., Jr. *Building the Next Ark: How NGOs Work to Protect Biodiversity*. Hanover, N.H.: Dartmouth College Press, 2004.

Hage, Wayne. *Storm over Rangelands: Private Rights in Federal Lands*. Bellevue, Wash.: Free Enterprise Press, 1989.

Hannaford, Peter. *Presidential Retreats: Where They Went and Why They Went There*. New York: Threshold Editions, 2012.

Hannaford, Peter. *Ronald Reagan and His Ranch: The Western White House, 1981–89*. Bennington, Vt.: Images from the Past, 2002.

Hannibal, Mary Ellen. *Citizen Scientist: Searching for Heroes and Hope in an Age of Extinction*. New York: The Experiment, 2016.

Hartzog, George B., Jr. *Battling for the National Parks*. Mt. Kisco, N.Y.: Moyer Bell, 1988.

Hausknecht, Murray. *The Joiners: A Sociological Description of Voluntary Association Membership in the United States*. New York: Bedminster Press, 1962.

Havlick, David G. *No Place Distant: Roads and Motorized Recreation on America's Public Lands*. Washington, D.C.: Island Press, 2002. https://doi.org/10.1046/j.1526-100X.2003.rec1142.x

Hayashi, Brian Masaru. *Democratizing the Enemy: The Japanese American Internment*. Princeton, N.J.: Princeton University Press, 2004.

Hays, Samuel P. *Beauty, Health, and Permanence: Environmental Politics in the United States, 1955–1985*. New York: Cambridge University Press, 1987. https://doi.org/10.1017/CBO9780511664106

Hays, Samuel P. *A History of Environmental Politics since 1945*. Pittsburgh: University of Pittsburgh Press, 2000. https://doi.org/10.2307/j.ctt6wrcjm

Hirt, Paul W. *The Wired Northwest: The History of Electric Power, 1870s–1970s*. Lawrence: University Press of Kansas, 2012.

Hoberg, George. *Pluralism by Design: Environmental Policy and the American Regulatory State*. New York: Praeger, 1992.

Hoberman, J. *Make My Day: Movie Culture in the Age of Reagan*. New York: New Press, 2019.

Hodel, Donald Paul, and Robert Deitz. *Crisis in the Oil Patch: How America's Energy Industry Is Being Destroyed and What Must Be Done to Save It*. Washington, D.C.: Regnery Publishing, 1993.

Horten, Gerd. *Radio Goes to War: The Cultural Politics of Propaganda during World War II*. Berkeley: University of California Press, 2002. https://doi.org/10.1525/9780520930735

Houser, Sue. *Hot Foot Teddy: The True Story of Smokey Bear*. Evansville, Ind.: M. T. Publishing Company, 2006.

Hoy, Suellen. *Chasing Dirt: The American Pursuit of Cleanliness*. New York: Oxford University Press, 1995.

Jackall, Robert, and Janice M. Hirota. *Image Makers: Advertising, Public Relations, and the Ethos of Advocacy*. Chicago: University of Chicago Press, 2000.

Jackson, Nancy Beth. *The Junior League: 100 Years of Volunteer Service*. New York: Association of Junior Leagues International, 2001.

Jeffords, Susan. *Hard Bodies: Hollywood Masculinity in the Reagan Era*. New Brunswick, N.J.: Rutgers University Press, 1994.

Johnson, Christopher. *This Grand and Magnificent Place: The Wilderness Heritage of the White Mountains*. Durham: University of New Hampshire Press, 2006.

Jones, John Bush. *All-Out for Victory! Magazine Advertising and the World War II Home Front*. Waltham, Mass.: Brandeis University Press, 2009. https://doi.org/10.26812/9781584657682

Jordan, Benjamin René. *Modern Manhood and the Boy Scouts of America: Citizenship, Race, and the Environment, 1910–1930*. Chapel Hill: University of North Carolina Press, 2016. https://doi.org/10.5149/northcarolina/9781469627656.001.0001

Jørgensen, Finn Arne. *Making a Green Machine: The Infrastructure of Beverage Container Recycling*. New Brunswick, N.J.: Rutgers University Press, 2011.

Jubenville, Allan. *Outdoor Recreation Planning*. Philadelphia: W. B. Saunders Co., 1976.

Julyan, Robert. *Hiking to History: A Guide to Off-Road New Mexico Historic Sites*. Albuquerque: University of New Mexico Press, 2016.

Kabaservice, Geoffrey. *Rule and Ruin: The Downfall of Moderation and the Destruction of the Republican Party*. New York: Oxford University Press, 2012.

Keim, Robert P. *A Time in Advertising's Camelot: The Memoirs of a Do-Gooder*. Madison, Conn.: Longview Press, 2002.

Keiter, Robert B. *Keeping Faith with Nature: Ecosystems, Democracy, and America's Public Lands*. New Haven, Conn.: Yale University Press, 2003. https://doi.org/10.12987/yale/9780300092738.001.0001

Keller, Morton, and R. Shep Melnick, eds. *Taking Stock: American Government in the Twentieth Century*. New York: Cambridge University Press, 1999.

Kengor, Paul, and Patricia Clark Doerner. *The Judge: William P. Clark, Ronald Reagan's Top Hand*. San Francisco: Ignatius Press, 2007.

Kennedy, Greg. *An Ontology of Trash: The Disposable and Its Problematic Nature*. Albany: State University of New York Press, 2007.

Kennedy, Robert F., Jr. *Crimes Against Nature: How George W. Bush and His Corporate Pals Are Plundering the Country and Hijacking Our Democracy*. New York: HarperCollins, 2004.

Kimble, James J. *Mobilizing the Home Front: War Bonds and Domestic Propaganda*. College Station: Texas A&M University Press, 2006.

Klyza, Christopher McGrory. *Who Controls Public Lands? Mining, Forestry, and Grazing Policies, 1870–1990*. Chapel Hill: University of North Carolina Press, 1996.

Klyza, Christopher McGrory, and David J. Sousa. *American Environmental Policy: Beyond Gridlock*. Updated and expanded ed. Cambridge, Mass.: MIT Press, 2013.

Knapp, Jeanne M. *Don Belding: A Career of Advertising and Public Service*. Lubbock: Department of Mass Communications, Texas Tech University, 1983.

Kodas, Michael. *Megafire: The Race to Extinguish a Deadly Epidemic of Flame*. Boston: Houghton Mifflin Harcourt, 2017.

Kopper, Philip. *Volunteer! O Volunteer! A Salute to the Smithsonian's Unpaid Legions*. Washington, D.C.: Smithsonian Institution Press, 1983.

Koppes, Clayton R., and Gregory D. Black. *Hollywood Goes to War: How Politics, Profits, and Propaganda Shaped World War II Movies*. New York: Free Press, 1987.

Kosek, Jake. *Understories: The Political Life of Forests in Northern New Mexico*. Durham, N.C.: Duke University Press, 2006. https://doi.org/10.1215/9780822388302

Kouwenhoven, John A. *The Beer Can by the Highway: Essays on What's American about America*. Garden City, N.Y.: Doubleday, 1961.

Krech, Shepard, III. *The Ecological Indian: Myth and History*. New York: W. W. Norton, 1999.

Kruse, Kevin M., and Julian E. Zelizer. *Fault Lines: A History of the United States since 1974*. New York: W. W. Norton, 2019.

Lacey, Michael J., ed. *Government and Environmental Politics: Essays on Historical Developments since World War Two*. Washington, D.C.: Wilson Center Press, 1989.

Ladd, Everett Carll, and Karlyn H. Bowman. *Attitudes toward the Environment: Twenty-Five Years after Earth Day*. Washington, D.C.: AEI Press, 1995.

Laird, Pamela Walker. *Advertising Progress: American Business and the Rise of Consumer Marketing*. Baltimore: Johns Hopkins University Press, 1998.

Landy, Marc K., Marc J. Roberts, and Stephen R. Thomas. *The Environmental Protection Agency: Asking the Wrong Questions*. New York: Oxford University Press, 1990.

Langton, Stuart, ed. *Environmental Leadership: A Sourcebook for Staff and Volunteer Leaders of Environmental Organizations*. Lexington, Mass.: Lexington Books, 1984.

Lash, Jonathan, Katherine Gillman, and David Sheridan. *A Season of Spoils: The Reagan Administration's Attack on the Environment*. New York: Pantheon Books, 1984.

Lawter, William Clifford, Jr. *Smokey Bear 20252: A Biography*. Alexandria, Va.: Lindsay Smith Publishers, 1994.

Layzer, Judith A. *The Environmental Case: Translating Values into Policy*. 3rd ed. Washington, D.C.: CQ Press, 2012.

Layzer, Judith A. *Open for Business: Conservatives' Opposition to Environmental Regulation*. Cambridge, Mass.: MIT Press, 2012. https://doi.org/10.7551/mitpress/8550.001.0001

Lazarus, Richard J. *The Making of Environmental Law*. Chicago: University of Chicago Press, 2004.

Lears, Jackson. *Fables of Abundance: A Cultural History of Advertising in America*. New York: Basic Books, 1994.

Lee, Debbie, and Kathryn Newfont, eds. *The Land Speaks: New Voices at the Intersection of Oral and Environmental History*. New York: Oxford University Press, 2017.

Lee, Mordecai. *Promoting the War Effort: Robert Horton and Federal Propaganda, 1938–1946*. Baton Rouge: Louisiana State University Press, 2012.

Lees, John D., and Michael Turner, eds. *Reagan's First Four Years: A New Beginning?* Manchester, U.K.: Manchester University Press, 1988.

Le Master, Dennis C. *Decade of Change: The Remaking of Forest Service Statutory Authority during the 1970s*. Westport, Conn.: Greenwood Press, 1984.

Leshy, John D. *Debunking Creation Myths about America's Public Lands*. Salt Lake City: University of Utah Press, 2018.

Lester, James P., ed. *Environmental Politics and Policy*. Durham, N.C.: Duke University Press, 1989.

Levantrosser, William, and Rosanna Perotti, eds. *A Noble Calling: Character and the George H. W. Bush Presidency*. Westport, Conn.: Praeger, 2004.

Loomis, John B. *Integrated Public Lands Management: Principles and Applications to National Forests, Parks, Wildlife Refuges, and BLM Lands*. New York: Columbia University Press, 1993.

Lykins, Daniel L. *From Total War to Total Diplomacy: The Advertising Council and the Construction of the Cold War Consensus*. Westport, Conn.: Praeger, 2003.

Manning, Robert E. *Studies in Outdoor Recreation: Search and Research for Satisfaction*. 3rd ed. Corvallis: Oregon State University Press, 2011.

Manning, Robert E., Laura E. Anderson, and Peter R. Pettengill. *Managing Outdoor Recreation: Case Studies in the National Parks*. 2nd ed. Boston: CABI International, 2017. https://doi.org/10.1079/9781786391025.0000

Marchand, Roland. *Advertising the American Dream: Making Way for Modernity, 1920–1940*. Berkeley: University of California Press, 1985. https://doi.org/10.1525/9780520342668

Marchand, Roland. *Creating the Corporate Soul: The Rise of Public Relations and Corporate Imagery in American Big Business*. Berkeley: University of California Press, 1998.

Marshall, Will, and Marc Porter Magee, eds. *The AmeriCorps Experiment and the Future of National Service*. Washington, D.C.: Progressive Policy Institute, 2005.

Mason, David E. *Voluntary Nonprofit Enterprise Management*. New York: Plenum Press, 1984. https://doi.org/10.1007/978-1-4684-4679-1

McAllister, Matthew P., and Emily West, eds. *The Routledge Companion to Advertising and Promotional Culture*. New York: Routledge, 2013. https://doi.org/10.4324/9780203071434

McCarthy, Kathleen D. *American Creed: Philanthropy and the Rise of Civil Society, 1700–1865*. Chicago: University of Chicago Press, 2003. https://doi.org/10.7208/chicago/9780226561998.001.0001

McCarthy, Kathleen D., ed. *Lady Bountiful Revisited: Women, Philanthropy, and Power*. New Brunswick, N.J.: Rutgers University Press, 1990.

McClellan, Harry "Punky." *Remember . . . Only You! A History of Forest Fire Prevention Outdoor Advertising*. Evansville, Ind.: M. T. Publishing Company, 2010.

McCloskey, J. Michael. *In the Thick of It: My Life in the Sierra Club*. Washington, D.C.: Island Press/Shearwater Books, 2005.

McCray, W. Patrick. *Keep Watching the Skies! The Story of Operation Moonwatch and the Dawn of the Space Age*. Princeton, N.J.: Princeton University Press, 2008.

McEvoy, James, III. *The American Public's Concern with the Environment: A Study of Public Opinion*. Davis: Institute of Governmental Affairs, University of California, 1971.

McMillon, Bill, Doug Cutchins, and Anne Geissinger. *Volunteer Vacations: Short-Term Adventures That Will Benefit You and Others*. 11th ed. Chicago: Chicago Review Press, 2012.

Meiners, Roger E., and Bruce Yandle, eds. *Regulation and the Reagan Era: Politics, Bureaucracy, and the Public Interest*. New York: Holmes and Meier, 1989.

Melillo, Wendy. *How McGruff and the Crying Indian Changed America: A History of Iconic Ad Council Campaigns*. Washington, D.C.: Smithsonian Books, 2013.

Melosi, Martin V. *Garbage in the Cities: Refuse, Reform, and the Environment*. Rev. ed. Pittsburgh: University of Pittsburgh Press, 2005. https://doi.org/10.2307/j.ctt5vkf00

Merchant, Carolyn. *Earthcare: Women and the Environment*. New York: Routledge, 1995.

Merchant, Carolyn, ed. *Green Versus Gold: Sources in California's Environmental History*. Washington, D.C.: Island Press, 1998.

Meyer, Jack A., ed. *Meeting Human Needs: Toward a New Public Philosophy*. Washington, D.C.: American Enterprise Institute for Public Policy Research, 1982.

Mikesh, Robert C. *Japan's World War II Balloon Bomb Attacks on North America*. Washington, D.C.: Smithsonian Institution Press, 1973. https://doi.org/10.5479/si.AnnalsFlight.9

Milazzo, Paul Charles. *Unlikely Environmentalists: Congress and Clean Water, 1945–1972*. Lawrence: University Press of Kansas, 2006.

Miles, John C. *Guardians of the Parks: A History of the National Parks and Conservation Association*. Washington, D.C.: Taylor & Francis, 1995.

Miller, Char. *Not So Golden State: Sustainability vs. the California Dream*. San Antonio, Tex.: Trinity University Press, 2016.

Miller, Char. *Public Lands, Public Debates: A Century of Controversy*. Corvallis: Oregon State University Press, 2012.

Mintz, Joel A. *Enforcement at the EPA: High Stakes and Hard Choices*. Austin: University of Texas Press, 1995.

Mittlefehldt, Sarah. *Tangled Roots: The Appalachian Trail and American Environmental Politics*. Seattle: University of Washington Press, 2013.

Mock, James R., and Cedric Larson. *Words That Won the War: The Story of the Committee on Public Information, 1917–1919*. Princeton, N.J.: Princeton University Press, 1939.

Moniz, Amanda B. *From Empire to Humanity: The American Revolution and the Origins of Humanitarianism*. New York: Oxford University Press, 2016. https://doi.org/10.1093/acprof:oso/9780190240356.001.0001

Morris, Andrew J. F. *The Limits of Voluntarism: Charity and Welfare from the New Deal through the Great Society*. New York: Cambridge University Press, 2009.

Morrison, Ellen Earnhardt. *Guardian of the Forest: A History of the Smokey Bear Program*. New York: Vantage Press, 1976.

Musick, Marc A., and John Wilson. *Volunteers: A Social Profile*. Bloomington: Indiana University Press, 2008.

Nash, Roderick, ed. *The American Environment: Readings in the History of Conservation*. Reading, Mass.: Addison-Wesley, 1968.

Nelson, Daniel. *Nature's Burdens: Conservation and American Politics, the Reagan Era to the Present*. Logan: Utah State University Press, 2017. https://doi.org/10.7330/9781607325703

Newman, Kathy M. *Radio Active: Advertising and Consumer Activism, 1935–1947*. Berkeley: University of California Press, 2004.

Nie, Martin. *The Governance of Western Public Lands: Mapping Its Present and Future*. Lawrence: University Press of Kansas, 2008.

Norris, James D. *Advertising and the Transformation of American Society, 1865–1920*. Westport, Conn.: Greenwood Press, 1990.

O'Connell, Brian. *Effective Leadership in Voluntary Organizations: How to Make the Greatest Use of Citizen Service and Influence*. New York: Association Press, 1976.

Oehser, Paul H. *The Smithsonian Institution*. New York: Praeger, 1970.

Orr, David W. *The Last Refuge: Patriotism, Politics, and the Environment in an Age of Terror*. Washington, D.C.: Island Press, 2004.

Ott, J. Steven, and Lisa A. Dicke, eds. *The Nature of the Nonprofit Sector*. 3rd ed. Boulder, Colo.: Westview Press, 2016.

Ottman, Jacquelyn A. *Green Marketing: Opportunity for Innovation*. 2nd ed. Lincolnwood, Ill.: NTC Business Books, 1998.

Paletz, David L., Roberta E. Pearson, and Donald L. Willis. *Politics in Public Service Advertising on Television*. New York: Praeger Publishers, 1977.

Palmer, John L., and Isabel V. Sawhill, eds. *The Reagan Record: An Assessment of America's Changing Domestic Priorities*. Cambridge, Mass.: Ballinger, 1984.

Palmer, Tim, ed. *California's Threatened Environment: Restoring the Dream*. Washington, D.C.: Island Press, 1993.

Papritz, Carew, ed. *100 Watts: The James Watt Memorial Cartoon Collection*. Auburn, Wash.: Khyber Press, 1983.

Pease, Otis. *The Responsibilities of American Advertising: Private Control and Public Influence, 1920–1940*. New Haven, Conn.: Yale University Press, 1958.

Peck, Janice, and Inger L. Stole, eds. *A Moment of Danger: Critical Studies in the History of U.S. Communication since World War II*. Milwaukee, Wis.: Marquette University Press, 2011.

Pendley, William Perry. *Sagebrush Rebel: Reagan's Battle with Environmental Extremists and Why It Matters Today*. Washington, D.C.: Regnery Publishing, 2013.

Pendley, William Perry. *War on the West: Government Tyranny on America's Great Frontier*. Washington, D.C.: Regnery Publishing, 1995.

Pennock, J. Roland, and John W. Chapman, eds. *Voluntary Associations*. New York: Atherton Press, 1969.

Perlstein, Rick. *Reaganland: America's Right Turn, 1976–1980*. New York: Simon & Schuster, 2020.

Perry, James L., and Ann Marie Thomson. *Civic Service: What Difference Does It Make?* Armonk, N.Y.: M. E. Sharpe, 2004.

Peterson, Gene. *Pioneering Outdoor Recreation for the Bureau of Land Management*. McLean, Va.: Public Lands Foundation, 1996.

Peterson, Tarla Rai, ed. *Green Talk in the White House: The Rhetorical Presidency Encounters Ecology*. College Station: Texas A&M University Press, 2004.

Pfiffner, James P. *The Strategic Presidency: Hitting the Ground Running*. Chicago: Dorsey Press, 1988.

Pope, Carl, and Paul Rauber. *Strategic Ignorance: Why the Bush Administration Is Recklessly Destroying a Century of Environmental Progress*. San Francisco: Sierra Club Books, 2004.

Pope, Daniel. *The Making of Modern Advertising*. New York: Basic Books, 1983.

Porter, Glenn, and Harold C. Livesay. *Merchants and Manufacturers: Studies in the Changing Structure of Nineteenth Century Marketing*. Baltimore: Johns Hopkins University Press, 1971.

Portney, Paul R., ed. *Natural Resources and the Environment: The Reagan Approach*. Washington, D.C.: Urban Institute Press, 1984.

Proctor, Tammy M. *Scouting for Girls: A Century of Girl Guides and Girl Scouts*. Santa Barbara, Calif.: Praeger, 2009.

Putnam, Robert D. *Bowling Alone: The Collapse and Revival of American Community*. New York: Simon & Schuster, 2000. https://doi.org/10.1145/358916.361990

Pyne, Stephen J. *Fire in America: A Cultural History of Wildland and Rural Fire*. Seattle: University of Washington Press, 1995. https://doi.org/10.2307/j.ctv550ch1

Pyne, Stephen J. *Here and There: A Fire Survey*. Tucson: University of Arizona Press, 2018.

Pyne, Stephen J. *Tending Fire: Coping with America's Wildland Fires*. Washington, D.C.: Island Press, 2005.

Radford, Jeff. *The Chaco Coal Scandal: The People's Victory over James Watt*. Corrales, N.M.: Rhombus Publishing Company, 1986.

Raphael, Timothy. *The President Electric: Ronald Reagan and the Politics of Performance*. Ann Arbor: University of Michigan Press, 2009. https://doi.org/10.3998/mpub.331702

Rathlesberger, James, ed. *Nixon and the Environment: The Politics of Devastation*. New York: Village Voice, 1972.

Reeves, Richard. *Infamy: The Shocking Story of the Japanese American Internment in World War II*. New York: Henry Holt, 2015.

Reeves, T. Zane. *The Politics of the Peace Corps and VISTA*. Tuscaloosa: University of Alabama Press, 1988.

Reiger, John F. *American Sportsmen and the Origins of Conservation*. 3rd ed. Corvallis: Oregon State University Press, 2001.

A Retrospective of Advertising Council Campaigns: A Half Century of Public Service. New York: Museum of Television & Radio, 1991.

Rettie, Dwight F. *Our National Park System: Caring for America's Greatest Natural and Historic Treasures*. Urbana: University of Illinois Press, 1995.

Rice, Gerard T. *The Bold Experiment: JFK's Peace Corps*. Notre Dame, Ind.: University of Notre Dame Press, 1985.

Ridenour, James M. *The National Parks Compromised: Pork Barrel Politics and America's Treasures*. Merrillville, Ind.: ICS Books, 1994.

Riley, Glenda. *Women and Nature: Saving the "Wild" West*. Lincoln: University of Nebraska Press, 1999.

Riley, Glenda, and Richard W. Etulain. *Presidents Who Shaped the American West*. Norman: University of Oklahoma Press, 2018.

Robinson, Greg. *A Tragedy of Democracy: Japanese Confinement in North America*. New York: Columbia University Press, 2009. https://doi.org/10.7312/robi12922

Roche, Jeff, ed. *The Political Culture of the New West*. Lawrence: University Press of Kansas, 2008.

Rogers, Heather. *Gone Tomorrow: The Hidden Life of Garbage*. New York: New Press, 2005.

Rollins, Peter C., and John E. O'Connor, eds. *Hollywood's Indian: The Portrayal of the Native American in Film*. Expanded ed. Lexington: University Press of Kentucky, 2003.

Rome, Adam. *The Genius of Earth Day: How a 1970 Teach-in Unexpectedly Made the First Green Generation*. New York: Hill and Wang, 2013.

Roney, Jessica Choppin. *Governed by a Spirit of Opposition: The Origins of American Political Practice in Colonial Philadelphia*. Baltimore: Johns Hopkins University Press, 2014.

Rosenbaum, Walter A. *Environmental Politics and Policy*. 2nd ed. Washington, D.C.: CQ Press, 1991.

Rothman, Hal K. *The Greening of a Nation? Environmentalism in the United States since 1945*. Fort Worth, Tex.: Harcourt Brace, 1998.

Russell, Sharman Apt. *Diary of a Citizen Scientist: Chasing Tiger Beetles and Other New Ways of Engaging the World*. Corvallis: Oregon State University Press, 2014.

Rutkow, Eric. *American Canopy: Trees, Forests, and the Making of a Nation*. New York: Scribner, 2012.

Sabin, Paul. *The Bet: Paul Ehrlich, Julian Simon, and Our Gamble over Earth's Future*. New Haven, Conn.: Yale University Press, 2013.

Sagawa, Shirley. *The American Way to Change: How National Service and Volunteers Are Transforming America*. San Francisco: Jossey-Bass, 2010.

Salzman, Ed, ed. *California Environment and Energy: Text and Readings on Contemporary Issues*. Sacramento: California Journal Press, 1980.

Sandage, C. H., ed. *The Promise of Advertising*. Homewood, Ill.: Richard D. Irwin, 1961.

Saphire, David. *Case Reopened: Reassessing Refillable Bottles*. New York: Inform, 1994.

Sauerhaft, Stan, and Chris Atkins. *Image Wars: Protecting Your Company When There's No Place to Hide*. New York: John Wiley & Sons, 1989.

Schaller, Michael. *Reckoning with Reagan: America and Its President in the 1980s*. New York: Oxford University Press, 1992.

Scott, Anne Firor. *Natural Allies: Women's Associations in American History*. Urbana: University of Illinois Press, 1991.

Sellars, Richard West. *Preserving Nature in the National Parks: A History*. New Haven, Conn.: Yale University Press, 1997.

Shabecoff, Philip. *A Fierce Green Fire: The American Environmental Movement*. Rev. ed. Washington, D.C.: Island Press, 2003.

Shafie, David M. *Eleventh Hour: The Politics of Policy Initiatives in Presidential Transitions*. College Station: Texas A&M University Press, 2013.

Shafie, David M. *Presidential Administration and the Environment: Executive Leadership in the Age of Gridlock*. New York: Routledge, 2014. https://doi.org/10.4324/9780203102558

Shanks, Bernard. *This Land Is Your Land: The Struggle to Save America's Public Lands*. San Francisco: Sierra Club Books, 1984.

Short, C. Brant. *Ronald Reagan and the Public Lands: America's Conservation Debate, 1979–1984*. College Station: Texas A&M University Press, 1989.

Siehl, George H. *The Policy Path to the Great Outdoors: A History of the Outdoor Recreation Review Commissions*. Background Study 08-44. Washington, D.C.: Resources for the Future, 2008.

Silverstein, Michael. *The Environmental Economic Revolution: How Business Will Thrive and the Earth Survive in Years to Come*. New York: St. Martin's Press, 1993.

Simon, Julian L., and Herman Kahn, eds. *The Resourceful Earth: A Response to Global 2000*. New York: Basil Blackwell, 1984.

Simon, Ted. *The River Stops Here: How One Man's Battle to Save His Valley Changed the Fate of California*. New York: Random House, 1994.

Skillen, James R. *The Nation's Largest Landlord: The Bureau of Land Management in the American West*. Lawrence: University Press of Kansas, 2009.

Skillen, James R. *This Land Is My Land: Rebellion in the West*. New York: Oxford University Press, 2020. https://doi.org/10.1093/oso/9780197500699.001.0001

Skinner, Kiron K., Annelise Anderson, and Martin Anderson, eds. *Reagan, in His Own Hand*. New York: Free Press, 2001.

Slotkin, Richard. *Gunfighter Nation: The Myth of the Frontier in Twentieth-Century America*. New York: Antheneum, 1992.

Smith, Constance, and Anne Freedman. *Voluntary Associations: Perspectives on the Literature*. Cambridge, Mass.: Harvard University Press, 1972.

Smith, Thomas G. *Green Republican: John Saylor and the Preservation of America's Wilderness*. Pittsburgh: University of Pittsburgh Press, 2006. https://doi.org/10.2307/j.ctt7zw993

Smith, Thomas G. *Stewart L. Udall: Steward of the Land*. Albuquerque: University of New Mexico Press, 2017.

Snow, Donald. *Inside the Environmental Movement: Meeting the Leadership Challenge*. Washington, D.C.: Island Press, 1992.

Snow, Donald, ed. *Voices from the Environmental Movement: Perspectives for a New Era*. Washington, D.C.: Island Press, 1992.

Soden, Dennis L., ed. *The Environmental Presidency*. Albany: State University of New York Press, 1999.

Spezio, Teresa Sabol. *Slick Policy: Environmental and Science Policy in the Aftermath of the Santa Barbara Oil Spill*. Pittsburgh: University of Pittsburgh Press, 2018. https://doi.org/10.2307/j.ctvqhv2d

Spitz, Bob. *Reagan: An American Journey*. New York: Penguin Press, 2018.

Spring, Dawn. *Advertising in the Age of Persuasion: Building Brand America, 1941–1961*. New York: Palgrave Macmillan, 2011. https://doi.org/10.1057/9780230339644

Stanton, Richard L. *Potomac Journey: Fairfax Stone to Tidewater*. Washington, D.C.: Smithsonian Institution Press, 1993.

Stauber, John C., and Sheldon Rampton. *Toxic Sludge Is Good for You: Lies, Damn Lies, and the Public Relations Industry*. Monroe, Maine: Common Courage Press, 1995.

Stearns, Peter N. *Be a Man! Males in Modern Society*. 2nd ed. New York: Holmes & Meier, 1990.

Stebbins, Robert A. *Amateurs, Professionals, and Serious Leisure*. Montreal: McGill-Queens University Press, 1992.

Stole, Inger L. *Advertising at War: Business, Consumers, and Government in the 1940s*. Urbana: University of Illinois Press, 2012. https://doi.org/10.5406/illinois/9780252037122.001.0001

Strasser, Susan. *Satisfaction Guaranteed: The Making of the American Mass Market*. New York: Pantheon Books, 1989.

Sullivan, Robert. *The Meadowlands: Wilderness Adventures at the Edge of a City*. New York: Scribner, 1998.

Swain, Donald C. *Wilderness Defender: Horace M. Albright and Conservation*. Chicago: University of Chicago Press, 1970.

Swift, Ernest. *A Conservation Saga*. Washington, D.C.: National Wildlife Federation, 1967.

Switzer, Jacqueline Vaughn. *Green Backlash: The History and Politics of Environmental Opposition in the U.S.* Boulder, Colo.: Lynne Rienner Publishers, 1997.

Teles, Steven M. *The Rise of the Conservative Legal Movement: The Battle for Control of the Law*. Princeton, N.J.: Princeton University Press, 2008. https://doi.org/10.1515/9781400829699

Thomas, Harold B. *The Background and Beginning of the Advertising Council*. New York: Advertising Council, 1952.

Todd, Anne Marie. *Communicating Environmental Patriotism: A Rhetorical History of the American Environmental Movement*. New York: Routledge, 2013.

Train, Russell E. *Politics, Pollution, and Pandas: An Environmental Memoir*. Washington, D.C.: Island Press/Shearwater Books, 2003.

Turner, James Morton. *The Promise of Wilderness: American Environmental Politics since 1964*. Seattle: University of Washington Press, 2012.

Turner, James Morton, and Andrew C. Isenberg. *The Republican Reversal: Conservatives and the Environment from Nixon to Trump*. Cambridge, Mass.: Harvard University Press, 2018. https://doi.org/10.4324/9780203521694

Udall, Stewart L. *The Quiet Crisis*. New York: Holt, Rinehart and Winston, 1963.

Unger, Nancy C. *Beyond Nature's Housekeepers: American Women in Environmental History*. New York: Oxford University Press, 2012.

Vale, Thomas R. *The American Wilderness: Reflections on Nature Protection in the United States*. Charlottesville: University of Virginia Press, 2005.

Vaughn, Jacqueline, and Hanna J. Cortner. *George W. Bush's Healthy Forests: Reframing the Environmental Debate*. Boulder: University Press of Colorado, 2005.

Vaughn, Jacqueline, and Hanna J. Cortner. *Philanthropy and the National Park Service*. New York: Palgrave Macmillan, 2013. https://doi.org/10.1057/9781137353894

Vaughn, Stephen. *Holding Fast the Inner Lines: Democracy, Nationalism, and the Committee on Public Information*. Chapel Hill: University of North Carolina Press 1980.

Vig, Norman J., and Michael E. Kraft, eds. *Environmental Policy in the 1980s: Reagan's New Agenda*. Washington, D.C.: Congressional Quarterly, 1984.

Vig, Norman J., and Michael E. Kraft, eds. *Environmental Policy in the 1990s: Reform or Reaction?* 3rd ed. Washington, D.C.: CQ Press, 1997.

Vogel, David. *California Greenin': How the Golden State Became an Environmental Leader*. Princeton, N.J.: Princeton University Press, 2018. https://doi.org/10.2307/j.ctvc77k1p

Wallace, Mike. *Mickey Mouse History and Other Essays on American Memory*. Philadelphia: Temple University Press, 1996.

Watkins, T. H. *Righteous Pilgrim: The Life and Times of Harold L. Ickes, 1874–1952*. New York: Henry Holt, 1990.

Watt, James G. *The Courage of a Conservative*. New York: Simon & Schuster, 1985.

Watt, Leilani. *Caught in the Conflict: My Life with James Watt*. With Al Janssen. Eugene, Ore.: Harvest House Publishers, 1984.

Webb, Robert H., and Howard G. Wilshire, eds. *Environmental Effects of Off-Road Vehicles: Impacts and Management in Arid Regions*. New York: Springer-Verlag, 1983. https://doi.org/10.1007/978-1-4612-5454-6

Weber, Samantha, ed. *Protected Areas in a Changing World: Proceedings of the 2013 George Wright Society Conference on Parks, Protected Areas, and Cultural Sites*. Hancock, Mich.: George Wright Society, 2014.

Weisbrod, Burton A. *The Voluntary Nonprofit Sector: An Economic Analysis*. Lexington, Mass.: Lexington Books, 1977.

Weisenfeld, Judith. *African American Women and Christian Activism: New York's Black YWCA, 1905–1945*. Cambridge, Mass.: Harvard University Press, 1997. https://doi.org/10.4159/harvard.9780674862661

Wellock, Thomas R. *Preserving the Nation: The Conservation and Environmental Movements, 1870–2000*. Wheeling, Ill.: Harland Davidson, 2007.

Wenner, Lettie M. *The Environmental Decade in Court*. Bloomington: Indiana University Press, 1982.

Wennersten, John R. *Anacostia: The Death and Life of an American River*. Baltimore: Chesapeake Book Company, 2008.

Whitaker, John C. *Striking a Balance: Environment and Natural Resources Policy in the Nixon-Ford Years*. Washington, D.C.: American Enterprise Institute for Public Policy Research, 1976.

Whitnah, Donald Robert. *A History of the United States Weather Bureau*. Urbana: University of Illinois Press, 1961.

Wiebe, Robert H. *The Search for Order, 1877–1920*. New York: Hill and Wang, 1967.

Wiebe, Robert H. *The Segmented Society: An Introduction to the Meaning of America*. New York: Oxford University Press, 1975.

Wilbur, Ray Lyman, and William Atherton Du Puy. *Conservation in the Department of the Interior*. Washington, D.C.: GPO, 1931.

Williams, Gerald W. *The Forest Service: Fighting for Public Lands*. Westport, Conn.: Greenwood Press, 2007.

Williams, Gerald W. *The U.S. Forest Service in the Pacific Northwest: A History*. Corvallis: Oregon State University Press, 2009.

Williams, Terry Tempest. *The Hour of Land: A Personal Topography of America's National Parks*. New York: Sarah Crichton Books, 2016.

Wilson, Randall K. *America's Public Lands: From Yellowstone to Smokey Bear and Beyond*. Lanham, Md.: Rowman & Littlefield, 2014.

Winkler, Allan M. *The Politics of Propaganda: The Office of War Information, 1942–1945*. New Haven, Conn.: Yale University Press, 1978.

Winks, Robin W. *Laurance S. Rockefeller: Catalyst for Conservation*. Washington, D.C.: Island Press, 1997.

Wolch, Jennifer R. *The Shadow State: Government and Voluntary Sector in Transition*. New York: Foundation Center, 1990.

Wolf, Peter. *Land in America: Its Value, Use, and Control*. New York: Pantheon Books, 1981.

Wood, James Playsted. *The Story of Advertising*. New York: Ronald Press, 1958.

Woodhouse, Keith Makoto. *The Ecocentrists: A History of Radical Environmentalism*. New York: Columbia University Press, 2018. https://doi.org/10.7312/wood16588

Wyckoff, William, and Lary M. Dilsaver. *The Mountainous West: Explorations in Historical Geography*. Lincoln: University of Nebraska Press, 1995.

Yellin, Emily. *Our Mothers' War: American Women at Home and at the Front during World War II*. New York: Free Press, 2004.

Yochim, Michael J. *Yellowstone and the Snowmobile: Locking Horns over National Park Use*. Lawrence: University Press of Kansas, 2009.

Young, Terence. *Heading Out: A History of American Camping*. Ithaca, N.Y.: Cornell University Press, 2017. https://doi.org/10.7591/9781501712838

Zakin, Susan. *Coyotes and Town Dogs: Earth First! and the Environmental Movement*. New York: Viking, 1993.

Zaslowsky, Dyan, and T. H. Watkins. *These American Lands: Parks, Wilderness, and the Public Lands*. Rev. ed. Washington, D.C.: Island Press, 1994.

Zinger, Clem L., Richard Dalsemer, and Helen Magargle. *Environmental Volunteers in America*. Washington, D.C.: National Center for Voluntary Action, 1973.

Zinser, Charles I. *Outdoor Recreation: United States National Parks, Forests, and Public Lands*. New York: John Wiley & Sons, 1995.

JOURNAL ARTICLES AND BOOK CHAPTERS

Adams, David S. "Ronald Reagan's 'Revival': Voluntarism as a Theme in Reagan's Civil Religion." *Sociological Analysis*, 48 (Spring 1987): 17–29. https://www.jstor.org/stable/3711680

Aberbach, Joel D. "Transforming the Presidency: The Administration of Ronald Reagan." In *Ronald Reagan and the 1980s: Perceptions, Policies, Legacies*, ed. Cheryl Hudson and Gareth Davies, pp. 191–207. New York: Palgrave Macmillan, 2008. https://doi.org/10.1057/9780230616196_12

Aleiss, Angela. "Iron Eyes Cody: Wannabe Indian." *Cineaste*, 25, no. 1 (1999): 30–31.

Anderson, Robin. "The 'Crying Indian,' Corporations, and Environmentalism: A Half-Century of Struggle over Environmental Messaging." In *The Routledge Companion to Advertising and Promotional Culture*, ed. Matthew P. McAllister and Emily West, pp. 404–419. New York: Routledge, 2013.

Armitage, Kevin C. "Commercial Indians: Authenticity, Nature, and Industrial Capitalism in Advertising at the Turn of the Twentieth Century." *Michigan Historical Review*, 29 (Fall 2003): 70–95. https://doi.org/10.2307/20174034

Aronczyk, Melissa. "Public Relations, Issue Management, and the Transformation of American Environmentalism, 1948–1992." *Enterprise and Society*, 19 (December 2018): 836–863. https://doi.org/10.1017/eso.2017.69

Ashley, Bob. "'Take Pride in America' Program Back in Action." *RV Business*, 53 (June 2003): 45.

Audette, Rose Marie. "The Bush Men: First Steps on the Environment from the New President, Hopeful Signs and Danger Warnings." *Environmental Action*, 20 (March/April 1989): 12–17.

Babbitt, Bruce. "The Future Environmental Agenda for the United States." *University of Colorado Law Review*, 64, no. 2 (1993): 513–522.

Benson, Etienne S. "A Centrifuge of Calculation: Managing Data and Enthusiasm in Early Twentieth-Century Bird Banding." *Osiris*, 32 (2017): 286–306. https://doi.org/10.1086/694172

Betz, Carter J., Donald B. K. English, and H. Ken Cordell. "Outdoor Recreation Resources." In *Outdoor Recreation in American Life: A National Assessment of Demand and Supply Trends*, H. Ken Cordell, Carter Betz, J. Michael Bowker, Donald B. K. English, Shela H. Mou, John C. Bergstrom, R. Jeff Teasley, Michael A. Tarrant, and John Loomis, pp. 39–182. Champaign, Ill.: Sagamore Publishing, 1999.

Blumm, Michael C. "The Bush Administration's Sweetheart Settlement Policy: A Trojan Horse Strategy for Advancing Commodity Production on Public Lands." *Environmental Law Reporter*, 34 (May 2004): 10397–10420.

Bright, Deborah. "Of Mother Nature and Marlboro Men: An Inquiry into the Cultural Meanings of Landscape Photography." *Exposure*, 23 (Winter 1985): 5–18.

Brough, Aaron R., James E. B. Wilkie, Jingjing Ma, Matthew S. Isaac, and David Gal. "Is Eco-Friendly Unmanly? The Green-Feminine Stereotype and Its Effect on Sustainable Consumption." *Journal of Consumer Research*, 43 (December 2016): 567–582. https://doi.org/10.1093/jcr/ucw044

Buttel, Frederick H., and William L. Flinn. "The Structure of Support for the Environmental Movement, 1968–1970." *Rural Sociology*, 39 (Spring 1974): 56–69.

Calvert, Jerry W. "Party Politics and Environmental Policy." In *Environmental Politics and Policy*, ed. James P. Lester, pp. 158–178. Durham, N.C.: Duke University Press, 1989.

Caplan, Ruth. "From the Director." *Environmental Action*, 20 (January/February 1989): 2.

Cawley, R. McGreggor, and William Chaloupka. "Federal Land Policy: The Conservative Challenge and Environmentalist Response." In *Federal Lands Policy*, ed. Phillip O. Foss, pp. 21–31. New York: Greenwood Press, 1987.

Chamberlin, Silas. "'To Ensure Permanency': Expanding and Protecting Hiking Opportunities in Twentieth-Century Pennsylvania." *Pennsylvania History*, 77 (Spring 2010): 193–216.

Cobb, Tom. "So Long, Smokey." *American Forests*, 81 (August 1975): 30.

Coggins, George Cameron, and Doris K. Nagel. "'Nothing Beside Remains': The Legal Legacy of James G. Watt's Tenure as Secretary of the Interior on Federal Land Law and Policy." *Boston College Environmental Affairs Law Review*, 17 (Spring 1990): 473–550.

"Corporate Advertising and the Environment." *Economic Priorities Report*, 2 (September–October 1971): 1–40.

Cox, J. Robert. "The (Re)Making of the 'Environmental President': Clinton/Gore and the Rhetoric of U.S. Environmental Politics, 1992–1996." In *Green Talk in the White House: The Rhetorical Presidency Encounters Ecology*, ed. Tarla Rai Peterson, pp. 157–175. College Station: Texas A&M University Press, 2004.

Cross, Gary. "Origins of Modern Consumption: Advertising, New Goods, and a New Generation, 1890–1930." In *The Routledge Companion to Advertising and Promotional Culture*, ed. Matthew P. McAllister and Emily West, pp. 11–23. New York: Routledge, 2013.

Cuff, Robert D. "Herbert Hoover, the Ideology of Voluntarism and War Organization during the Great War." *Journal of American History*, 64 (September 1977): 358–372. https://doi.org/10.2307/1901829

Culhane, Paul J. "Sagebrush Rebels in Office: Jim Watt's Land and Water Politics." In *Environmental Policy in the 1980s: Reagan's New Agenda*, ed. Norman J. Vig and Michael E. Kraft, pp. 293–314. Washington, D.C.: Congressional Quarterly, 1984.

Curti, Merle. "American Philanthropy and the National Character." *American Quarterly*, 10 (Winter 1958): 420–437. https://doi.org/10.2307/2710584

Daynes, Byron. "Bill Clinton: Environmental President." In *The Environmental Presidency*, ed. Dennis L. Soden, pp. 259–302. Albany: State University of New York Press, 1999.

Dilsaver, Lary M. "Resource Conflict in the High Sierra." In *The Mountainous West: Explorations in Historical Geography*, William Wyckoff and Lary M. Dilsaver, pp. 281–302. Lincoln: University of Nebraska Press, 1995.

"Directors Announce New Role for NCVA." *Voluntary Action News*, 6 (September/October 1975): 7.

"Don Hodel, President Reagan's Point Man for Parks and Recreation: A Conversation with the Secretary of the Interior." *Parks and Recreation*, 21 (August 1986): 52–58, 64.

Donovan, Geoffrey H., and Thomas C. Brown. "Be Careful What You Wish For: The Legacy of Smokey Bear." *Frontiers in Ecology and the Environment*, 5 (March 2007): 73–79. https://doi.org/10.1890/1540-9295(2007)5[73:BCWYWF]2.0.CO;2

Drake, Brian Allen. "The Skeptical Environmentalist: Senator Barry Goldwater and the Environmental Management State." *Environmental History*, 15 (October 2010): 587–611. https://doi.org/10.1093/envhis/emq086

Dunaway, Finis. "Gas Masks, Pogo, and the Ecological Indian: Earth Day and the Visual Politics of American Environmentalism." *American Quarterly*, 60 (March 2008): 67–99. https://doi.org/10.1353/aq.2008.0008

Dunlap, Riley E., and Rik Scarce. "Poll Trends: Environmental Problems and Protection." *Public Opinion Quarterly*, 55 (Winter 1991): 651–672. https://doi.org/10.1086/269288

Elliott, Jock. "Advertising Agencies in the Public Service." In *A Retrospective of Advertising Council Campaigns: A Half Century of Public Service*, pp. 13–16. New York: Museum of Television & Radio, 1991.

Faich, Ronald G., and Richard P. Gale. "The Environmental Movement: From Recreation to Politics." *Pacific Sociological Review*, 14 (July 1971): 270–287. https://doi.org/10.2307/1388642

Feliciano, D. V. "President Reagan's Cabinet Councils: It's No Secret, Environment Is Second Priority to Natural Resources Development." *Journal (Water Pollution Control Federation)*, 54 (March 1982): 210–212.

Friedman, Gail. "Dumping the Pump: Bucks County, Pennsylvania, Community Activism and Eco-Politics in the Age of Reagan." *Pennsylvania History*, 85 (Summer 2018): 299–332. https://doi.org/10.5325/pennhistory.85.3.0299

Fuller-Bennett, Harald, and Iris Velez. "Woodsy Owl at 40." *Forest History Today*, 18 (Spring 2012): 22–27.

Gamm, Gerald, and Robert D. Putnam. "The Growth of Voluntary Associations in America, 1840–1940." *Journal of Interdisciplinary History*, 29 (April 1999): 511–557. https://doi.org/10.1162/002219599551804

Ganzel, Richard. "Maximizing Public Land Resource Values." In *Western Public Lands: The Management of Natural Resources in a Time of Declining Federalism*, ed. John G. Francis and Richard Ganzel, pp. 129–148. Totowa, N.J.: Rowan & Allanheld, 1984.

Getches, David H. "The Legacy of the Bush II Administration in Natural Resources: A Work in Progress." *Ecology Law Quarterly*, 32, no. 2 (2005): 235–248.

Gilbert, Bil. "Where There's Smokey, There's Fire." *Sports Illustrated*, 36 (12 June 1972): 88–92, 94, 97, 100–102, 104.

Gillroy, John M., and Robert Y. Shapiro. "The Polls: Environmental Protection." *Public Opinion Quarterly*, 50 (1986): 270–279. https://doi.org/10.1086/268981

Goldberg, Robert A. "The Western Hero in Politics: Barry Goldwater, Ronald Reagan, and the Rise of the American Conservation Movement." In *The Political Culture of the New West*, ed. Jeff Roche, pp. 13–50. Lawrence: University Press of Kansas, 2008.

Goldin, Milton. "Ronald Reagan and the Commercialization of Giving." *Journal of American Culture*, 13 (Fall 1990): 31–36. https://doi.org/10.1111/j.1542-734X.1990.1303_31.x

"Good Sam Leads the Way with Take Pride Program." *Highways*, 38 (March 2004): 10.

Gregg, Frank. "Public Land Policy: Controversial Beginnings for the Third Century." In *Government and Environmental Politics: Essays on Historical Developments since World War Two*, ed. Michael J. Lacey, pp. 141–177. Washington, D.C.: Wilson Center Press, 1989.

Grese, Robert E., Rachel Kaplan, Robert L. Ryan, and Jane Buxton. "Psychological Benefits of Volunteering in Stewardship Programs." In *Restoring Nature: Perspectives from the Social Sciences and Humanities*, ed. Paul H. Gobster and R. Bruce Hull, pp. 265–280. Washington, D.C.: Island Press, 2000.

Griffith, Robert. "The Selling of America: The Advertising Council and American Politics, 1942–1960." *Business History Review*, 57 (Autumn 1983): 388–412. https://doi.org/10.2307/3114050

Gross, Rachel. "From Buckskin to Gore-Tex: Consumption as a Path to Mastery in Twentieth-Century American Wilderness Recreation." *Enterprise and Society*, 19 (December 2018): 826–835. https://doi.org/10.1017/eso.2018.95

Hall, Peter Dobkin. "A Historical Overview of Philanthropy, Voluntary Associations, and Nonprofit Organizations in the United States, 1600–2000." In *The Nonprofit Sector: A Research Handbook*, 2nd. ed., ed. Walter W. Powell and Richard Steinberg, pp. 32–65. New Haven, Conn.: Yale University Press, 2006.

Hanshew, Annie. "Sky-Fighters of the Forest: Conscientious Objectors, African American Paratroopers, and the US Forest Service Smokejumping Program in World War II." In *The Land Speaks: New Voices at the Intersection of Oral and Environmental History*, ed. Debbie Lee and Kathryn Newfont, pp. 175–192. New York: Oxford University Press, 2017.

Hartwig, Bill. "Volunteers Vital to Refuges." *Wildlife Refuge Magazine*, 1 (Autumn 2005): 19.

Hendee, John C. "Membership in Conservation Groups and Outdoor Clubs." In *The Forest Recreation Symposium*, ed. E. vH. Larson, pp. 123–127. Upper Darby, Pa.: Northeastern Forest Experiment Station, Forest Service, U.S. Department of Agriculture,1971.

Hendee, John C., and Randall C. Pitstick. "The Growth of Environmental and Conservation-Related Organizations: 1989-1991." *Renewable Resources Journal*, 10 (Summer 1992): 6–19.

Hodel, Donald. "Foreword." In *Audubon Wildlife Report 1986*, pp. xv–xvi. New York: National Audubon Society, 1986.

Hoffman, Paul G. "Introduction." In *The Promise of Advertising*, ed. C. H. Sandage, p. ix–xiii. Homewood, Ill.: Richard D. Irwin, 1961.

Holden, Constance. "Public's Fear of Watt Is Environmentalists' Gain." *Science*, 212 (24 April 1981): 422. https://doi.org/10.1126/science.212.4493.422-a

Holden, Constance. "The Reagan Years: Environmentalists Tremble." *Science*, 210 (28 November 1980): 988–989. https://doi.org/10.1126/science.210.4473.988

Howard, Bruce. "The Advertising Council: Selling Lies." *Ramparts*, 13 (December 1974–January 1975): 25–26, 28–32.

Howlett, Michael, and Rebecca Raglon. "Constructing the Environmental Spectacle: Green Advertisements and the Greening of the Corporate Image, 1910–1990." *Environmental History Review*, 16 (Winter 1992): 53–68.

Hughes, Melinda. "NWF Becomes a Partner of the Take Pride in America Initiative." *Volunteer Spirit*, 14 (July/August 2006): 1.

"Interior Department and State Launch Take Pride in Florida Project to Help Hurricane Ravaged Public Lands." *CEQ E-Notes*, 2, no. 42 (27 October 2004).

Kellner, Douglas. "Presidential Politics: The Movie." *American Behavioral Scientist*, 46 (December 2002): 467–486. https://doi.org/10.1177/0002764202238058

King, Samantha. "Offensive Lines: Sport-State Synergy in an Era of Perpetual War." *Cultural Studies ↔ Critical Methodologies*, 8 (November 2008): 527–539. https://doi.org/10.1177/1532708608321575

Kraft, Michael E. "A New Environmental Policy Agenda: The 1980 Presidential Campaign and Its Aftermath." In *Environmental Policy in the 1980s: Reagan's New Agenda*, ed. Norman J. Vig and Michael E. Kraft, pp. 29–50. Washington, D.C.: Congressional Quarterly, 1984.

Kraft, Michael E. "U.S. Environmental Policy and Politics: From the 1960s to the 1990s." *Journal of Policy History*, 12, no. 1 (2000): 17–42. https://doi.org/10.1353jph.2000.0006

LaFaille, Tom. "The Ad Council: Gatekeepers for PSA's." *Access*, no. 34 (17 May 1976): 17–19.

Langton, Stuart. "The New Voluntarism." *Nonprofit and Voluntary Sector Quarterly*, 10 (January 1981): 7–20. https://doi.org/10.1177/089976408101000104

Lanoue, David J. "Retrospective and Schematic Assessments of Presidential Candidates: The Environment and the 1988 Election." *Polity*, 25 (Summer 1993): 547–563. https://doi.org/10.2307/3235121

Layzer, Judith A. "Environmental Policy from 1980 to 2008: The Politics of Prevention." In *Conservatism and American Political Development*, ed. Brian J. Glenn and Steven M. Teles, pp. 223–260. New York: Oxford University Press, 2009.

Lazerson, Barbara Hunt. "Spokes-Terms." *American Speech*, 70 (Spring 1995): 107–110. https://doi.org/10.2307/455877

Leshy, John D. "The Babbitt Legacy at the Department of the Interior: A Preliminary View." *Environmental Law*, 31 (2001): 199–227. https://doi.org/10.2139/ssrn.1600431

Leshy, John D. "Natural Resource Policy." In *Natural Resources and the Environment: The Reagan Approach*, ed. Paul R. Portney, pp. 13–46. Washington, D.C.: Urban Institute Press, 1984.

Lewis, Dylan. "Unpaid Protectors: Volunteerism and the Diminishing Role of Federal Responsibility in the National Park Service." In *Protected Areas in a Changing World: Proceedings of the 2013 George Wright Society Conference on Parks, Protected Areas, and Cultural Sites*, ed. Samantha Weber, pp. 95–100. Hancock, Mich.: George Wright Society, 2014.

Lewis, James G. "Smokey Bear: From Idea to Icon." *Forest History Today*, 24 (Spring/Fall 2018): 13–16.

Lock, Reinier. "Interview: Donald P. Hodel." *Natural Resources and Environment*, 2 (Spring 1986): 40–43, 75–76.

Lorenz, Jack. "Developing the Complete Volunteer." In *Voices from the Environmental Movement: Perspectives for a New Era*, ed. Donald Snow, pp. 205–216. Washington, D.C.: Island Press, 1992.

Lynch, F. Bradley. "A Short History of the Advertising Council." In *A Retrospective of Advertising Council Campaigns: A Half Century of Public Service*, pp. 6–9. New York: Museum of Television & Radio, 1991.

Macleod, David. "Original Intent: Establishing the Creed and Control of Boy Scouting in the United States." In *Scouting Frontiers: Youth and the Scout Movement's First Century*, ed. Nelson R. Block and Tammy M. Proctor, pp. 13–27. Newcastle upon Tyne, U.K.: Cambridge Scholars, 2009.

Manchester, Albert E. "An American Original." *American Forests*, 87 (October 1981): 16–17, 47–48.

Mander, Jerry. "EcoPornography: One Year and Nearly a Billion Dollars Later, Advertising Owns Ecology." *Communication Arts Magazine*, 14, no. 2 (1972): 45–47, 54–55.

Marchand, Roland. "The Fitful Career of Advocacy Advertising: Political Protection, Client Cultivation, and Corporate Morale." *California Management Review*, 29 (Winter 1987): 128–156. https://doi.org/10.2307/41165244

Martin, Emilie. "Student Volunteers in the National Parks and Forests." *National Parks and Conservation Magazine*, 47 (February 1973): 24–27.

Matthews, Christopher J. "Your Host, Ronald Reagan: From G.E. Theater to the Desk in the Oval Office." *New Republic*, 190 (26 March 1984): 15–18.

Mattoon, John. "How the Johnny Horizon Program Came to Be." In *Pioneering Outdoor Recreation for the Bureau of Land Management*, by Gene Peterson, pp. 60–62. McLean, Va.: Public Lands Foundation, 1996.

McDowell, Jeanne. "The Greening of Hollywood." *Time*, 133 (12 June 1989): 76.

McPhee, John. "Balloons of War." *New Yorker*, 71 (29 January 1996): 52–60.

Melnick, R. Shep. "Risky Business: Government and the Environment after Earth Day." In *Taking Stock: American Government in the Twentieth Century*, ed. Morton Keller and R. Shep Melnick, pp. 156–184. New York: Cambridge University Press, 1999.

Mervin, David. "An Evaluation of the Presidency of George Bush." In *A Noble Calling: Character and the George H. W. Bush Presidency*, ed. William Levantrosser and Rosanna Perotti, pp. 101–118. Westport, Conn.: Praeger, 2004.

Miller, Char. "In the Sweat of Our Brow: Citizenship in American Domestic Practice during WWII—Victory Gardens." *Journal of American Culture*, 26 (September 2003): 395–409. https://doi.org/10.1111/1542-734X.00100

Miller, James Nathan. "What Really Happened at EPA." *Reader's Digest*, 123 (July 1983): 59–64.

Miller-Rushing, Abraham, Richard Primack, and Rick Bonney. "The History of Public Participation in Ecological Research." *Frontiers in Ecology and the Environment*, 10 (August 2012): 285–290. https://doi.org/10.1890/110278

Mitzman, Barry. "Abusing Public Power." *Environmental Action*, 7 (24 April 1976): 7–11.

Nash, Roderick. "The Potential of Conservation History." In *The American Environment: Readings in the History of Conservation*, ed. Roderick Nash, pp. ix–xiv. Reading, Mass.: Addison-Wesley, 1968.

"National Congress on Volunteerism and Citizenship." *Voluntary Action News*, 6 (September/October 1975): 2.

Nelson, Robert H. "Privatization of Federal Lands: What Did Not Happen." In *Regulation and the Reagan Era: Politics, Bureaucracy, and the Public Interest*, ed. Roger E. Meiners and Bruce Yandle, pp. 132–165. New York: Holmes and Meier, 1989.

"'NRPA Members Are Engaged in a Very Important Enterprise': Part Two of an Interview with Interior Secretary Don Hodel." *Parks and Recreation*, 21 (September 1986): 66–72.

O'Toole, John. "The Advertising Council's Oldest Customer." In *A Retrospective of Advertising Council Campaigns: A Half Century of Public Service*, pp. 24–27. New York: Museum of Television & Radio, 1991.

Pimlott, J. A. R. "Public Service Advertising: The Advertising Council." *Public Opinion Quarterly*, 12 (Summer 1948): 209–219. https://doi.org/10.1086/265942

Pope, Daniel. "The Advertising Industry and World War I." *The Public Historian*, 2 (Spring 1980): 4–25. https://doi.org/10.2307/3376987

Portney, Paul R. "Natural Resources and the Environment: More Controversy Than Change." In *The Reagan Record: An Assessment of America's Changing Domestic Priorities*, ed. John L. Palmer and Isabel V. Sawhill, pp. 141–175. Cambridge, Mass.: Ballinger, 1984.

Prausa, Robert L. "Multiple-Use Management for Recreation in the East." In *The Forest Recreation Symposium*, ed. E. vH. Larson, pp. 96–102. Upper Darby, Pa.: Northeastern Forest Experiment Station, Forest Service, U.S. Department of Agriculture, 1971.

Reilly, William K. "The New Environmental Policy: Preventing Pollution." *Domestic Affairs*, 1 (Summer 1991): 73–98.

Rotolo, Thomas. "Trends in Voluntary Association Participation." *Nonprofit and Voluntary Sector Quarterly*, 28 (June 1999): 199–212. https://doi.org/10.1177/0899764099282005

"Rules for Nominations for the National Volunteer Awards for 1975." *Voluntary Action News*, 6 (September/October 1975): 14.

Schindler-Rainman, Eva. "Trends and Changes in the Volunteer World." *Nonprofit and Voluntary Sector Quarterly*, 11 (April 1982): 157–163. https://doi.org/10.1177/089976408201100216

Schlesinger, Arthur M. "Biography of a Nation of Joiners." *American Historical Review*, 50 (October 1944): 1–25. https://doi.org/10.2307/1843565

Schneider, Gary. "From the Publisher." *Inspire Your World: Celebrating the People, Companies and Causes That Inspire Us to Give Back*, 1 (April/May 2004): 4.

Schulman, Bruce J. "The Privatization of Everyday Life: Public Policy, Public Services, and Public Space in the 1980s." In *Living in the Eighties*, ed. Gil Troy and Vincent J. Cannato, pp. 167–180. New York: Oxford University Press, 2009.

Scott, Anne Firor. "Women's Voluntary Associations: From Charity to Reform." In *Lady Bountiful Revisited: Women, Philanthropy, and Power*, ed. Kathleen D. McCarthy, pp. 35–54. New Brunswick, N.J.: Rutgers University Press, 1990.

"Secretary Norton Announces the Designation of Estes Park, Colo. as a Take Pride in America City." *CEQ E-Notes*, 2, no. 30 (28 July 2004).

"Secretary Norton Commends 2004 National Take Pride in America Award Winners at Department of Interior Ceremony." *CEQ E-Notes*, 2, no. 37 (22 September 2004).

Short, C. Brant. "Conservation Reconsidered: Environmental Politics, Rhetoric, and the Reagan Revolution." In *Green Talk in the White House: The Rhetorical Presidency Encounters Ecology*, ed. Tarla Rai Peterson, pp. 134–150. College Station: Texas A&M University Press, 2004.

Sinclair, Bruce. "Gustavus A. Hyde, Professor Espy's Volunteers, and the Development of Systematic Weather Observation." *Bulletin of the American Meteorological Society*, 46 (December 1965): 779–784. https://doi.org/10.1175/1520-0477-46.12.779

Skocpol, Theda, Marshall Ganz, and Ziad Munson. "A Nation of Organizers: The Institutional Origins of Civic Volunteerism in the United States." *American Political Science Review*, 94 (September 2000): 527–546. https://doi.org/10.2307/2585829

Smith, J. Morgan. "The Story of Smokey Bear." *Forestry Chronicle*, 32 (June 1956): 183–188. https://doi.org/10.5558/tfc32183-2

Sousa, David J., and Christopher McGrory Klyza. "'Whither We Are Trending': Interrogating the Retrenchment Narrative in U.S. Environmental Policy." *Political Science Quarterly*, 132 (September 2017): 467–494. https://doi.org/10.1002/polq.12659

Staehle, Marjory Houston. "He Gave Us Smokey the Bear." *American Legion Magazine*, 102 (January 1977): 10, 48.

Stanfield, Rochelle L. "Tilting on Development: Interior Secretary Donald P. Hodel." *National Journal*, 19 (7 February 1987): 313–318.

Stine, Jeffrey K. "Environmental Policy during the Carter Presidency." In *The Carter Presidency: Policy Choices in the Post-New Deal Era*, ed. Gary M Fink and Hugh Davis Graham, pp. 179–201. Lawrence: University Press of Kansas, 1998.

Stine, Jeffrey K. "Natural Resources and Environmental Policy." In *The Reagan Presidency: Pragmatic Conservatism and Its Legacies*, ed. W. Elliot Brownlee and Hugh Davis Graham, pp. 233–256. Lawrence: University Press of Kansas, 2003.

Stole, Inger L. "Consumer Protection in Historical Perspective: The Five-Year Battle over Federal Regulation of Advertising, 1933 to 1938." *Mass Communication and Society*, 3, no. 4 (2000): 351–372. https://doi.org/10.1207/S15327825MCS0304_02

Stole, Inger L. "Persuasion, Patriotism and PR: US Advertising in the Second World War." *Journal of Historical Research in Marketing*, 5, no. 1 (2013): 27–46. https://doi.org/10.1108/17557501311293343

Stole, Inger L. "Politics as Patriotism: Advertising and Consumer Activism during World War II." In *A Moment of Danger: Critical Studies in the History of U.S. Communication since*

World War II, ed. Janice Peck and Inger L. Stole, pp. 13–34. Milwaukee, Wis.: Marquette University Press, 2011.

Strand, Ginger. "The Crying Indian: How an Environmental Icon Helped Sell Cans—and Sell Out Environmentalism." *Orion*, 27 (November/December 2008): 20–27.

Stumpf, Gary. "Cultural Resource Management in Arizona." In *Opportunity and Challenge: The Story of BLM*, James Muhn and Hanson R. Stuart, p. 252. Washington, D.C.: GPO, 1988.

Sutton, Victoria. "The George W. Bush Administration and the Environment." *Western New England Law Review*, 25, no. 2 (2003): 221–242.

"Taking Pride in the Dunes." *In the Dunes*, 6 (May 2006): 19.

Tatalovich, Raymond, and Mark J. Wattier. "Opinion Leadership: Elections, Campaigns, Agenda Setting, and Environmentalism." In *The Environmental Presidency*, ed. Dennis L. Soden, pp. 147–187. Albany: State University of New York Press, 1999.

Thompson, Barton H., Jr. "Conservative Environmental Thought: The Bush Administration and Environmental Policy." *Ecology Law Quarterly*, 32, no. 2 (2005): 307–347.

Train, Russell E. "The Environmental Record of the Nixon Administration." *Presidential Studies Quarterly*, 26 (Winter 1996): 185–196.

Turner, Michael. "The Reagan White House, the Cabinet, and the Bureaucracy." In *Reagan's First Four Years: A New Beginning?*, ed. John D. Lees and Michael Turner, pp. 39–67. Manchester, U.K.: Manchester University Press, 1988.

Vig, Norman J. "Presidential Leadership and the Environment: From Reagan to Clinton." In *Environmental Policy in the 1990s: Reform or Reaction?* 3rd. ed., ed. Norman J. Vig and Michael E. Kraft, pp. 95–118. Washington, D.C.: CQ Press, 1997.

Viscusi, W. Kip. "The Misspecified Agenda: The 1980s Reforms of Health, Safety, and Environmental Regulation." In *American Economic Policy in the 1980s*, ed. Martin Feldstein, pp. 453–504. Chicago: University of Chicago Press, 1994.

"Vols Help Smokey the Bear." *Voluntary Action News*, 3 (November 1972): 5.

Wade, Bill. "A New Tragedy for the Commons: The Threat of Privatization to National Parks (and Other Public Lands)." *George Wright Forum*, 22, no. 2 (2005): 61–67.

Wallace, Mike. "Ronald Reagan and the Politics of History." In *Mickey Mouse History and Other Essays on American Memory*, pp. 249–268. Philadelphia: Temple University Press, 1996.

Warshaw, Shirley Anne. "White House Control of Domestic Policy Making: The Reagan Years." *Public Administration Review*, 55 (May/June 1995): 247–252. https://doi.org/10.2307/3110243

"Watt . . . We Worry!" *Mad*, no. 234 (October 1982): back cover.

Williams, Ted. "The Metamorphosis of Keep America Beautiful." *Audubon*, 92 (March 1990): 124–134.

Wilson, John. "Volunteering." *Annual Review of Sociology*, 26 (2000): 215–240. https://doi.org/10.1146/annurev.soc.26.1.215

Wojtowciz, Carol. "Philadelphia, 1736: Ben Franklin Organizes His Volunteers." *Firehouse*, 3 (April 1978): 53, 56, 72.

Yang, Mei-ling. "Selling Patriotism: The Representation of Women in Magazine Advertising in World War II." *American Journalism*, 12 (Summer 1995): 304–320. https://doi.org/10.1080/08821127.1995.10731745

Young, Dannagal Goldthwaite. "Sacrifice, Consumption, and the American Way of Life: Advertising and Domestic Propaganda during World War II." *Communication Review*, 8 (March 2005): 27–52. https://doi.org/10.1080/10714420590917352

NEWSPAPER ARTICLES

Albuquerque Journal. "Goldie Bear Heads for Red-Carpet U.S. Capital Reception, 'Wedding'." 8 September 1962.

Barker, Karlyn. "Ad Rules Don't Apply for NFL Bash." *Washington Post*, 4 September 2003.

Barker, Karlyn. "Canal, Towpath Flood Damage Set at $9.3 Million." *Washington Post*, 15 November 1985.

Barker, Karlyn. "NFL Tries Play for Fans on Mall." *Washington Post*, 31 August 2003.

Barr, Stephen. "Advisory Panels Nosing Out: Tea Sniffers and Others Bow to Budget Agency's Thriftiness." *Washington Post*, 31 March 1994.

Boyd, Gerald M. "Reagan Is Reported Set to Name Energy Secretary to Interior Post." *New York Times*, 10 January 1985.

Bukro, Casey. "Harbor Taints Dukakis' Record on Pollution." *Chicago Tribune*, 2 September 1988.

Callahan, David. "The Billionaires' Park." *New York Times*, 1 December 2014.

Cowgill, Pete. "Some Fires Help, Not Hurt, Forests." *Arizona Daily Star*, 11 November 1976.

Cronon, William. "When the G.O.P. Was Green." *New York Times*, 8 January 2001.

Cumberland (Md.) *News*. "Stanton Will Address Society during Dinner." 15 October 1986.

DeSilva, Bruce, and Charles F. J. Morse. "Bush Promises Cleanup: Candidate Decries Pollution in Sound and Boston Harbor." *Hartford Courant*, 2 September 1988.

Dougherty, Philip H. "Advertising: Doner Gets 'Good Guys' for Pride in America." *New York Times*, 10 April 1987.

Evening Star (Washington, D.C.). "Volunteers Pour In: 'We Need You' Ads Work." 22 January 1973.

Fisher, Eric. "Live Show Kicks Off NFL Year." *Washington Times*, 4 September 2003.

Francis, David R. "Encouraging Volunteers: A Thousand Points of Light to Shine." *Christian Science Monitor*, 7 November 1989.

Gay, Lance. "U.S. Parks Director Calls System Too Big." *Washington Star*, 1 February 1981.

Gilford, Jim. "Helping Clean Up the Canal." *Frederick* (Md.) *Post*, 12 February 1986.

Goldstein, Amy, and Lois Romano. "Earth Day's Point, Counterpoint." *Washington Post*, 23 April 2004.

Goodwin, Derek V. "Raiders of the Sacred Sites." *New York Times*, 7 December 1986.

Greene, Deni. "To the Beaches! Oil Rigs Are Coming!" *New York Times*, 19 July 1982.

Greenhouse, Steven. "The 1992 Campaign: The Economy; Despite Recession's End, Bush May Face Unusually Harsh Public Judgment." *New York Times*, 11 May 1992.

Hamilton, John Maxwell. "How Our Information Wars Began—in WWI." *Washington Post*, 3 August 2014.

Harris, David. "Asking Too Much of the 'Spirit of Volunteerism.'" *New York Times*, 10 October 1981.

Harris, Lyle V. "Volunteers Help Clean C&O Canal." *Washington Post*, 31 July 1986.

Hornaday, Ann. "America Loves a Vigilante, Until We Meet One." *Washington Post*, 8 April 2012.

Isaacs, Stan. "Smokey the Bear Is Just Like Tom Seaver." *Newsday*, 4 February 1970.

Jehl, Douglas. "Norton Record Often at Odds with Laws She Would Enforce." *New York Times*, 13 January 2001.

Johnson, Kirk. "Bill Opening Wilderness to Biking Also Opens Debate on Conservation." *New York Times*, 20 August 2016.

Johnson, Steve. "Make That Smokey Bear." *Chicago Tribune*, 30 August 1990.

King, Wayne. "New Ad Drive: Call It a Fistful of Leaves." *New York Times*, 10 April 1987.

Landler, Mark. "At White House Homecoming, Former President's 'Points of Light' Shine On." *New York Times*, 16 July 2013.

Larmer, Paul. "Norton Departs: A Look at Interior's Counterrevolution—And Its Unintended Consequences." *High Country News*, 3 April 2006.

Levy, Claudia. "Stretch of Canal Closed for Cleanup." *Washington Post*, 6 March 1986.

Lindsey, Robert. "U.S. Oil Lease Sale in Coast's Waters Blocked in Court." *New York Times*, 28 July 1981.

Los Angeles Times. "The Meaning of the Victory of Bill Clinton and Al Gore: Agonized by Recession and Gridlock, America Asks for Change." 4 November 1992.

Montague, Zach. "Manuel Luján Jr., Former Congressman and Interior Secretary, Is Dead at 90." *New York Times*, 27 April 2019.

Montgomery, David. "The NFL's New Turf." *Washington Post*, 1 September 2003.

New York Times. 1947. "Ad Council Plans Campaign." 24 January.

New York Times. 1973. "Lists of White House 'Enemies' and Memorandums Relating to Those Named." 28 June.

New York Times. 1982. "Watt Is Slowed on Oil Leasing." 11 October.

New York Times. 1982. "Watt Unleashes Oil Explorers, to Some Dismay." 25 July.

New York Times. 1983. "To Interior, a One-Way Secretary." 15 October.

New York Times. 1983. "Watt Says Foes Want Centralization of Power." 21 January.

New York Times. 1983. "What James Watt Said—and Did." 11 October.

New York Times. 1993. "Bush's 'Points of Light' Volunteerism Burns On, with Clinton's Aid." 22 April.

New York Times. 2006. "Gale Norton Resigns." 12 March.

Oakes, John B. "Clark's Low Wattage." *New York Times*, 18 October 1983.

Pasztor, Andy. "Reagan Policies Spur Big Revival of the Environmental Movement." *Wall Street Journal*, 9 August 1982.

Pasztor, Andy. "White House Acts to Change Image on Environment." *Wall Street Journal*, 11 March 1983.

Peterson, Bill. "In Boston, Bush Sails into Dukakis." *Washington Post*, 2 September 1988.

Phillips, Harry A. "Smokey Bear Dies: Creator from Norwich." *Bulletin* (Norwich, Conn.), 14 November 1976.

Radcliffe, Donnie. "Honoring Deeds Well Done." *Washington Post*, 16 April 1982.

Randolph, Eleanor. "'Hook and Bullet Boys' vs. Environmentalists: Watt Courts Sportsmen to Back Policies." *Los Angeles Times*, 10 June 1981.

Rich, Frank. "How Dirty Harry Turned Commie." *New York Times*, 13 February 2005.

Robbins, Jim. "Bears and Bikers Meet in Uncharted Territory." *New York Times*, 8 October 2019.

Rogers, Paul. "Clint Eastwood on Parks and Recreation Commission." *San Jose Mercury News*, 2 December 2001.

Rosenthal, Jack. "Nixon Submits Plan to Merge 9 Volunteer Programs." *New York Times*, 25 March 1971.

Sabin, Paul. "The Decline of Republican Environmentalism." *Boston Globe*, 31 August 2013.

Shabecoff, Philip. "Environmental Groups Angered by Reagan Choice for Interior Job." *New York Times*, 14 October 1983.

Shabecoff, Philip. "Environmentalism Back in Spotlight as Activists and Administration Battle." *New York Times*, 19 September 1982.

Shabecoff, Philip. "Environmentalists Say Either Bush or Dukakis Will Be an Improvement." *New York Times*, 1 September 1988.

Shabecoff, Philip. "Many Are Divided on Watt's Legacy." *New York Times*, 12 October 1983.

Shabecoff, Philip. "Nearing Complete Renovation of Interior Department Rules." *New York Times*, 23 January 1983.

Shabecoff, Philip. "Politics and the E.P.A. Crisis: Environment Emerges as a Mainstream Issue." *New York Times*, 29 April 1983.

Shabecoff, Philip. "Questions Arise Not Just over Watt's Words." *New York Times*, 2 October 1983.

Shabecoff, Philip. "Wildlife Unit Asks Watt's Ouster." *New York Times*, 15 July 1981.

Shabecoff, Philip. "Working Profile: Donald P. Hodel; Watt's Goals at Interior, but in a Different Style." *New York Times*, 3 March 1986.

Smith, Marie. "Volunteer Plan." *Washington Post*, 7 January 1970.

Smith, Terence. "Peace Corps: Alive but Not So Well." *New York Times*, 25 December 1977.

Soskis, Benjamin. "Republicans Used to Celebrate Voluntarism and Service. What Happened?" *Washington Post*, 3 August 2018.

Toner, Robin. "Bush, in Enemy Waters, Says Rival Hindered Cleanup of Boston Harbor." *New York Times*, 2 September 1988.

Troxell, Ted. "About 20,000 Scouts to Spearhead C&O Canal Park Cleanup." *Sunday Times* (Cumberland, Md.), 2 March 1986.

Turan, Kenneth. "Smokey's Enduring Appeal." *Washington Post*, 10 November 1976.

Wald, Matthew L. "Key Player for President Is Resigning as Head of the Interior Dept." *New York Times*, 11 March 2006.

Washington Post. 2003. "Marketing the Mall." 3 September.

Washington Post. 2003. "Pitching in for Parks." 19 April.

Washington Post. 2018. "National Mall and Memorial Park's Volunteers-In-Parks." 4 January.

Weinraub, Bernard. "The Shuttle Explosion: Reagan Postpones State of Union Speech." *New York Times*, 29 January 1986.

Weisman, Steven R. "Reagan, Assailing Critics, Defends His Environmental Policy as 'Sound'." *New York Times*, 12 June 1983.

Yardley, William. "In State Parks, the Sharpest Ax Is the Budget's." *New York Times*, 7 June 2011.

ONLINE RESOURCES

"ALF—1989 Department of Interior PSA." https://www.youtube.com/watch?v=vrWDlNAM_f8 (accessed 6 May 2021).

American Association of Museum Volunteers. Who We Are. https://aamv.wildapricot.org/Who-We-Are (accessed 16 December 2019).

American Horse Council. Take Pride in America. http://www.horsecouncil.org/issues/2005%20 summer%20fall%20issues/TAKE%20PRIDE (accessed 20 June 2007; no longer available).

American Sand Association. *In the Dunes* (newsletter). https://americansandassociation.org/all-downloads/newsletters-2/whats-new-archive (accessed 16 April 2019).

Bennicoff, Tad. "Bearly Survived to Become an Icon." *Bigger Picture*, 27 May 2010. https://siarchives.si.edu/blog/bearly-survived-become-icon (accessed 29 April 2019).

Brough, Aaron R., and James E. B. Wilkie. "Men Resist Green Behavior as Un-Manly: A Surprising Reason for Resistance to Environmental Goods and Habits." *Scientific American Mind* (Behavior & Society), 26 December 2017. https://www.scientificamerican.com/article/men-resist-green-behavior-as-unmanly/ (accessed 5 May 2019).

Charles Bronson "Take Pride in America" Commercial. 1987. https://www.youtube.com/watch?v=wfxp6HR6KwI (accessed 5 May 2021).

Clint Eastwood Take Pride in America PSA. 1987. https://www.youtube.com/watch?v=TTEteDDJu10 (accessed 14 January 2020).

D'Angelo, Chris. "Smokey Bear Is 75: Is It Time for Him to Retire?" *HuffPost*, 12 November 2019. https://www.huffpost.com/entry/smokey-bear-75th-birthday-legacy_n_5dc5cf48e4b0fcfb7f662fda (accessed 27 November 2019).

Dreyfus, Susan N. "Volunteerism and US Civil Society." *Stanford Social Innovation Review*, 29 August 2018. https://ssir.org/articles/entry/volunteerism_and_us_civil_society (accessed 15 January 2021).

"Eastwood Asks Fellow Seniors to Help Improve Public Recreational Areas." *SeniorJournal.com*, 18 August 2005. http://www.seniorjournal.com/NEWS/Volunteers/5-08-18EastwoodVolunteers.htm (accessed 30 June 2007; no longer available).

Heritage of Splendor [film documentary]. Los Angeles: Richfield Oil Corporation, 1963. https://archive.org/details/Heritage1963 (accessed 1 June 2019).

Hodel, Donald. Address to the National Conference of State Legislatures. C-SPAN. 22 February 1985. https://www.c-span.org/video/?125324-1/national-conference-state-legislatures (accessed 9 May 2019).

Hodel, Donald P. Interview by Bruce Collins, with questions phoned in by the public. C-SPAN. 9 April 1985. https://www.c-span.org/video/?72472-1/department-interior (accessed 9 May 2019).

Hodel, Donald. Interview by Bruce Collins. *The Reagan Legacy*. C-SPAN. 22 November 1988. https://www.c-span.org/video/?5721-1/interview-donald-hodel (accessed 9 May 2019).

Keep America Beautiful. Crying Indian [public service announcement featuring Iron Eyes Cody]. 1971. https://www.youtube.com/watch?v=8Suu84khNGY (accessed 6 August 2019).

Keep America Beautiful. Crying Indian on Horseback [public service announcement featuring Iron Eyes Cody]. 1975. https://www.youtube.com/watch?v=8_QGBWaD-A4 (accessed 6 August 2019).

Keep America Beautiful. It Happens in the Best of Places [public service announcement featuring Susan Spotless]. 1961. https://www.youtube.com/watch?v=-BCnGP-ktrQ (accessed 6 August 2019).

Khatami, Elham. "Trump Seeks to Get Rid of Service Programs Like AmeriCorps, Senior Corps in Budget Proposal." *Think Progress*, 13 March 2019. https://archive.thinkprogress.org/trump-white-house-2020-budget-scraps-americorps-senior-corps-799fd69177e0/ (accessed 11 December 2020).

King, Robert. "Celebrating Earth Day with the Legacy of Johnny Horizon, 1968–1977." *My Public Lands*, 28 September 2013. https://mypubliclands.tumblr.com/johnnyhorizon (accessed 27 March 2020).

Lewis, James. "Forgotten Characters from Forest History: Johnny Horizon." *Peeling Back the Bark*, 17 March 2011. https://foresthistory.org/forgotten-characters-from-forest-history-johnny-horizon/ (accessed 29 April 2019).

Linda Evans Discusses Her "Take Pride in America" Ad [7 June 1990 interview aired on *Entertainment Tonight*]. https://m.youtube.com/watch?v=pw_9MJTRrIQ (accessed 3 October 2019).

Lou Gossett Jr. Take Pride in America PSA. 1987. https://m.youtube.com/watch?v=tUdf7y2cN7c (accessed 12 December 2020).

National Wildlife Federation. Volunteer Handbook. 2007. https://www.nwf.org/~/media/PDFs/Volunteers/NWF-Volunteer-Handbook-2007.ashx (accessed 9 May 2019).

O'Neil, Megan. "Volunteer Numbers Surge after Trump Election." *Chronicle of Philanthropy*, 2 February 2017. https://www.philanthropy.com/article/volunteer-numbers-surge-after-trump-election/ (accessed 16 December 2020).

"Park Rangers Outside the Woods: A Q&A with Park Ranger Jason Cangelosi." 4 May 2018. https://www.thesca.org/connect/blog/park-rangers-outside-woods-qa-park-ranger-jason-cangelosi (accessed 13 May 2019).

Ronald Reagan Library. President Reagan's Photo Opportunities on 21–23 July 1987. https://www.youtube.com/watch?v=3T9CvC3rYg8 (accessed 15 April 2019).

"6 Excerpts from the Original 1957 SCA Crew Journals." 8 June 2017. Student Conservation Association. https://www.thesca.org/connect/blog/6-excerpts-original-1957-sca-crew-journals (accessed 24 May 2019).

Smithsonian's National Zoo. History. https://nationalzoo.si.edu/about/history (accessed 13 April 2019).

Smokey Bear Museum and Gift Shop. Village of Capitan website. https://www.villageofcapitan.org/smokey-bear (accessed 5 May 2021).

Souris, Elena. "Volunteering as Civic Engagement at Home and Abroad." *New America*, 23 October 2017. https://www.newamerica.org/political-reform/participatory-democracy-project/civic-engagement/volunteering-civic-engagement-home-and-abroad/ (accessed 11 December 2020).

"The Student Conservation Association Turns 60: Part 1, a Look Back. 8 June 2017." Student Conservation Association. https://www.thesca.org/connect/blog/student-conservation-association-turns-60-part-1-look-back (accessed 24 May 2019).

"Super Bowl Ratings History (1967–present)." http://www.sportsmediawatch.com/super-bowl-ratings-historical-viewership-chart-cbs-nbc-fox-abc/ (accessed 30 August 2018).

U.S. Department of the Interior, Bureau of Land Management. https://www.blm.gov/get-involved/volunteers/volunteer-opportunities (accessed 5 May 2021).

U.S. Department of the Interior, Fish and Wildlife Service. Volunteers. https://www.fws.gov/volunteers/ (accessed 22 August 2018).

U.S. Department of the Interior, Office of Service/Take Pride in America. http://www.takepride.gov/aboutus.html (accessed 22 April 2004; no longer available).

U.S. Department of the Interior Museum. Portrait of an Agency, 2017. https://artsandculture.google.com/exhibit/portrait-of-an-agency%C2%AO-us-department-of-the-interior/WQLCE7mvTPURKQ?hl=en (accessed 14 December 2020).

U.S. Forest Service Graphics. https://www.nal.usda.gov/exhibits/speccoll/exhibits/show/smokey-bear/us-forest-service-graphics (accessed 16 November 2020).

INDEX

environmental policy of, 79–82, 91–94, 95–96, 170n3, 171n6

5,000th Daily Point of Light Award, 188n77

presidential campaign and election of, 79–80

reelection and policies of, 95–96

Take Pride in America awards program and ceremony, 76, 85–86

Thousand Points of Light initiative, 82–87, 88–89, 98, 188n77

Bush, George W.
  election of, 98
  environmental policy of, 99–100, 111–113
  reelection campaign and victory, 110–112
  reelection of, 112
  Take Pride in America campaign reactivation and focus under, 99–115
  USA Freedom Corps initiative, 98–99, 100–101, 111

C&O Canal National Historical Park, 71–73

Cangelosi, Michelle L., 186–187n67, 187–188n74

Carter, Jimmy, 39, 40, 41, 50

celebrity spokespersons
  Ad Council campaigns, 58
  Johnny Horizon campaign, 16
  Take Pride in America campaign, x, 58–65, 74, 85, 87–88, 89, 90, 93, 104, 109–110, 112–113, 117, 118, 161–162n34, 175n30
  Voluntary Action campaign, 37

Clark, William P., 47–48, 52, 154n36

Clean Air Act, 95

Clean-up Camporee, 71–73

Clinton, Bill, 95–98, 99

Clusen, Charles M., 156n3

Coles, Laveranues, 106

Committee on Public Information (CPI), 1–2

Congress, U.S.
  Clean Air Act, 95
  depression and calls for advertising regulation by, 2
  National Tree Trust Act, 82
  National Wildlife Refuge Volunteer Improvement Act, 34
  Reagan relationship with, 39–40
  Smokey Bear Act, 10–11, 129n36
  Take Pride in America Act, 90, 116
  Take Pride in America campaign scrutiny by, 73–74
  Take Pride in America promotion and defense by Hodel, 56–57, 73–74, 160n25, 168n19
  Volunteer and Community Partnership Enhancement Act, 34
  Volunteers in the National Forest Act, 34

conservation
  budgets for, 118
  competing visions of public lands use and, 67–71, 166n8, 167n11

contributions of volunteers, 28–29, 139nn18–19

philanthropic support for, 28–29, 139nn18–19

responsibility for, 53–58, 119

Cooperative Forest Fire Prevention Program, 8, 128n30, 129–130n37

Crandall, Derrick A.
  American Recreation Coalition role of, 68
  assistance with Take Pride in America events by, 103
  Bush relationship with, 174n23
  Spirit of Take Pride in America award for, 111
  Take Pride in America Advisory Board appointment, 91
  Take Pride in America support by, 68, 98, 100, 102, 180–181n11, 182n23

Crying Indian (Iron Eyes Cody) campaign, 19–22, 117, 133–134n19

Cushman Titus, Elizabeth, 31–32, 159n13

Davis, Gray, 112

de Tocqueville, Alexis, 25

Dunlap, Louise, 47

Earth Day, 16, 19, 30, 82, 110–111

Eastwood, Clint
  background and selection for campaign, 61, 163n43
  public service announcements by and script for, 59–65
  Take Pride in America awards program and ceremony, 75–77, 168–169n24
  Take Pride in America role of, x, 74, 85, 90, 93, 104, 109–110, 112–113, 117

Energy, U.S. Department of, 7, 42, 43, 51, 52, 157n7

Environmental Defense Fund, 7, 23

environmental policy
  bipartisan support for, ix, 39, 50
  Bush (George H. W.) policies, 79–82, 91–94, 95–96, 170n3, 171n6
  Bush (George W.) policies, 99–100, 111–113
  Carter policies, 39, 40, 41
  Clinton policies, 96–98, 99
  Nixon policies, 39, 40
  Obama policies, 115–116
  public relations efforts of environmental organizations and, 50
  Reagan first-term legacy and, 49–50
  Reagan gubernatorial record of, 40–41
  Reagan policies, ix–x, 39, 40–47, 118–119
  Reagan second-term policies, 50, 52–53, 157–158n8
  Trump policies, 116

Environmental Protection Agency (EPA)
  Bush (George H. W.) policies, 81
  Gorsuch Burford as administrator of, ix–x, 48

impact of, 25–27, 118
motivations for, 29, 113
Obama initiatives, 115–116
public land stewardship and, 29–34, 35,
100–102, 108–110, 111–113, 116, 142–143n32,
143n34, 143–144n36, 144–145n42
Reagan and Republican Party focus on
individual rather than government action, 38,
53–56, 158n11, 159n13
science and, 27–29, 139nn18–19
Trump on, 116, 188–189n80
Voluntary Action campaign, 35–38, 145n48
Volunteer and Community Partnership Enhancement Act, 34
Volunteers in Forests program, 34, 144n40
Volunteers in Parks (VIP) program, 33–34, 113,
143–144n36
Volunteers in the National Forest Act, 34
voluntourism program, 114

War Advertising Council
benefits to corporations and advertising
agencies, 4
creation of, 2–3, 125n7
focus of campaigns and purpose of, 2–4
membership of, 3
volunteer-based work of, 2–3
War Information, Office of (OWI), 3
water
campaigns for clean water supplies, 7
"Clean Water" magazine ad, 20
Watt, James
anti-environmental proclivities of, ix–x, 43–47,
166n8
background of, 42–43, 51
confrontational style of, 43

Hodel relationship with, 51, 52, 156n1, 157n6
Interior Department changes under, 43
Interior secretary position of, ix–x, 42–43
Norton relationship with, 99
resignation of, 47
unpopularity of and reelection of Reagan, 46–
47, 153n32
Wendelin, Rudolph "Rudy," 10, 11
Western States Tour, 111
Wilderness Society, 44, 47, 156n3
wildfire suppression and forest ecologies, 131n42
wildlife refuges
expansion under America the Beautiful
program, 81–82
National Wildlife Refuge Volunteer
Improvement Act, 34
visitors to, 55
Wilson, Woodrow, 1–2
Wonderful Outdoor World (WOW), 108–109,
185n50
Wooden, Ruth, 24
Woodsy Owl anti-littering campaign, 16
World War I
support for and the Committee on Public
Information, 1–2
volunteer opportunities during, 26
World War II
advertising campaigns to win support for, 2–4
forest fire prevention campaign during, 7–10
public service campaigns during, 7
volunteer opportunities during, 26, 136–
137n6
WOW (Wonderful Outdoor World), 108–109,
185n50

Young, Lisa, 115, 188n78

ABOUT THE AUTHOR

JEFFREY K. STINE is curator for environmental history at the Smithsonian Institution's National Museum of American History. He founded and coedited the University of Akron Press book series *Technology and the Environment* and has served as president of the American Society for Environmental History and the Public Works Historical Society. His publications include *America's Forested Wetlands: From Wasteland to Valued Resource, Mixing the Waters: Environment, Politics, and the Building of the Tennessee-Tombigbee Waterway*, and the coedited volume *Living in the Anthropocene: Earth in the Age of Humans*.